A305 D

THE OPEN UNIVERSITY

Arts: A third level Course
History of architecture and design 1890 - 1939
Documents

Documents

The Open University
Arts: a third level course
History of architecture and design 1890–1939
Documents

Documents

A collection of source material on the Modern Movement

Edited by Charlotte Benton
for the Course Team

The Open University Press

The Open University Press,
Walton Hall, Milton Keynes.

First published 1975.

Designed by the Media Development Group of the Open University.

Printed in Great Britain by
Martin Cadbury, a specialized division of Santype International,
Worcester and London.

ISBN 0 335 00713 9

This text forms part of an Open University course. The complete list
of units in the course appears at the end of this text.

For general availability of supporting material referred to in this text
please write to the Director of Marketing, The Open University, P.O.
Box 81, Walton Hall, Milton Keynes, MK7 6AT.

Further information on Open University courses may be obtained from
the Admissions Office. The Open University, P.O. Box 48, Walton
Hall, Milton Keynes, MK7 6AB.

1.1

Contents

Introduction

This anthology of writings on architecture and design of the period 1914–39 has been assembled with two main aims in mind: one was to fill in some of the most glaring omissions in the main set book reading (which contains, for example, nothing on Russia and very little on Britain of this period); the other was to supplement the documentary component already represented by *Form and Function*.[1] In fact, not surprisingly, several of the extracts selected here come from the mass of material from which we made our final selection for *Form and Function*. But this collection does differ considerably in kind from *Form and Function*. Our two main aims give it a certain arbitrariness as a collection; that is to say, it does not have the kind of overall formal cohesion we tried to aim for in *Form and Function*. Nevertheless, the material did fall fairly naturally into groups, either by specific subject-matter (e.g. Parts 1, 2 and 3) or by theme (Parts 4 and 5) and most of the parts *can* be read as self-contained blocks, although some (e.g. Parts 4 and 5) are less homogeneous than others.

We hope that—as with *Form and Function*—you will use *Documents* both when directed (in the units) to a particular article and independently, in your own time, to search out connections and contrasts over the whole range of the course. I do not want to establish any hard-and-fast rules for the use of *Documents*, but I offer the following general guidelines to the appropriate stages at which to read various items or whole parts. I have deliberately not mentioned every item in each part. The detailed cross-referencing of authors, architects, designers, and subject-matter with the other elements of the course (and broadcasting should be remembered here at least as much as the units and *Form and Function*) is up to you.

Part 1

The 1914 Deutscher Werkbund Congress material (1.1 to 1.4) is of special relevance to Units 5–6 and radio vision programmes 11 and 12, but the issues raised here are of continuing importance throughout the rest of the period.

Giedion's article (1.5) gives a critical overview, from the vantage point of 1926, of the post-war and newly emerging tendencies in (mainly) German architecture and would best be read while you are working through Units 9–10.

Part 2

Is entirely concerned with the Deutscher Werkbund housing exhibition, the Weissenhof Siedlung built in Stuttgart in 1927. While this section can be read most appropriately when you are working on Units 13–14 (and especially for television programme 10), the issues raised here are crucial to an understanding of the wider social and political issues provoked by the International Style. You should also watch out here for participants from the 1914 Werkbund Congress—have their positions hardened or modified?

Part 3

Is essential reading for Unit 14 and the radio programmes associated with this unit. Like Part 2 it is also essential reading for an appreciation of the implications of the International Style, most particularly for the interpretation of its forms and the transformation of their meaning in a different social and political context.

Part 4

Fits no particular units. But 4.1 might usefully be read in the context of Units 10, 13 and 17. 4.2 fills out some of the background to the early parts of Units 5–6, and 4.3 extends the public-housing concerns touched on in Units 9–10, 11–12 and 17–18 to the field of programmatic planning.

Part 5

5.1 and 5.2 are directly connected with the section on Behrens in Units 5–6 and with television programme 4. But the specific issues raised here, of the resolution of a functional programme for an industrial building in an aesthetically acceptable architectural form, have echoes and variations in other parts of the course and you should be on the look-out for these. 5.3 examines the issues of an aesthetic of industrial building and could usefully be read concurrently with Units 5–6 and 9–14.

Part 6

Is of obvious relevance to Units 18 and 19–20 and to a number of radio and television programmes in the latter part of the course. But it is also intended to help you to prepare for one of the main themes of the Summer School (Architecture and Design in Britain during the 1920s and 1930s), and to fill out the background against which your special project may well be set.

Those are some key examples and they are fairly straightforward; but I would like to stress again that the more sophisticated cross-referencing of the different component parts of the course is up to you. The main value of the material in this booklet (and in *Form and Function*) should be that it gives you a measure of independence from the correspondence texts and the set books, that it provides you with some 'raw' material with which to form your own assessment—and to accept, modify or reject other people's judgements as and where necessary.

[1] A 305 Course Anthology, *Form and Function*, ed. C. A. and T. J. Benton with D. Sharp, Crosby Lockwood Staples/The Open University Press, 1975

Part 1 Arts and Crafts and Architecture in Germany

1.1–1.4

All these items come from the congress of the Deutscher Werkbund held on the occasion of the Deutscher Werkbund exhibition in Cologne in July 1914. Muthesius circulated to the delegates his *Propositions* (1.1), defining the main themes of his speech, a few days in advance of the speech itself for consideration and debate. *The Task of the Werkbund in the Future* (1.3), delivered on 3rd July, basically resumes the theme of *Where do we stand?* (*Form and Function* no. 24) given at the 1911 congress: standardization in architecture and industrial design. But whereas in 1911 Muthesius's ideas had seemed to offer the Werkbund a progressive definition of its future policy, his re-statement and elaboration of the principle of standardization in 1914 was found highly provocative and divisive by many of the architect and artist members of the Werkbund. Muthesius seemed to them to be attacking the very idea of artistic freedom and the rôle of the creative designer. Their response is best summarized in Van de Velde's *Counter Propositions*, delivered on 3rd July, and in some of the individual contributions to the ensuing debate of 4th July (1.4) which includes contributions by, amongst others, Peter Behrens, August Endell and Bruno Taut.

1.5

This article was occasioned by an exhibition organized by Hartlaub, Platz and Strübing entitled 'New Types of Architecture' which was held in Mannheim Art Gallery in 1926. The main bias of the exhibition was towards recent German architecture, although it also included a small section on recent Dutch architecture. The exhibition was organized, as the title of the article suggests, by building types, the largest section being devoted to functional buildings of all kinds.

In this article Giedion analyses the changes in architectural attitudes which have taken place over the last few years, from the individualism of Expressionism to the emerging *neue Sachlichkeit* (New Objectivity) of the twenties.

1.1 Propositions by Hermann Muthesius

1 Architecture, and with it the whole area of the Werkbund's activities, is striving towards standardization and only through standardization can it recover that universal significance which was a characteristic of architecture in times of harmonious culture.

2 Standardization, which is the result of a beneficial concentration, will alone make possible the development of universally valid, unfailing good taste.

3 As long as a universal high level of taste has not been achieved, we cannot count on German arts and crafts making their influence effectively felt abroad.

4 The world will demand our products only when they are the vehicles of a convincing stylistic expression. The foundations for this have now been laid by the German movement.

5 The most urgent task is to develop creatively what has already been achieved. Upon it, the movement's ultimate success will depend. Any relapse and deterioration into imitation would today mean the squandering of a valuable possession.

6 Starting from the conviction that it is a matter of life and death for Germany constantly to improve its production, the Deutscher Werkbund, as an association of artists, industrialists, and merchants, must concentrate its attention upon creating the preconditions for the export of its industrial arts.

7 Germany's advances in applied art and architecture must be brought to the attention of foreign countries by effective publicity. Next to exhibitions the most obvious means of doing this is by illustrated periodical publications.

8 Exhibitions by the Deutscher Werkbund are only meaningful when they are restricted radically to the best and most exemplary. Exhibitions of arts and crafts abroad must be looked upon as a national matter and hence require public subsidy.

9 The existence of efficient large-scale business concerns with reliable good taste is a prerequisite of any export. It would be impossible to meet even internal demands with an object designed by the artist for individual requirements.

10 For national reasons, large distributive and transport undertakings whose activities are directed abroad ought to link up with the new movement, now that it has shown what it can do, and consciously represent German art in the world.

1.2   **Counter-Propositions** by Henry Van de Velde

1   So long as there are still artists in the Werkbund and so long as they exercise some influence on its destiny, they will protest against every suggestion of the establishment of a canon and of standardization. By his innermost essence the artist is a burning idealist, a free spontaneous creator. Of his own free will, he will never subordinate himself to a discipline that imposes upon him a type, a canon. Instinctively he distrusts everything that might sterilize his actions and everyone who preaches a rule that might prevent him from thinking his thoughts through to their own free end, or that attempts to drive him into a universally valid form, in which he sees only a mask that seeks to make a virtue out of incapacity.

2   Certainly the artist who practises a beneficial concentration has always recognized that currents which are stronger than his own will and thought demand of him that he should acknowledge what essentially corresponds to the spirit of his age. These currents may be very manifold; he absorbs them unconsciously and consciously as general influences; there is something materially and morally compelling about them for him. He willingly subordinates himself to them and is full of enthusiasm for the idea of a new style *per se*. And for twenty years many of us have been seeking forms and decorations entirely in keeping with our epoch.

3   Nevertheless it has not occurred to any of us that henceforth we ought to try to impose upon others as standards, these forms and decorations which we have sought or found. We know that several generations will have to work upon what we have started before the physiognomy of the new style is established, and that we can talk of standards and standardization only after the passage of a whole period of endeavour is over.

4   But we also know that as long as this goal has not been reached our endeavours will still have the charm of creative impetus. Gradually the energies, the gifts of all, begin to combine together, antitheses become neutralized and at precisely that moment when individual strivings begin to slacken, the physiognomy will be established. The era of imitation will begin and decorations will be used, the production of which no longer calls for any creative impulse; the age of infertility will then have commenced.

5   The desire to see a standard type come into being before the establishment of a style is exactly like wanting to see the effect before the cause. It would be to destroy the embryo in the egg. Is anyone really going to let themselves be dazzled by the apparent possibility of thereby achieving quick results? These premature effects have all the less

prospect of enabling German arts and crafts to exercise an effective influence abroad, because foreign countries are a jump ahead of us in the old tradition and the old culture of good taste.

6   Germany, on the other hand, has the great advantage of still possessing gifts which other, older, wearier peoples are losing—the gifts of invention, of brilliant personal inspiration—and it would be nothing short of castration to tie down so soon this rich, many-sided creative *élan*.

7   The efforts of the Werkbund should be directed towards cultivating precisely these gifts, as well as the gifts of individual manual skill, joy and belief in the beauty of highly differentiated execution, not toward inhibiting them by standardization at the very moment when foreign countries are beginning to take an interest in German work. As far as fostering these gifts is concerned, almost everything still remains to be done.

8   We do not deny anyone's good will and we are very aware of the difficulties that have to be overcome in carrying this out. We know that the workers' organization has done a very great deal for the workers' material welfare, but it can hardly find an excuse for having done so little towards arousing enthusiasm for consummately fine workmanship in those who ought to be our most joyful collaborators. On the other hand, we are well aware of the need to export that lies like a curse upon our industry.

9   And yet nothing, nothing good and splendid, was ever created out of mere consideration for exports. Quality will not be created out of the spirit of export. Quality is always first created exclusively for a quite limited circle of connoisseurs and those who commission the work. These gradually gain confidence in their artists; slowly there develops first a narrower, then a national clientele, and only then do foreign countries, does the world, slowly take notice of this quality. It is a complete misunderstanding of the situation to make the industrialists believe that they would increase their chances in the world market if they produced *a priori* standardized types for this world market before these types had become well-tried common property at home. The wonderful works being exported to us now were none of them originally created for export; think of Tiffany glasses, Copenhagen porcelain, jewellery by Jensen, the books of Cobden-Sanderson, and so on.

10   The purpose of every exhibition must be to show the world this native quality and it is quite true that the Werkbund exhibitions will have meaning only when, as Herr Muthesius so rightly says, they restrict themselves radically to the best and most exemplary.

1.3   The Task of the Werkbund in the Future by Hermann Muthesius

The Deutscher Werkbund would be in a pretty bad way if it were to feel entirely satisfied with its first exhibition. The weaknesses of a first effort are only too apparent . . . and the prevailing impression given by our rather over-stocked display is of a certain reserve and indecision, not to say downright dullness. . . .

But even in these terms the current exhibition leaves room for not altogether unfruitful considerations. Any ambitious undertaking such as the modern architecture and Arts and Crafts movement, which the Werkbund represents, tends to develop in two directions; one is to make its activities more and more widespread and the other is to strive to achieve ever-higher standards. As far as the Werkbund is concerned, the upward trend is purely artistic while the broad outward sweep is more closely bound to economics. . . .

Leaving aside the higher aspirations for a moment, the present exhibition is certainly a fair reflection of the breadth of influence our movement has acquired. . . .

Its success has shown that commercial circles as a whole and the great majority of industrial manufacturers definitely wish to collaborate with us today. It is of the utmost importance that this should be acknowledged because it could to some extent outweigh the perfectly justified reproach that our new achievements have actually been few in number. In fact people are beginning to wonder exactly what it is the Werkbund wants.

In so far as we are an association of artists, industrialists, manufacturers and merchants our foremost goal must be the popularizing and practical diffusion of the activities which for the past fifteen years we have been accustomed to calling artistic. But if art had been our sole concern, we should have founded an artists' association from the very beginning and left out the manufacturers. No, for us it was always a question of making art useful, of reconciling artistic aims with industrial and commercial ends, and trying to bring about a kind of partnership of artistic, industrial and administrative forces. In any case art is far too pretentious a word for many sectors of our activities, where it is simply a question of good taste, good decent forms and good proportions. So many catch phrases have been engendered over the last ten years, such as 'art in the home', 'art in the street', 'shop-window art', 'student-living art' and 'art in a man's suit'—practically every word has to have 'art' tagged on—that the situation seems almost comic. In the past, when all expressions of daily life bore the stamp of unity and good taste, no one would have dreamed of coming out with the word 'art' at the slightest opportunity in every corner of business and domestic life. The eighteenth-century writers scarcely ever refer to it in their descriptions of interiors, the decorative arts and utensils. In those days it was taken for granted that forms were pleasing and that craftsmen, buyers and merchants had good taste and there was no need to point out these qualities specially. The fact that the word 'art' began to be increasingly employed from about the middle of the nineteenth century onwards is simply a sign that society as a whole was suddenly afflicted with a loss of confidence and almost a feeling of spiritual void in matters of taste. All the activities which have been labelled arts and crafts since the time of Gottfried Semper and which the Werkbund has taken up are basically a means of trying to compensate for this lack. It is essential for us to recover an innate feeling for good taste, just as in earlier periods, which is a natural thing after all. If some look upon this as modifying the nature of the Werkbund's crusade, it in no way diminishes the general significance of our work. The natural application of good taste in the life of an individual may be a private affair, but where a whole people is concerned the private matter can soon become a national characteristic which not only colours the cultural composition of the country as a whole but also has a far-reaching effect on its economy. . . .

Despite the individualistic characteristics of different values there can no longer be any doubt that a unified expression of style has already been achieved in modern arts and crafts. This may not be quite as obvious to us as to observers from abroad, because we see things at such very close range. But foreigners have already regarded the German exhibits in St Louis[1] and Brussels[2] as possessing a strong personality of their own in comparison with the usual type of display organized by other countries. Since then we have made more progress along the salutary road towards unification and this alone should make us proud, because unity means strength. The transfer from the individual to the typical is an organic process of development which not only broadens and popularizes but also has a deepening and refining effect. A gradual, even flow of unified achievements distinguishes every period of cultural flowering, especially the peak periods of architecture. In a sense whole generations have worked together on the same task and each individual artist has done his part towards realizing the whole result, just as today in factories and building concerns every effort is increasingly directed towards perfecting and improving the manufactured article (cameras, telescopes, steamers, turbines . . .). The tendency to develop towards a type should be an especially characteristic feature of the architectural arts. The fundamental difference between the so-called liberal arts, poetry, music, painting and sculpture, and architecture is that the

[1] 1904 (International Exhibition).

[2] 1910 (International Exhibition).

(ed.)

liberal arts are self-fulfilling whereas architecture has a practical purpose to serve. The liberal arts are almost exceptions in daily life because we turn to them when we seek relief from routine. But architecture, conceived as providing a rhythmical framework for everyday needs, on the contrary provides the backcloth of tranquillity which is indispensable if anything outstanding is to be accomplished. It is a well-known fact that eccentricities in architecture give more cause for regrets than in any other art. Nowadays, for instance, most of the so-called 'modern' works scarcely bear looking at after about five years. The arts and crafts museums which bought up pieces of decorative arts in Paris in 1900, the heyday of individualism, have since had to store them away in dark corners of their cellars. People become especially sensitive about anything abnormal in tectonics, anything that departs from the peaceful course of development. The peculiar quality of architecture is that it tends towards the type and typifying supposes the normal, not what is out of the ordinary. . . .

Now, though I have described this process of standardization as having already begun and have pointed out its advantages, I must make it plain straightaway, to guard against any misunderstandings, that I am not trying to ask creative artists to aim for a maximum of uniformity. This would not only be completely wrong, it would fail. Genuine artists have always followed their inner convictions and must be completely free, because they cannot create anything valid unless they are. But it is generally recognized that architecture is the one art which has the most difficulty in severing its ties with tradition and as far as I can see there seems little reason why it should. But there is certainly a great difference between old themes being simply reworked in new combinations and a whole generation using the new equipment provided by the changing conditions of the times to develop the tradition further with new works of art. The habit of working over old elements was usual in the days when architects and craftsmen claimed to be 'versed in all the styles'. And today too, even though a new and vital movement has set in, meanwhile in architecture, which we must acclaim as one of the finest

achievements of the age, a Biedermeier tendency still persists, as ready as ever to satisfy the public's weakness for idolatry.

Running parallel to some of the freshest and most creative designs, especially in factory and commercial building, is a very obvious reactionary trend which claims that all the modern movement has achieved in the last fifteen years is regrettable and dishonest. Even many of those who originally took part in our exciting but rigorous campaigns have now found their way back to the cosy four walls of traditional style, insisting that the only reality lies in staying at home and that to venture out of doors is madness. . . . The fields chiefly affected are those where new needs have arisen, such as transport, commerce, factory-design and domestic building.

It is already easy to see that a new means of expression is growing up which faithfully reflects the character of the times. And we must on no account lose sight of the precept that an age like ours, where living conditions have totally changed in comparison with earlier periods, where international exchange in cultural and material respects has replaced prejudiced provincialism, where technology has broken down the barriers of time and space and unprecedented inventions have transformed our environment, that such an age deserves its own form of expression in art too. The internationalization of our lives, moreover, will inevitably bring about a certain uniformity in architecture all over the globe. We might even say that this is already apparent in our dress, the tectonic medium which most immediately affects us. Today the same jackets and shirts are being worn from the north to the south pole.

The Deutscher Werkbund's particular province has always been handicrafts, but seen in the special sense of dignifying the conception of form and promoting quality. Such activities aim at an ideal, just as the Werkbund itself can be defined as a product of German idealism. It is thus fundamental to our nature to continue to strive for the highest and the best, never to rest on our laurels, always to feel dissatisfied with what we have achieved and to be ever alert for new sources of enrichment. . . .

1.4   Extracts from the Werkbund debate, Cologne

Peter Behrens

I must honestly confess that I was not altogether clear what Herr Muthesius meant by standardization [Typisierung]. And it did not immediately occur to me to think of it as a canon. My first reaction was to imagine typical art, which I regard as the highest goal of any artist's activity. In this

sense it means the ultimate and most powerful expression of a deep personality and also the most mature and intelligent resolution of the object to be created, of the object conceived, purified of all its accessories. In both respects an artist's best works will always be types. It is quite evident, for instance, that if a department store is strikingly designed so as to express its purpose, it will be a better piece of architecture than if it looks like a castle. Formerly, the constant striving for perfection led to a situation where the ground plan of a house could not be better rendered than by filling all its functional and aesthetic needs; and the outcome was the type of town house which has been repeated so often with occasional slight variations. That is what I understand by typical art. Limiting the freedom of the artist does not come into it. On the contrary the Werkbund must regard the preservation of the artist's liberty as one of its most sacrosanct laws. . . .

August Endell

. . . if we now have to add a doubtful word like 'standardization' [*Typisierung*] to the unfortunate 'quality', which I should really prefer to replace by 'beauty', our programme is going to be completely ruined; this is an expression which has never even existed before and it could scarcely be more obscure.

It would be very rash to admit such a word into our list of aims without giving it a little more thought. It is our duty, though, to state what we want clearly and frankly. The previous speaker has very skilfully outlined just how difficult it is to grasp the notions of type and 'standardization', so I can now limit my remarks to the more positive side of the suggestions. In fact we are really saying that we must try to export on a grand scale and therefore ought to standardize. . . .

It is a matter of indifference to me whether or not my achievements produce a unity. How can I create something typical if ten thousand others are doing the same? How am I supposed to influence the others? Uniformity of artistic work will lead to stamped out goods. And it is not even true that earlier periods were able to establish that kind of unity. We think they did because we do not know enough about the past and are influenced by the conception of art history which has been generally accepted since Hegel. . . .

Karl Ernst Osthaus

The word 'types' is not quite so devoid of meaning as Herr Endell suggests, because the Werkbund movement sees it in a rather special light. In my opinion, the notion of type originated with workers' housing schemes. It was found that the cost of building an estate could be considerably reduced if specific elements such as windows, doors, heating installations and so on were designed in a standard way, which restricted the use of basic forms. Metzendorf used one type of window 4000 times, and another 7000 times, in one year for instance, in his estate in Essen. It is perfectly obvious that the application of standard elements signifies considerable economy in the case of very large estates and that is what ultimately justifies standardization. Only we did not stop there; we went on to transfer the notion of 'type' to furniture design as well. As far as I

know, this has been a favourite practice in the Dresden workshops. There too it has become a question of employing standard elements such as carcase frames with different component parts for pieces of furniture designed for quite a variety of purposes. Riemerschmid has discovered some very ingenious ways of assembling standard forms for different types of furniture (beds, chests of drawers, cupboards, tables . . .). Once again the designs are based on economic considerations and it is obvious that this type of manufacture will produce articles which can be sold at a lower price than others. The social advantages deriving from this are plain. If the types are really well designed, a comparatively large number of people will be able to benefit from the new opportunities the Werkbund can provide.

That is how the notion of 'type' arose, ladies and gentlemen, and I doubt if anyone will deny that 'standardization' in this sense has its positive side.

But I also agree with the remarks made by Van de Velde and Endell in that I certainly do not believe that standardization can be regarded as significant artistically. I think that Endell is right when he says that the appearance of unity in the past is largely an illusion arising from a wrong approach to art history. Types grow up wherever they match local needs. The very fact that types first appeared in Germany in the designs for workers' houses is ample illustration of the fact. If contemporary living conditions show unity, there will be matching unified forms. In any case, the spirit of the times at present is scarcely likely to produce much unity of form. . . .

Everything is still in the course of being generated and it would be anticipating the future to try to discern or ask for standardization so soon. And as standardization has absolutely nothing to do with art. . . .

We must regard our movement as an ethical one and worry not so much about our exports as about whether our work is really worthy of us. We must work conscientiously because we cannot do anything else, because we love working and we love beauty, because beauty makes us 'mad' and we want only to see beautiful things around us. That is all that is important and that is where the strength of our movement lies. Please do not forget it. . . .

Richard Riemerschmid

Some people have been saying that we were talking at cross purposes yesterday. I have the feeling that we are doing the same today. (*Hear, hear!*) In fact we are discussing two totally different things. On the one hand we are talking about mass production in association with industry—which I should like to split into two broad groups—and on the other about individual works of art. Obviously there are a great many connections between the two, but for practical purposes it is important to try to make the distinction as clear as possible and not continually disguise one as the other and mix them up so that no one knows which one is being discussed. One person is talking about the ground to be ploughed and the other about the flowering tree which must be allowed to grow. They are not the same thing at all!

Now why exactly was the Werkbund founded? If I remember rightly, its purpose was defined more or less as the dignifying of labour with the collaboration of art, industry and handwork. Both aims should be kept in view, not just one at a time. At this meeting I have often had the impression that the various supporters look upon their particular aim as the only one that exists.

A great deal has been said about 'standardization'. I completely agree with the view that a type must evolve naturally and cannot be sought, that it cannot and should not be aimed at deliberately, particularly if standardization is to be understood as a canon. But as far as I know and can tell, Herr Muthesius never once said that he was referring to a canon. I feel—and I should like to insist on this—that on the contrary, it was wrong of those who hold other views suddenly to replace the word 'standardization or canon'. That is a different thing altogether and with such methods. . . .

(*The last words are drowned by the applause*)

Bruno Taut

. . . How do we establish a high standard? What exactly is a high standard? In my opinion it is a means of popularizing the chief ideas. Art sets up a kind of pyramid which widens out towards the bottom. The most competent, that is the artists with ideas, are at the top. The broader lower portion is thus nothing more than a kind of flattening of these ideas. I cannot conceive of standardization in any other way and I find it very distressing to hear that the solution to our problems is not simply to have faith in the peak. I feel that this exhibition is a good illustration of such an outlook. People tend to believe that if they leave something out of this or simplify that, they will obtain something standard. And I am not only speaking of higher matters, or rather so-called pure art. The same applies to every single article. If a great artist, say Van de Velde, makes a beautiful teaspoon, it will inevitably attract a certain public and will be copied over and over again until in the end it cannot be distinguished from an ordinary one. . . . In any case the Werkbund has no choice in the matter; the path it follows obliges it to recognize that nothing has ever been created by committees and that a multiplicity of heads, no matter how talented, never produce anything of quality, least of all anything artistic such as an exhibition, which has to be cast in a single mould. I thus propose that we elect a dictator with artistic matters. His period of office could be limited to about three years, for instance. But I honestly believe, after hearing the opinions of Endell, Obrist, Van de Velde and the others that this is the only possible way to

achieve good work and encourage artistic quality. I should like to suggest Van de Velde or Poelzig for such a dictator-ship. . . . (*Applause*)

Walter Riezler

Herr Endell mentioned that the rapture produced by the sight of a beautiful object is the state which also produces great art. I should like to claim the opposite view. It may be true that this 'sacred madness' is the original state of chaos out of which art develops, but as far as architectural creations are concerned at any rate, it cannot be an indi-vidual experience; at the most it will be a kind of collective condition. It was not the individual who built the Gothic cathedrals who was mad but the period. (*Hear, hear!*) In his day, the gifted individual always distinguished himself through his alertness, clarity of vision and calm. This is how architecture and everything connected with it has been produced for hundreds and thousands of years. Buildings which are the result of an individual state of madness all too often bear the stamp of lunacy on their brow.

I should also like to refer to another remark made by one of the previous speakers, who claimed that the way a form is applied can make it extraordinarily characteristic for certain people and that such a view ultimately makes it absurd. He likened art to a pyramid and said, not that everything builds up to the peak, but that everything depends on the peak. 'We must start at the top.' Now, ladies and gentlemen, just try to imagine a pyramid which starts at the top. It is indicative of the views of such circles to believe that an individual organism floating in the air can provide a basis for art and forms. (*Warm applause*)

I am convinced that it is the other way round. If the foundations are lacking, a complete solution can never be found, at least not as far as these notions are concerned. Such foundations can only be laid along the lines Herr Muthesius is referring to when he speaks of 'standardi-zation'. (*Long warm applause*) . . .

On the other hand—and I must make this plain—there are a number of specific things which can be achieved within an association like the Werkbund. I am convinced that our fate depends on carrying out these very real obligations which have nothing to do with artistic individuality or mysticism or anything else of the kind and it is the duty of each one of us to join in. I am absolutely convinced that the Werkbund's rôle lies in carrying out these very everyday tasks. It would be ridiculous to dream of anything else. An association such as ours is not designed for drawing up or imposing rules for artistic culture or anything else that signifies a peak. (*Applause*) What Herr Riemerschmid said is perfectly right. The Werkbund must learn to be responsible for its own future. Our activities do not need to dazzle the outside world, they could even remain totally unknown if it were not necessary occasionally to draw people's attention to them and organize an exhibition.

(*Hear, hear!*) Our true duties are not to be found in the exhibition halls, but in the quiet painstaking labour defined when we founded our association which Riemerschmid has just cited. The Werkbund must persevere humbly and steadily in its declared attempt to raise the level of mechanical work. Our competence and even the very existence of our association can only be justified in so far as these real tasks are fulfilled. (*Long deafening applause*)

Robert Bremer

Ladies and gentlemen; I do not know whether we are allowed to refer to sexual problems on an occasion like this, but I feel that what we are experiencing here today would fit into that category. We are really going through a form of conjugal crisis as a result of the unnatural marriage we arranged between schoolmasters and artists.

When Endell said just now that the sight of a beautiful shape could send us crazy, the majority laughed. And they were perfectly right to laugh at such a shameless unveiling of the aesthetic experience. (*Applause*) It would have been most embarrassing if they had not laughed. And in fact it would have been impossible and even undesirable for the majority to feel so sensitive about their feelings for art that they were unable to laugh. The majority here have nothing to do with art. . . .

The question now is whether or not there should be a divorce. I tend to think there should and I imagine that most artists would agree with me. But the marriage has been successful in a number of respects even so, because

there has been a whole crowd of affectionate children. Up to now nothing has gone wrong. But there suddenly seems to be a kind of rebellion brewing among certain of the schoolmasters, not the pupils. It is obviously essential to make it quite clear that if the marriage is to last, it will depend on the Werkbund's infinite respect for its artists. . . .

Herr Riezler has just outlined a kind of sociology of art, and made it quite clear that art grows up from below. No doubt he thought he was making a claim for socialism with that remark. Now I certainly have not much to say for the aristocracy but I do feel that views like this are pure demagogy. Art cannot grow out of the masses; it never has and never will. (*Bravo!*) It is certainly true that in the modern state the progress of art in general depends on the ruling power and therefore on the masses, but the creative process has its own origins and it largely works against the general will. Even when socialism has conquered the world, as I hope it will, art will still come into conflict with the opinion of the masses. The artists will still have to fight, before the public at large is brought to heel. (*Bravo!*) If the masses give their commissions, as the kings and popes did when they built their castles and churches, this does not mean that the artist can at last lead a free existence. It will still be a matter of life and death and madness. (*Hear, hear!*) The artist is never wrong and the majority, when not wholly opposed to what he does, is very seldom right. The majority must listen or at the most advise; it has absolutely no right to criticize or attempt to influence the artist. . . .

1.5   The State of German Architecture by Sigfried Giedion

Taking 1912–20 as roughly the time during which German Expressionism was at the height of its power, we must recognize that this was also the period (at least in Germany) when architecture counted as one of the minor arts. What is the use of architecture, whose purpose is to cover our external life, when the clarion cry rings out: Look inwards! Free us from material objects! Give us inspiration! Paint the essence of humanity! Paint our mistreated generation in swirling colours glowing with the rays of eternity!

Expressionist architecture in the proper sense of the term does not exist, for architecture can flower only where it can be master. It is almost inherent in the terms of German Expressionism that architecture should be excluded. Some of Poelzig's individual works could be regarded as symbolic of Expressionist architecture, but we should not ascribe a style to them.

When Expressionism first became widespread, its inspiration came not from architecture but from the applied arts. Colours flowed from pictures on to walls and objects.

1925: Many people now find themselves confronted with a transformed situation. A new form of architecture is coming into existence: inartistic, unfashionable. Related phenomena are being produced from Russia to America at unheard-of speed. National boundaries are crossed so that all creative efforts can benefit mutually. For a while the so-called 'free' arts are relegated to the background while reality holds sway in this utopian current. The architect turns away from the painter, from the sculptor and, most emphatically, from the historian, so as to accept as his real brother and helper the sociologist, economist and statistician.

The architect deliberately strips off the last insulating layer of aestheticism which could separate him from real life, so that, almost forgetting himself, he can subject himself to the ruling commands as thoroughly as possible: the traffic movements of a town have become more important than form or monumentality.

One should not fear that a total aridity may suddenly

occur. Until architecture has totally assimilated the whole standard of our changed way of life, it will be unable to find formulas whose obvious rightness will be indispensable material for future generations. We demand a continuity. Architecture formulates, and must formulate anew so as to be able fully to embody within itself the new conditions.

At this crucial point, one asks involuntarily: Where does German architecture stand at the moment?

Summary: It must be realized that in the movement at the beginning of the century—which included architecture—and in whose wake the mainstream still flows to this day, decorative art was in the ascendancy. The sequel to this was that decoration, rather than architecture, became of prime importance. It is not mere chance that most of the leading architects of this period came from a background in the crafts or interior design. Let us attempt to clarify the advantages and disadvantages of this artistic infiltration. Decorative art proceeded from form; it purified it by putting into practice the war-cry: 'Expediency versus style, to clear Germany from imitations of style which had become stereotyped, and to do this more radically than in any of the neighbouring countries.' A certain standard of interior decoration and objects has become the norm to such an extent that, for instance, even the worst German philistine would have felt a sense of superiority when faced with the Art Nouveau productions at the Paris Exhibition.

But suddenly the problem has changed, and architecture is taking over. Expediency versus style is no longer the question. People have stopped racking their brains over how to find a formal style—which was frequently the case in the wake of artistic statements of the problem. After all, the search for a common style is still going on, as different modes are employed concurrently, and the search can be traced back to the 1830s. The new architect is governed by necessity, the cost of building, and calculations,

almost to the point of total indifference to form. Of course these factors are always the most help in searching for a new style.

We grew up with what we called the 'artistic' movement, and can freely admit what it gave us: purification of household objects, a more refined sense of interiors, and a new life for almost all materials, metal, wood and textiles—from the surface decoration on ceramics, to the finishing on a wall. The architectural purification of the house should not be forgotten, even though it did not escape from an over-lavishly cushioned boudoir atmosphere.

Yet it must be stated clearly that the decorative movement has petered out, and not just recently. The *Werkstätten* culture, which complied with the tastes of a refined bourgeoisie, has come to an end. This is most clearly shown in the case of the *Wiener Werkstätten*, which although achieving some significance at first, has been moving for years in the direction of the rococo, from which there can be no progression.

So a playful and irrelevant quality has entered into even such refined products as these. Articles in silver look as though one could crumple them like tissue paper, ceramics are often treated in an inappropriate way which denies the inherent qualities of the clay—the curves of a nervous feminism. All the world seems to be disintegrating into toys.

This must be stated here, for architecture, especially in Germany, infiltrated as it was by artistic currents, did not manage to avoid the rush into a premature rococo state after a promising start. And this is where we stand today in some confusion. Poelzig should be named here as the most representative architect of this tendency. From his promising factories, shops and water towers he has turned all too quickly to a baroque theatricality, similar to that found in industrial art, which gave movement to simple profiles, like that of Behrens in 1910. No-one knows better than

Figure 1   Hans Poelzig, Design for Festival Theatre, Salzburg, 3rd version, 1922

Figure 2 Peter Behrens, I.G. Farben, Hoechst-am Main, 1920-4

Poelzig how to mould an inflexible brick wall and make it malleable, so that it is emotionally charged, as in the case of the administrative offices built for the Meyer Brothers in Hanover. The future confronts this type of architecture (the Salzburg Festival Theatre Scheme) with its monumental appearance (**Fig. 1**) and is foreign to it. We should not evade the question: 'Can we permit the existence of such ineffective architecture today, when we are still only groping for the smallest element (the house) without being sure of finding a solution?'

It is strange how the earlier industrial spans, such as Peter Behrens's hangar built in Hanover in 1915, still hold their ground and—against all odds—still remain monuments which are part of the development. In the last few years Behrens has given vague indications of a romantic line of approach. There is a clear progression from his problematical brick church in the Munich Industrial Show of 1922, through the coloured domed hall for the Hoechst Farbwerke (**Fig. 2**), with its Gothic stalactite-like pillars, to the romantic imagery of ruins in his conservatory in the Paris Exhibition. This romantic approach is more a personal attribute of Behrens's temperament—and can be seen too in some of his speeches—than a far-reaching symptom of the age, as is, for example, Poelzig's exuberant

baroque style. Behrens's splendid buildings, with their romantic lines, can be considered symptomatic only in so far as they demonstrate the influence of decorative art.

Even the two greatest talents of the preceding generation were not able to escape the artistic infiltration of German architecture. This can only serve to complicate progress towards a purified architecture. It is generally considered that Germany will be in the forefront of future developments, but this is still by no means certain. It is easy to sneer at the Art Nouveau movement in France, or at the prominent Gobelins-mania in America, but such formal matters lose their importance when, as today, one looks first at the unspoiled skeleton which lies beneath. For it is sometimes possible to overlook the ludicrous decoration which has been stuck on—as in the case of *La Samaritaine*, the Parisian store designed by F. Jourdain—and it is possible to sense the constructive, uncorroded framework.

Certainly to limp in pursuit of France's artistic trends is grotesquely false, since the whole situation has now changed. Besides, there is a new movement in France (Le Corbusier, Lurçat, Leclerc,[1] etc.), which has the advantage that it does not have to fight so strongly as in Germany against an adjustment of taste, which is all the more dangerous. In the polarization between those forces which are clearly advancing and the unrepentant traditionalists, radical solutions are fundamentally easier, since in the great divide between action and reaction there does not always exist in the latter a readiness for external assimilation. In this way a movement stays almost safe from fashionable dilution. Until now France has not had such compromisers, who shave off their high roofs at the first gust, who suddenly squeeze the height of a window into a wide format, who provide the garden hedge with horizontal stakes and use shapes attached externally in the style of Frank Lloyd Wright.

Nothing is so crushing to a movement such as the new architecture—which must struggle out of the ground so as to be able to transmit to later generations a workable vocabulary—as facile imitation which, through mimicry, hides an unchanged inner core.

At its outset, the decorative art movement of 1900 firmly intensified the feeling for materials which had been lost. Now that movement has lost its impetus, for this feeling for materials has now been transformed into an almost voluptuous handling of material surfaces instead of the actual reality of the thing itself.

In architectural terms this means that in Germany and the cultural circles dependent on it, a tremendous virtuosity has been achieved in the handling of the surface of a wall. The favourite is a brick wall. Poelzig is merely the chief representative of a series of active architects, in whose hands the wall achieves almost the flexibility of fabric.

It is possible to turn one's heavy artillery against the historicist façades which are common in France and America today. Yet the refined manner of handling

[1] Probably a misprint in the original for Le Coeur. (ed.)

*Figure 3   Jacob Koerfer, Multi-storey block on the Hansaring,
Cologne, 1925*

*Figure 4   Wilhelm Kreis, Wilhelm-Marx-Haus office building,
Düsseldorf, 1924*

surfaces, which is common practice in Germany, is much
more dangerous and obstructive for new forms of architecture, since it allows quite false effects to insinuate themselves into new buildings.

This is most clearly seen in the problem which arises
with skyscrapers in Germany. Though this problem has
been all too frequently discussed in the newspapers, it
remains one of the 'monumental tasks' which has still to be
confronted properly. Not one of the skyscrapers already
built is the work of an architect who can guarantee a
solution to the problem. The only solution to have materi-
alized so far is a multi-storey house. That is still the best
example instance (see for instance Koerfer's problem with
skyscrapers on the Cologne Hansaring (**Fig. 3**)).

The skyscraper problem has reached this impasse through
the artistic infiltration which took control over it. The
skyscraper has particular features which make it unique:
a framework, concrete and iron. Its construction is an
uncluttered outer wall supported on an inner framework.

The cantilevering of the building, which achieves expression
through its outer surface, is intimately related to the new
role of architecture. If the skeleton of the skyscraper is not
properly apparent in a homogeneous form, then its purpose
is misunderstood.

Obviously some of the solutions in Germany do create a
voluntary or involuntary compromise with the expression
of the constructive central core. But still, as has sometimes
been the case, skyscrapers have been designed in which the
impact of the façade has been achieved by arranging the
layers of brick in a special manner and by using different
materials to bring out the contrast in these layers; this is
more dangerous than a skyscraper which an American
architect ornamented with a frieze of pillars like the Parthenon. Because of the vast dimensions of American
skyscraper building, the presence of the inner framework is
able to make itself felt despite any excrescence put on the
outside. The dilemma of German architecture is shown in
a skyscraper in Düsseldorf, where at one point the upward

thrust of the walls has been broken by a decorative moulding in filigree (**Fig. 4**). This, with its pointed zig-zag lines, is nothing more than an enormously enlarged sketch from the studio of some Expressionist artist. These latest rival trends seem even further from a solution than the ones which were already established.

It cannot be denied that through artistic infiltration the skyscraper problem has reached a dead end. It is discredited. Surely there is some architect who could handle the problem decisively; they managed to find Messel to build the Wertheim store, and Behrens for AEG's factories. Certainly such architects exist; it just happens that they are not given anything to build. They make sketches, provide material for their imitators who dilute their ideas, and are then themselves left out in the cold. Perhaps the situation will change. Until then, however, no one will build a skyscraper that can be said to have a 'character' of its own.

We have cited the skyscraper problem, since it shows the general level of today's production at its most blatant. One would have thought that Europe, which is constantly asserting its cultural superiority over America, would at least be capable of finding a suitable form of housing for its economic system. But 'artistic aestheticism' is not the way.

The second, and more important, problem which architecture faces and must soon solve, is in direct opposition to 'artistic aestheticism'. The price of individual housing units must be brought down through the mechanical production of components. Even though the now defunct Arts and Crafts Movement created first-class workers' housing estates, its significance lay in the creation of a cultivated middle-class environment. The rather over-cultivated feeling for the surface charm of materials linked up with *soigné* and somewhat effeminate feeling for plushy furnishings, which was a seductive element of the previous era's good interior design. How tempting it is to fall back into the plump soft cushions on an armchair on a thick carpet behind long drawn curtains and think: Life should resemble this sheltered island. But is it life? Is it our life?

The new architecture, which remains bleak to the point of coarseness, throws such feelings to the winds as it empties the rooms. Where the earlier movement contracted a secret union with luxury, the new architecture joins hands with the many, with those of limited means, with 99% of the populace. The bourgeois way of life with a variety of rooms is downright hostile to this new creative movement. New solutions to the housing problem show that one large room is all that is needed; any others are extraneous and should be limited as far as possible. This is the link between above and below, this is the link with tradition, with the large room in a peasant's house, with even more remote forms of dwellings. For the first time

in the history of building the creative desire of architecture is at one with the possibilities of the lower classes. Indeed, it is dependent on them.

Clearly from here onwards the move today is to build barrack-like complexes to house the masses. Public transport makes it possible to decentralize. But people want single units, single homes. What is generally possible today only for the well-off because of the craftsman methods of building, will become general practice. But simultaneously it has been recognized that the whole problem is one of economics. Without cheaper methods of housing through the industrialization of production methods, no solution will be found. One would almost like to say that the country which in ten years' time has the most factories producing houses, will be the country that leads in future architectural development.

Behind these advances, which today have become almost universal, hides at the same time the desire for a structure for the architecture of the future. This is a desire for standardization, for the best utilization of space, for exterior simplification of form. Forms with mechanically produced sections: doors, furniture, objects (not hand-made luxury individual articles) will become identical with today's demands for form.

While this aesthetic infiltration remains more-or-less limited at the moment to German cultural circles and their spheres of influence (its most durable monument must surely be the Stockholm City Hall[1]), the new forms of architecture are also taking root in Russia and America.

In every area today we are scattered to an almost inconceivable degree. It is striking however that it is precisely the new architectural creations that show a definite and homogeneous sense of purpose, which we can find otherwise only in dance forms and in the production of cars.

It is by no means clear which country will work out a decisive solution—perhaps they will work on it together. The German soil will doubtless be very fertile, only we must recognize exactly where we stand. As in 1900, at the start of the earlier movement, power was firmly entrenched with the pattern book architects, so now it lies almost totally with the representatives of 'artistic aestheticism'. (We will keep silent about the disastrous Arts and Crafts attitude which manifests itself today in the verdicts of juries.) Certainly the pattern book architects, who often broke away quite abruptly from the historical pattern, had less taste than is usual today, when forms are more heavily disguised, more remote and less controllable. But today we object precisely to this 'taste' which so easily lets architectural matters slip into dangerously fashionable realms. Now is the time to attempt once again to break away from superficial attraction and to re-establish architecture as a functional art.

[1] Ragnar Ostberg. Built 1909–23. (ed).

2.1

Walter Riezler was the editor of *Die Form*, the official journal of the Deutscher Werkbund, from 1927 (see also 1.4). The following extract from Riezler's article on the Weissenhof exhibition shows the difficulties the exhibition posed for the apologists of the new architecture.

2.2

This is an extract from an article by the Swiss architect Hans Schmidt (better known, perhaps, for his work in the partnership of Schmidt and Artaria). Schmidt's attitude towards the exhibition is basically sympathetic. He grasps the aesthetic qualities of Le Corbusier's houses particularly well and has many perceptive comments to make (for example his identification of the Arts and Crafts sources of many of the planning ideas). But, like Riezler, he also points out the problems the exhibition posed for its apologists. Most important of all, he counterbalances the exhibitors' claims for the major significance of the exhibition by pointing to the example of Bruno Taut's and Ernst May's proven and effective practice in low-cost modern housing.

2.3

Felix Schuster was an editor of the *Schwäbischer Heimatbuch*, a deeply traditionalist, regionalist magazine, committed to the preservation of Wurttemburgian traditions; he was also connected with a strong local chapel of the *Deutscher Bund für Heimatschutz*,[1] and was one of the abler critics of the International Style. These extracts are taken from an impressive collection published by Schuster in the *Schwäbischer Heimatbuch* of some one hundred pages of adverse criticism of the Weissenhof exhibition. Interestingly much of this criticism was drawn from the circle of the Werkbund itself, but it also includes statements by the influential Stuttgart architect Paul Bonatz (who was originally appointed architect-in-charge of the Weissenhof project, but was superseded by Mies van der Rohe) and Paul Schmitthenner, who was to become one of the fiercest opponents of the Modern Movement. One of the most interesting reactions comes from the *Deutscher Bund für Heimatschutz*; this should be compared with Schmitthenner's *Tradition and New Building* (*Form and Function*, no. 104). But the most damning criticism of the exhibition comes from Hermann Muthesius (writing in the year of his death) and it is an ironic adjunct to the Werkbund debate of 1914 that Muthesius should here be attacking Gropius.

2.1   The Dwelling House by Walter Riezler

A town council, guided by a committee of experts and as part of its normal building programme for this year, has asked leading architects, domestic and foreign, to build an estate. The aim is to demonstrate as clearly as possible the problems of building dwelling-houses which would take into account all the limiting and controlling economic and social factors, which have become so important in recent years. Moreover, these houses are to be sold or let, like any other newly-built house, after the exhibition closes. Thus instead of the individualistic patronage of princes we get

Figure 5   Weissenhof Siedlung, Stuttgart, 1927. Site plan

EXHIBITION   SITE

1   J. FRANK, VIENNA
2   J. OUD, ROTTERDAM
3   M. STAM, ROTTERDAM
4   LE CORBUSIER, GENEVA
5   P. BEHRENS, BERLIN
6   R. DÖCKER, STUTTGART
7   W. GROPIUS, DESSAU
8   L. HILBERSEIMER, BERLIN
9   MIES VAN DER ROHE, BERLIN
10 H. POELZIG, BERLIN
11 A. RADING, BRESLAU
12 H. SCHAROUN, BRESLAU
13 G. SCHNECK, STUTTGART
14 BRUNO TAUT, BERLIN
15 MAX TAUT, BERLIN

Figure 6   View of Weissenhof Siedlung

[1] German Society for the Preservation of the Homeland. (ed).

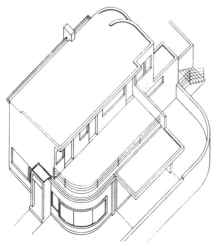

Figure 7   Hans Scharoun, House at Weissenhof Siedlung

Figure 8   Le Corbusier and P. Jeanneret, 2 houses, Weissenhof Siedlung

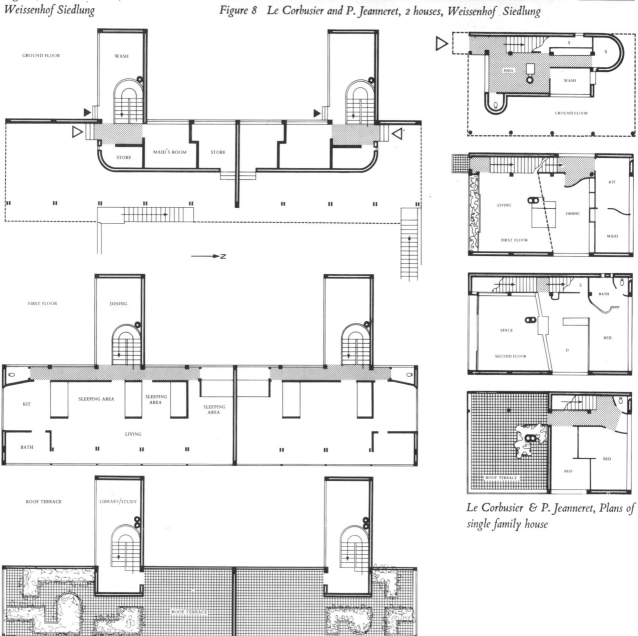

Le Corbusier & P. Jeanneret, Plans of single family house

Figure 9   Le Corbusier & P. Jeanneret, Plans of double house

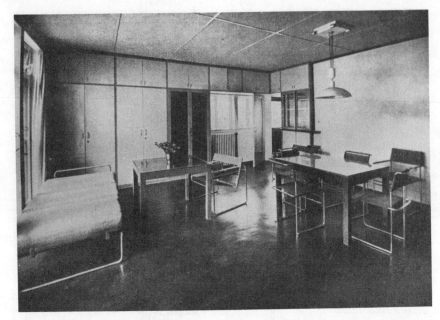

Figure 10 Weissenhof Siedlung, Interior of
house by Walter Gropius, furniture by
Marcel Breuer

Figure 11 Mart Stam, Row of three houses,
Weissenhof Siedlung, 1927

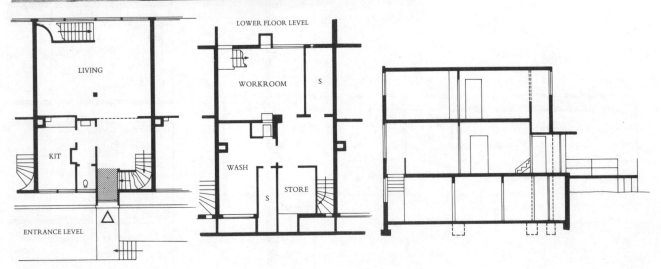

Figure 12 Mart Stam, Weissenhof Siedlung house

the collective work of the commune, instead of the particular and unique we get a striving after the universal, instead of the luxury of the artistic individual, rising above the spiritual and material needs of the masses, we get the social convictions for which at the moment only one problem exists: to provide model dwellings that will meet the requirements and the economic capacity of the masses. It would be surprising if this change in approach did not make itself visible. . . .

Even though it is not what those responsible for the project had in mind it must be said that what strikes one most in the whole exhibition is the superficial formal impact (**Fig. 6**). No one had expected to find that it was already possible today to get together more than a dozen architects from all parts of Europe to work together on a project, to give them complete freedom in the handling of all the exterior details (apart from the design of the roof) and still not detract from the unity of the general appearance. In this respect, at any rate, the bold experiment has succeeded —with the possible exception of the curious, certainly not unoriginal curved-romantic of Scharoun's small house (**Fig. 7**). We may leave it to the penetrating eye of particularly scrupulous and sensitive observers to pick out the national or racial differences still recognizable in a style so completely suited to the general concept of the 'International-European'. That an individualist form should have been followed so swiftly by an entirely non-personal form is something that grows out of the whole structure of the age we live in. And yet the first signs of it had already begun to appear even before the war, under the pressure of social conditions and especially in the building of garden cities and workers' estates. Perhaps the process of spontaneously natural design can be seen in action for the first time in the Weissenhof Siedlung. We can see that simplicity evolved directly out of the features of the terrain, the building materials, the economic factors, the ground plan. Clearly, this simplicity is the expression of an entirely appropriate, very impersonal feeling for form which is not at all motivated by notions of 'effect' or 'beauty'. . . .

. . . Both of Le Corbusier's houses call for, and deserve, special attention (**Figs. 8–9**). All visitors find them the most interesting features of the exhibition. While to the layman they are just objects of headshaking and laughter, to the radically-minded they represent the climax of the exhibition, the only really pure embodiment of the new 'attitude to building'. Certainly, as was only to be expected from Le Corbusier's books, they are evidence of a mature, bold and truly modern spirit. It is a brilliant idea to get the house off the ground by the use of all the building techniques available today and to combine with light, landscape and open space to form an absolutely new unity. It is extremely ingenious how, in the one house, every aspect of living is encompassed in the single, complex, very lively-shaped room which in turn spills out into the open

space outside through the huge window which fills the entire wall. It is even conceivable that, in a southern climate where the windows are open for most of the year and the splendid roof-garden can be used, a childless couple might pass their lives in such a house very easily and pleasantly. But it is entirely inconceivable that the house should be occupied in our climate by anyone but fanatical advocates of the 'new living'—who are even prepared to freeze if that will be the best offering they can make to the new idea. The huge room could certainly not be heated so that one could be able to use the lower part of the room in the cold climate we actually experience. Since the sleeping quarters are only separated from the other room by a half-wall, it will be impossible for the husband to sit with his friends over a cigar if his wife wants to sleep. And the wife won't enjoy having a bath when her husband has a visitor, for even the bath stands in the main room. None of the occupiers can be allowed to fall ill, for then the whole great room becomes a sick room and all life in the house comes to a halt. All these objections are so obvious that even the most superficial and favourably disposed observer can make them; that doesn't make them any less cogent. . . .

Hand in hand with the gradually and irresistibly increasing pressure of social obligations there goes a 'depersonalization' of our lives, which is bound to express itself in our homes and which has indeed already found appropriate expression in modern furniture. . . .

No one can avoid the impression of an absolutely 'clean' conception made by the rooms in Gropius's houses, designed as it were with an engineer's objectivity, worked out to the last detail (**Fig. 10**). And yet we don't know whether these rooms, with their objective coolness and impersonality (which suggested to so many visitors a comparison with an hotel or a nursing-home, or even a surgical clinic), may not go far beyond what the modern-minded man who has still to be convinced on these questions will put up with in his home. Perhaps the most fanatical followers of the new ideas in building will feel in a few years time the need to create a certain 'homeliness', which one might describe as an atmosphere of emotional warmth. Let us be clear about this: even the new man will still require emotional warmth, even when the process of depersonalization has gone still further! If in fact—and this is not yet proved—a house of that kind, fully standardized and mechanically constructed, turns out to be substantially cheaper than other kinds of house, then economic pressure may make many people order them. But they will certainly do all they can to get over this pressure as time passes and to achieve a genuine 'homeliness'. In parts of these dwellings it looks as if you were in a liner—not a present day liner but a liner of the future, for it will be a little time yet before the shipping lines stop fitting out their ships like palaces! In quite a lot of these modern houses you get the feeling that the room you are in has not been designed in the old sense, but that its shape has been forced on it by the structural features of the building. Sometimes the iron frame of the house appears suddenly in the living-room, naked and raw, uncovered and painted with oil paint. . . .

Often lack of resources or a serious concern to cut costs to the minimum and avoid anything 'superfluous' may be to blame. Often, too, one gets the feeling that the question of the actual execution of the work is approached with astonishing indifference. Most surprising in this respect are Le Corbusier's houses, despite the astonishing sensitivity of their design, in which the actual handling of materials and paintwork is of a meagre charmlessness which one hopes will never be exceeded. And even so they cost a packet! In these houses, and so often elsewhere too, we couldn't help thinking of the manufacture of a Ford car,

which is also knocked together as if it were too much trouble to worry about the proper finishing of each component and the proper use of materials. After a number of years of unparalleled success Ford has finally come to grief on this charmlessness—which is a highly gratifying proof that the feeling for form still persists intact—and it is unlikely that an architecture conceived on similar lines would achieve the same transient success. For even if that famous expression 'living-machine' is anything more than a clever phrase, it must be conceded that we shall demand rather more of this machine than that it should continue to function without going wrong. And think what a high level of loving performance we expect from a car today! It is indeed true that more care and love are lavished on the equipment and finish of a mail-van than can be seen in many of the Stuttgart houses.

2.2   The Housing Exhibition, Stuttgart by Hans Schmidt

The reader who has followed the description of this unusual layout[1] will wonder how such a house can be lived in (**Fig. 9**). And the answer is that a new kind of living is required. Its author has intentionally designed it in such a way that it cannot be inhabited in the usual bourgeois manner. To have the living room, dining room, stairs, study, bedroom, bath and bidet gathered within four walls, as it were, without any insulation against noise and odours, hardly expresses the current concept of gracious living. Will we in the future have to disregard noise and smells for the sake of an interesting use of space, just as with Schinkel, Semper and Poelaert one must overlook all kinds of discomforts for the sake of a monumental appearance? Will this uninterrupted flow of space from one room to the next impose its own pattern on the very life we lead? Or is it merely, as we suspect it is, a harmless exaggeration, an extension of the life style of the artist's studio, where an impromptu dinner is spread on a rickety table close to the artist's easel, where the clatter of crockery and the tinkling of the piano intrude agreeably on the writer's thoughts as he sits at his desk, where the bed stands ready for models and lady friends alike, with bath and bidet conveniently at hand? Or is our question too serious? Are we, perhaps, being too pedantic? Should we be content to admit that if we came across this house in Castagnola or Ospedaletti, we would eagerly rent it for a couple of months? But if you have written a book on the new architecture, boldly crossing out the past, one cannot get away with such trivial judgements.

And so we return to this house, in which almost unconsciously we find ourselves trying to get some idea of the League of Nations building as Le Corbusier planned it. We

forget all considerations of how and where, of cupboards and desks and bathrooms and beds. Instead we follow the lines, the values, the interplay of broad and narrow, low and high, of enclosing walls and liberating spaces. We walk round the house, delighting in the play of wall and window, of heavy mass and airy lightness. And step by step, room by room, we gain an ever increasing sense of a new kind of beauty. Not that the interior decoration and fittings seem particularly appealing. The colours are muddy, almost dirty—overtones of black pudding and graphite—the fittings are skimped and careless (at least they were in the middle of August when we visited the house). There is no beautiful setting of trees and shrubs to enhance the exterior. No, the entire effect comes from its own essential character, even though its finish is distinctly frugal by Swiss standards. The building has a very special kind of charm, and though we may doubt whether it affords what one might call gracious living, there can be no doubt that a new way of living, a new feeling for life pervades this remarkable structure. . . .

The first thing which strikes the Swiss observer is the finish of the buildings, which is careless, not to say sloppy, by any standards. Even taking into account the fact that they are built for exhibition purposes, they are nevertheless permanent buildings, the prototypes of buildings to be reproduced many hundreds of times. Even worse than the deplorable finish are the features which even with the best possible finish could not be cleanly executed or would not stand up to the rigours of daily use. The houses have no plinth at the base: instead the painted finish of the exterior walls goes straight down to the pavement or the earth of the adjoining flowerbeds. The windows, which are particularly

[1] Of Le Corbusier and Jeanneret's Single House. (ed.)

large, have no sills; the frequently used parapets on the walls have no form of capping, and so on. The hand rails on the terraces and balconies sacrifice safety to aesthetics, being made of widely-spaced horizontal iron bars. In the interests of the coming generation we can only hope that the first child to lose its life because of this ill-considered arrangement is the child of one of these architects. . . .

It is rather more difficult to excuse the planning of the spaces, indeed the whole layout of the houses. For it is surely here if anywhere that the new art which does not wish to be an art must show the progress it has made and convince the beholder of its effectiveness. All of the projects have clearly been spawned from the desire to create as large a space within these small houses as possible. The desire is comprehensible both in the architect, who wishes to show off his skills, and in the owner, who would like to have something decent in return for his hard-earned cash. As a result we have a series of endless combinations: dining room–living room–hall; study–living room–stairwell, and so on. Very nice to look at, but completely unusable. The houses are not made for a single old lady with her cats and a canary, but for an average sized family. Now the size of the average Central European family has been quoted for the past six years as 4.5 persons, that is two parents and two to three children. It seems natural enough to suppose that the inhabitants will include children, but one is horrified on inspecting the houses to discover that there is nowhere where one would be able to write a postcard in peace and quiet. The most blatant example of this is in the small houses designed by Mart Stam (**Figs. 11-12**). Here we find that on the ground floor the main living area is irrevocably linked with the working area on one side, and the stair-well is linked to the study on the other. Both of these units can be linked by opening a folding wall partition, and the space can be extended even further by opening up the wall of the bathroom. Obviously the small size of the houses, imposed by the conditions of the exhibition, imposes a natural limit on the amount of space which can be made available by combining the functions of different rooms. But what could be done was not enough, and so the architects had recourse to movable partitions: sliding walls, folding walls, sliding

glass doors, leather screens (even the double doors which we abandoned two decades ago), with all their attendant disadvantages: lack of sound insulation, lack of flat surfaces to stand things against, the discomfort of temporary furniture arrangements, and so on. The movable wall is a veritable trademark of the exhibition houses, and this again we can hardly regard as a sign of progress. On the contrary, we are most painfully reminded of the staircase halls and the suites of rooms inter-connected by double doors which were a feature of the 1890s.

One turns angrily away from these things—all the more so because these are not the harmless doodles of week-end painters, but the work of architects who consider themselves the 'leading' exponents of their art and who are prepared to step forward and fiercely defend their views.

How can one explain such things to the critical layman, as he wanders through the exhibition with a mocking and superior air? One would like to be able to have a brotherly word with such people, and tell them that all these follies would appear insignificant if they would only confine their attention to this or that important detail. But it is impossible.

The 'fifteen most celebrated architects' have, with few exceptions, made it extremely difficult for any friend of their youthful art to stand up in favour of the new way of living, for the new, objective, perfected, rational science of tectonics.

Fortunately, among the fragments on the 'Experimental Site', one project does stand out as a witness to the new spirit, and merits our serious attention. Councillor May, of the Frankfurt housing department, has erected one of his terrace houses there—in the improbably short time of five days, if our information is correct. It is constructed of large pre-fabricated concrete panels with Visitini reinforced floor slabs and, thankfully, a solid rough-cast plinth. The ground floor is finished and even furnished, while the upper floor is left unplastered so that the technically minded can find out for themselves all about the much discussed rationalization of construction methods and the possibilities of mass production. . . .

2.3   **Heimatschutz and New Building** by Felix Schuster

Professor Wetzel, of the Technische Hochschule, Stuttgart

A conglomerate of bare cubes, it sticks out like a sore thumb in the gentle, supple lines of the Sutttgart landscape. Memories of travel are awakened. Not of the fairy-tale cubic cities of the South—all that gives those their magic is missing here: the harshness of the structures, of the

vegetation, of the scenery, the rocks, the sea, above all the sun of the South, the glare of light that melts everything together. Here we get vivid memories of travel in America, of that country in the settlement phase of the great migration. Everything there is still improvised. Nothing has grown up out of the climate, out of the soil. Everything looks borrowed, accidental, foreign. And the same with the Weissenhof estate. It is no ornament to the Stuttgart scene. There is none of the restful, satisfying feeling of having grown up out of the soil, that infallible criterion for sound building creation at all times and in all countries. And what is the secret of everything really genuine? The architect's honest attempt to take account of the natural potential and amenities of the locality's special character and to take full advantage of them in a sensible and economical design. . . .

Professor Paul Bonatz, of the Technische Hochschule, Stuttgart, writing in the Schwäbische Merkur

A heap of stark cubes, uncomfortably crowded, pushes up the slope in a series of horizontal terraces, looking more like a suburb of Jerusalem than dwellings for Stuttgart. As a concession to the outward appearance the building elements are continually switched around with one another, so that each one looks at the back walls of the man in front a short distance away. . . .

Professor Paul Schmitthenner, of the Technische Hochschule, Stuttgart, writing in the Suddeutsche Zeitung

Today we have reached the point where the forces emerging from those various sources are becoming active. A generation of architects is emerging which thinks and builds practically, technically and economically instead of decorating formalistically.

And just as we reach this point, the beginning of reason in architecture, there starts up a sort of literary debate about the living-machine, about colour in building, about flat and pitched roofs. We are on the point of getting a prescription for the international style of the 20th Century.

The best kind of architects, the rationalists, know that you can build a good house with or without a roof. They even know that a house without a roof is nothing new. They choose to use one or the other (with good reason) according to the actual purpose of the project. For instance, they would build a small house with a pitched roof because the extra room in the roof is essential for keeping the house tidy and also for health; if they build with a flat roof as a concession to form they do not provide the extra space, and thus this becomes an uneconomical form. In the right place they can even build quite decently without roofs (see the main railway station in Stuttgart).[1] They know that a good building can be given a certain character with colour, but they know too that colour is not the essential point and that the best paint won't turn a bad house into a good one. They know that what is beautiful is what is right in its place. They know too that the requirements, for instance, for a flying-machine will be the same the world over, even in darkest Africa. The living-machine, on the contrary, is just a slogan to them; their houses are built on the ground. They know that there is an element of the international in

building—the eternally valid laws that determine the structure from the materials and form from the structure; hence buildings must be different in different parts of the world. But, finally, they know, being not merely craftsmen and technicians but also artists, that there are things that go beyond the 'ratio' without necessarily excluding reason, that there are irrational things that show up in their work, even as a rate. There are skilful architects throughout the world who, because they are architects, look on one another's work with respect. . . .

Fritz Stahl, the art critic, writing in Berliner Tageblatt

The exhibition . . . a deliberate propaganda exercise for a certain point of view, for a small clique. There is no need to deny or even underestimate the significance of this group, but it is by no means as great as its spokesmen, and the latest speeches to the listening artists and critics, make out.

'The dwelling-house'—says this exhibition—'only we moderns know anything about it, a dozen of us in Germany and two or three abroad.' Function and style are all muddled up. The fact that everywhere you look there are houses and estates being built, and homes furnished, which do not

Figure 13   Poster for the Werkbund Exhibition 'Die Wohnung', 1927

[1] By Paul Bonatz and F. E. Scholer; built 1911–14 and 1919–27. (ed.)

follow the new trends and yet fulfil all the practical needs just as well as they do, is simply ignored by them. I can't put it more politely than that. And those who produce these houses still put up with this fiction. And perhaps, though they are also organized now, they will even put up with that incredible poster, which goes well beyond the widest bounds of permissible propaganda—for it is really nothing but propaganda (**Fig. 13**). A thick, red cross strikes out (what is presented to the public as) the old style dwelling which these brilliant newcomers have now eliminated. And what kind of dwelling is it? Dark, dreary, with over-elaborate furniture, the dwelling-house of 1900. Oh, they still exist here and there, left over, some indeed newly built by the newly rich, whose ideals come from the same period. But anyone who claims that it is still valid to attack this dwelling-house is telling a barefaced lie. That kind of house was got rid of 20 years ago. The dwelling of today looks quite different. But of course, if you had illustrated a room by Bertsch, Pankok, Riemerschmid—I could name many, many more, but those three are honorary members of the Werkbund—if, I say, you had illustrated such a room, there would have been some danger that the public would have decided in favour of it and against the most modern, and that would never have done.

The obstinate puritanism of the new movement is an error which, like the errors of the latest aesthetic, benefits only those who have no talent. Austerity is a good thing, but it is meaningless by itself. A structure is no more a finished work than a skeleton is a body. There, in a nutshell, is the criticism of the modern movement.

In criticizing these houses we should always begin from a thoroughly spiritual standpoint. For only unheard-of practical advantages could justify the abandonment of the old form of house, could justify the admitted formlessness of the new houses; their greater cheapness is just not enough on its own.

And now we must look just a bit further. Is the general problem of the dwelling-house really no more than a practical and economic problem? And can it be solved internationally, as the supporters of the new architecture believe and as Councillor Bruckmann so astonishingly declared? No, a thousand times no. All that is not modern at all; it is left over from yesterday, from that period of materialism which is otherwise so heartily despised by this generation. We must admit that there is a shortage of homes, and that we must make do with the simplest and most quickly built. But there is a great difference between recognizing this need and deducing a dogma from it. For the German, at any rate, the home is, and will surely remain, an emotional matter. And if it can be shown that every one, apart from those few who have been converted, is still unenthusiastic about these new houses and homes, then it can only be professional obstinacy to disregard it. It will show a total disregard of the very people

who are told on special occasions that they are to be the true representatives of culture. A deeper and truer instinct demands that the new houses to be put up by this generation should conform to the old tradition of house-building. This tradition is the creation of the mass of the people of all generations, against which the individual has only a limited right. If anyone does not see that, then he has no right to complain about the historicizing architects of the nineteenth century, whose mistakes and faults lay in their deliberate readiness to destroy tradition. Tradition can only be changed gradually; in the nineteenth century, the traditions which had evolved over the years were sabotaged. In the last decades before the war we reached back beyond those bad times to the good tradition. And is this development, which should, and could, gradually restore coherence, now to be broken again? Home, and homeliness—these words, which embody the essence of the dwelling-house, are always associated with the old forms.

One of the distinctive features of the new style is the omission of the roof. There has been a strong reaction against this everywhere. Supporters of the style say: 'We don't need it any more.' (They also say: 'We can economize on it.' More of that later!) And they lay the flat top out as a roof-garden, which also serves the purpose of misleading the opposition. It can only serve that purpose for aesthetes. Everyone else knows that the roof is not only ostensibly an indispensable protection from rain, but also a room, a utility room, a lumber-room, and as such becomes more indispensable the smaller the house. The roof-garden, so seldom usable in our flats, is absolutely superfluous on a house in a garden suburb. Condemned to be left to go to waste by the inconvenience of climbing the stairs up to it, it is no substitute. It is an idea for the big city.

The German house, modified to meet the requirements of the new generation: that is what we should be looking for if the housing problem is to be regarded as a matter for the people and not just for architects.

Hermann Muthesius, 'The controversy about the shape of the roof', Baukunst und Bauhandwerk, 1927, no. 2

... Anyone who bothers to go into the matter in depth will perceive that what motivates the spirits of this group of architects today is the 'new form'. The new form influences it so powerfully that all other considerations are forced into the background. The new form has so tyrannical an effect on its disciples that both the other *leitmotif*—especially that one so strongly emphasized everywhere—rationalization—are submerged, almost crushed. It is the new form that calls for the flat roofs and puts up with the manifold disadvantages, still at present unforeseen, which go with it. It is the new form that gives us the tremendous over-lighting of the living-rooms, because it dictates to its disciples the absolute need to run unbroken lines of windows all round the house. It is the new form that leaves the outer walls defenceless against the weather, from which in the past, our climate being what it is, they had generally been protected by a projecting roof. All these are things that have nothing at all to do with rationalization or economy or structural requirements. It is simply a question of form. The ideal is to create cubic blocks. Simple cubes are shoved up against one another and combined in a more or less well-assembled composition, while anything other than cubic blocks is hardly even considered. What they don't notice is that this concentration on individual cubic blocks often takes them back to those crazily grouped building forms that were common as the German 'villa' 30 years ago, and that, meanwhile, the carefully achieved compactness of the house has got lost. For in general, though they would never admit it, the new architects are as strongly biased in favour of external formal motifs as were the architects of the old style. In just this search for composition that is now coming to the fore we shall later find the cause of the buildings' short life, and this is where, on practical grounds, we must put our first big question-mark. After a few years of the soaking unavoidable in our climate the buildings will presumably look like ruins, unless extraordinarily expensive repairs are constantly carried out to eliminate the damage from weathering and to maintain a clean appearance.

It would be easy, and it is certainly tempting, to pick out the practical faults and shortcomings that come to light in the houses in the exhibition. The estate positively teems with them. The experienced practitioner often gets the feeling that he is looking at the work of amateurs. . . .

Hermann Muthesius, writing in Wasmuths Monatshefte, 1927, no. 2

. . . But what is the object of all this justification of correct construction, functionalism, economy? What is the point of this defence of the flat roof, now an essential feature of the new architecture, on the grounds of its saving in costs? The essence of the cubist building style has nothing to do with reality.

Materials and the construction must serve as tools for the will to form which lives in human heads; not the other way round. Reinforced concrete cannot of itself create a new style. On the contrary, it only leads one astray into the creation of pure superficialities, as projecting cantilevered slabs everywhere bear witness. In the light of these monstrosities, these windows that are always carried round the corners, these flat roofs behind parapets, so unsuitable in our climate, this exaggerated use of great glass surfaces, one can only speak of a constructional romanticism, no less an extravagance than

was the *Jugendstil* with its fantastic traceries. Are there not strong echoes here of the endlessly changing fashions in clothes? Doesn't the comparison suggest itself immediately?

. . . Even if the fashion is a good one, we must still be quite clear that the latest 'new architecture', propagated with such keenness, is in fact nothing but a temporary style which will pass away with changing fashion. The features of the style which we can pick out in the works of the prophets of the new architecture today remind us only too strongly of the happily buried *Jugendstil* of 20 years ago. . . .

Professor Dr Högg, of the Technische Hochschule, Dresden

The Weissenhof estate in Stuttgart gives us a gratifying foretaste of how the new, the 'coming' architecture is meant to look, when it gives us 'living-machines' instead of the houses we have been used to: amateur games with technical innovations, mechanizations influenced by America with a touch of the Wild West, Bolshevistic egalitarianism, the promotion of untried substitute building materials on the grounds of efficiency, the absurd borrowing of building forms from industry, attempts to harmonize with the customs and outlook of people brought up differently and living under different skies—it is all up there in the Weissenhof estate, stirred up into a pretty tasteless brew. And, in spite of all the boastful words, it gives an impression of great confusion and impotence. There are a few very good and practical rooms that look as if they came from workshops in Dresden or Munich, but they do little to alter the overall effect.

There are serious people among us who think it their business to encourage such efforts, people who believe that something new will crystallize out of the hotch-potch of houses stuck up on piles, oriental rooflessness, disembodied glass architecture, inartistic iconoclasm and bogus socialism. Today, it is a sign of collapse that everything be new, different from before. Whether what is new is necessarily also better than the old thing it elbows aside is a question hardly ever considered. . . .

Draft of a paper prepared by the Deutscher Bund für Heimatschutz presenting guidelines for contemporary housing

The *Deutscher Bund für Heimatschutz* has, from the start, directed its activities particularly towards preservation and development of the traditional rural and urban building styles and to the struggle against muddle and false romanticism. Examples of the old building styles are vanishing faster than ever both in towns and in the country. It is seldom that anything of equal worth takes their place. The task is, moreover, made more difficult by all the modern problems, new styles of building, new residential and economic problems, the modern expansion of traffic, the ready availability of materials other than local building materials, and in many architectural circles an irrelevant hankering after novelty.

The DBH regards the production of buildings that betray every tradition as a serious danger to German culture. It does not however completely reject good new ideas—those which amount to something more than a passing fashion or a false internationalizing. It looks on tradition not as the objective of the art of building but as a starting-point for sound, practical progress. Native building culture is thus not the setting-up of permanently valid formal ideals, but active co-operation in the proper shaping of our environment by aid to a genuine conception of building. On these grounds it recognizes the following guidelines:

1   In dwelling-houses and shops no less than in engineering structures (factories and commercial buildings), economic considerations are paramount. They should be of a typical character, either following established local practices and well-tried building styles or based on experiments and conclusions worked out anew with the greatest care for new kinds of problems.

2   Good house-building and good engineering building, good craftsmanship and good manufacture are in no way opposed to each other. But there is one essential difference between them. Dwelling-houses (shops stand rather in between) have to meet essentially different requirements, which spring from landscape and scenery, climate, style of living and local characteristics. To aim at an international style would thus amount to a destruction of national values. For engineering structures, which in general are always concerned with similar problems, an internationally uniform style can well be allowed to develop.

3   Hence the DBH recognizes the vernacular building style as a starting-point for good new ideas.

4   An engineering building need not conflict with its surroundings if its designer takes those surroundings into account from the start in his choice of materials, construction, outline, scale and colour, and designs the building with consideration and understanding.

5   In the building of dwelling-houses and agricultural buildings the DBH also calls for the abandonment of building styles that are no longer appropriate. Of course today's advancing standardization and rationalization must take proper account of certain new requirements of living, of agriculture, of safety in operation and in case of fire, of the greater ease with which materials can be transported to sites, etc.

6   The standards committee of German industry has accepted the authoritative co-operation of the DBH in the drawing up of basic lines for the standardization of small house building. But it cannot be too strongly emphasized that rationalization and 'new building' are not synonymous. Originality is not a monopoly of the latest building form; it is possible, and indeed, in so far as it is economically advantageous, is even necessary to a great extent in every building form. In fact it is to be found in wide measure in even the oldest indigenous building styles. Only in the age of vulgarity and tastelessness, which the DBH has done most to combat, has it been lost.

7   The mass-produced, pre-fabricated dwelling-house does not by any means rule out the decent house-design that should always be the aim.

8   The flat roof cannot be regarded as the roof of the future for Germany. The flat roof will still appear as a disturbing foreign body in built-up areas whose appearance is dependent on well-designed pitched roofs, especially in sloping areas that give a view over the roofs, apart from some exceptions and deliberately planned single examples. For the rest the DBH has nothing against roof terraces and roof gardens, nor against flat roofs on buildings in large towns and so forth—after all, these are nothing new.

9   In every good building it is not only a matter of meeting the economic, technical, constructional requirements; the surroundings must also be taken into account. Only thus can the work take harmonious shape. Not only in buildings that follow established national styles but also in those whose conception is modern in aim and style, the harmony of building and landscape sought after by the DBH will be achieved so long as false modishness, false romanticism, and all sorts of muddle and incompetence are avoided. The new architecture will succeed through its own good qualities and, by remaining objective, will drive out bogus romanticism.

Part 3 Architecture and Town Planning in the USSR

3.1 and 3.2

These two items should be read in sequence. The VOPRA *Declaration* consists of an attack on other contemporary architectural tendencies, focusing on the formalist and idealist concerns of OSA, and going on to a statement of Vopra's own position. OSA's *VOPRA and OSA* is a counterblast refuting VOPRA's interpretation of the attitudes and practices of OSA.

3.3 and 3.4

These two articles on architecture and town planning in the USSR are probably the major articles of the period in English on these subjects. Although Lubetkin left the USSR in 1922 and worked in Western Europe through the rest of the decade (coming to England only in the early thirties) he kept closely in touch with developments in his native country. These articles are of interest not only because the breadth and factual accuracy of Lubetkin's survey is considerably greater than that of most other contemporary West European commentators but also because of their socio-political angle. Lubetkin not only establishes the general ideological and historical framework of the 'new architecture' in the USSR but he also tackles the various and sometimes conflicting ideological nuances of the different architectural groups (whose ideological differences are well illustrated in 3.1 and 3.2).

3.1 Declaration by VOPRA (Union of Proletarian Architects)

Throughout the periods when our society was divided by class, architecture served the interests of the ruling classes. Responding in the first place to utilitarian demands and conditioned more than any other art form by the economics and technology of the given era, it expressed the psychology of the ruling classes.

Architecture during the period of capitalism is characterized by ornamentalism, and a departure into self-indulgent formalism and preoccupation with technique. Architecture in the USSR under the conditions of the proletarian revolution and the building of socialism, is nevertheless still in the mainstream of bourgeois art—constructivism, formalism and especially eclecticism are the dominant tendencies in the architecture of our times. These tendencies, identical with such tendencies in the capitalist West, have been modified by and adapted to our conditions; influenced by our reality, they remain in their essence alien to it.

At the same time proletarian architecture is growing on the economic foundations of the transitional period. It is being built on the basis of a planned economy and an advanced technology and is dedicated to the resolution of those problems presented during the process of building a new socialist society.

The social role of architecture acquires a special significance in the hands of the proletariat. Proletarian architecture is not a weapon of enslavement and domination, not a passive, contemplative art, but an active art, which must become a means for the liberation of the masses, a powerful lever in the building of socialism and a new collectivist way of life, organizing the psyche and actively educating the will and feeling of the masses towards the struggle for communism.

We reject eclecticist architecture and the method of the eclectics, who mechanically copy the old architecture, and blindly follow classical canons and schemata. Eclecticism is especially prominent in the architecture of the era of industrial and trade capital. Under the anarchy of an economic system of production based on private ownership and competition, architecture, bearing all the marks of this economic system, is increasingly converted into a commodity. Eclecticism in the present day is reactionary in its attraction to outdated methods of construction, in its disregard for the properties of contemporary materials, constructions and building production methods, and in its opposition to the achievements of industrial technology. It is reactionary in its attraction to petty-bourgeois forms of life, it inhibits the burgeoning of a new, collectivistic way of life, it is reactionary and inimical to us ideologically with its resurrection of forms which belong to classes alien to us.

We reject formalism in architecture, which appeared in the period of the development of industrial capitalism, when in connection with the powerful development of industrial technology, a gap was revealed between ornamental forms (decoration 'in styles') and new constructions and materials (reinforced concrete, glass, etc.). The architects of this tendency reject eclecticism, but at the same time it is beyond their powers to harmonize their ideas with the investigations and the technology of the new age; they have departed into an abstract search for a 'new' architectural form. Formalism has appeared as a result of the clash of the psycho-ideology and habits of the petty-bourgeois intelligentsia with the monopolistic tendencies of the era of financial capital.

We reject formalism, which obtains abstract architectural forms exclusively by laboratory methods, which squeezes the content of a building into these preconceived forms, which disregards constructions, materials and the significance of technology in architecture. We reject formalism, which under our present conditions has lost contact with the social utilitarian problems put forward by the proletariat.

We reject particularly the groundless dreaming and utopianism of formalist architects in the sphere of the resolution of present-day social-existential problems, and the idealistic nature of their theories and working methods.

We recognize the positive historical role played by constructivism (and also formalism) in the process of the defeat of eclecticism and technological conservatism, in the advancement of the problems of the rationalization, mechanization and standardization of construction in its propaganda for industrial technology, and so on. But at the same time, we note that although constructivism produced positive results under Soviet conditions with its criticism of the eclectics, and of pre-industrial forms of architecture, it was, however, unable in its own theory and practice to go further than a leftist phrase and a 'revolutionary' posture.

We reject constructivism, which arose on the basis of financial capital. This form of architecture was defined by the basic features of monopolistic capital, the aspiration towards capitalist planning, rationalization and heavy industrialization. Constructivism which moved towards the negation of art and its replacement by technology and engineering, represented the architectural reflection of the psycho-ideology of big business elements in the bourgeoisie, an indication of which (psychology) was given by the technical intelligentsia's characteristic machine fetishism, anti-psychologism and vulgar materialism.

We reject the constructivism of the present day with its disregard for artistic content and for means of artistic effect. We repudiate constructivism with its abstract inventions, its blind imitation of Western technique, and mechanical transposition of that technique on to our own soil without consideration for local conditions, real possibilities, availability of materials and economic factors; and with its excessive anticipation in the resolution of social-existential problems. We repudiate constructivism, which on the one hand lapses into an aesthetic relish for constructions, and the imitation of the external forms of industrial technology, and on the other departs into a self-indulgent preoccupation with technique, and machine fetishism. We reject both constructivist theory, built on vulgar materialism, and the constructivists' formal, technical functionalism, as a method of work and of architectural analysis.

We regard as irrelevant and nihilistic the position of the constructivists who deny art any part in the design of an architectural organism. We consider that under our present conditions, architecture has a leading part to play in relation to the other forms of three-dimensional art,

and we particularly stress the need to find ways to use, in the process of architectural design, all forms of art, aiming towards their organic unity.

We reject any attempt to gloss over the class role of architecture, and to foist on to the proletariat a classless architecture, whose realization is only possible under the conditions of a communist society. In our view, during the period of the dictatorship of the proletariat, and the struggle for the socialist reconstruction of the world, architecture should have class forms and content, and should serve the concrete requirements of the proletariat in its role as leader of the workers and oppressed of the whole world; the architecture of this period must devote all its resources to the class struggle, on the side of the fighting proletariat.

We consider that proletarian architecture should be developed on the basis of the application of the method of dialectical materialism in its theory and practice.

We are in favour of an architecture with a modern scientific and technological foundation. In this period of industrialization and the building of socialism, architecture is unthinkable to us without the attainment of a higher level of technique, without the mastery of improved working methods.

In rejecting both conservatism and utopian dreaming, from which they would not result, we are in favour of the maximum progress in the realm of science and technology, a radical reorganization of construction methods, mechanization, standardization, etc.; the critical class-orientated utilization of all the achievements of European and American technology from the point of view of real expediency under our material conditions and within the range of real possibilities.

As a result of the basic problems of our economy, we must direct science and technology towards the maximum rationalization and reduction in the cost of our building. For us, questions of economy and rationalization are fundamental to our work.

The class interests of the proletariat under the conditions of the cultural and existential revolution have posed new problems for architects, and are making architecture one of the most important weapons in the struggle for a collectivist way of life and for cultural reconstruction.

The basic tendencies in our way of life are the movement towards collectivization in all spheres of life, the creation of vital, rational and cheerful conditions for communal living, work and leisure. A whole series of practical problems stands before the architect: the building not of residences of the smallholding sort, but of extended, communal types of dwelling; the building of factories, collective and state farms, as places where work is rationally organized in a healthy environment; the building of clubs for the intelligent use of leisure and for the education of the masses in the spirit of communism, rest homes, schools, crèches, etc. All these problems should be resolved not only from the standpoint of utilitarian, technical expediency (practicalism) and not only from the point of view of the narrow, local functions of a building (constructivism) but also, and principally, from the point of view of the broad social significance of a building.

We are in favour of a realistic stock-taking of the concrete requirements of our new way of life, for the maximum attention to its details, and for the complete satisfaction of all the demands of the mass consumer of architecture, for the active and not passive satisfaction of those demands: the architect should be a propagandist, an agitator, an organizer of new forms of work and living: neither cutting himself off from reality nor settling for a thing once it has been achieved, he should be in the vanguard of the proletarian movement.

All these everyday tasks of architecture: the house, the club the factory, etc.—are not only productive, existential, constructional and technical problems but also artistic problems, problems of the effect of architectural methods on man's emotional world, on his psyche.

We reject the tendency towards emptiness (aimlessness) the striving towards the organization of sensations only (formalism) and of feelings of admiration for 'beauty' (eclecticism and constructivism). We are in favour of proletarian art, whose content expresses the profoundest intentions and aspirations of the working class and embraces the whole sphere of sensations, the entire complex of man's emotions and thoughts.

We are in favour of a proletarian, class-based architecture, an art which is a constructional and formal whole, a cheerful art organized by the will of the masses towards struggle and work. We are against the separation of form from content and form from construction—we are for their organic unity. For us, form is not a canon or an abstract symbol and construction is not an aim in itself; they are the means for the expression of concrete content. The architect should possess a single expertise in formal composition and construction. We are in favour of mastering the architecture of the past, and studying it in accordance with the method of Marxist analysis, not for the purpose of imitation and mechanical copying (eclecticism) but for the critical use of a proletarian architecture. We are in favour of the use and application to architectural work of all the accomplishments of modern science concerning form, colour, etc.

Accordingly, our architectural method is based on a comprehensive view of the object of architecture, on an inventory of the greatest quantity of the elements which define architecture, with their mutual connections, contradictions, and effects on one another (socio-economic emotional and ideological, constructional and technical, and so on). We are against the isolated resolution of particular problems in the development of architecture. We are in favour of the organic resolution of all problems as a whole, going from the general to the particular and from the particular to the general, from the analysis of parts to a synthetic generalization corresponding to the unity of the whole. We are in favour of deriving the resolution of all our architectural problems from our general economic tasks, from present-day projects and future aspirations, from a comprehensive account of specific local conditions.

In each concrete task, we concentrate attention on the chief moments dictated for architecture as a whole at a given time by the class interests of the proletariat.

We are in favour of the method of dialectical materialism in design and research work.

Proletarian architecture must not be the preserve of a narrow circle of specialists, but must become the property of the millions, and develop under their participation, control and evaluation. The path of proletarian architecture, from 'art for the masses' towards 'the art of the masses' is not the path of a cloistered, exclusive caste of academics, but the path of an active worker in society and fighter for the cause of the working class.

Founder members of VOPRA: *Alabyan, Baburov, Deryabin, Fayfel', Ivanov, Kozelkov, Kochar, Krestin, Kryukov, Kunovsky, Mazmanyan, Matsa, Mikhaylov, Mordvinov, Polyakov, Simbirtsev, Solodovnik, Terekhin, Vlasov, Zapletin, Zaslavsky, Zil'berg*

3.2 F. Yalovkin, OSA (Association of Contemporary Architects) Vopra and OSA

'Study and master bourgeois culture, don't let yourself be deceived by fairy-tales about how proletarian culture had to some degree already grown up, however it may have matured.

'The birth of proletarian culture must be thought of dialectically. The essence of this process lies in the assimilation by millions of people of the achievements of bourgeois culture under the conditions of the Soviet State.'
Lenin.

The starting-point of the repudiation of constructivism in the VOPRA declaration is: 'we reject constructivism, which has arisen on the basis of financial capital'. If we repudiate everything that has arisen on the basis of financial capital, then evidently we should reject the building of tractors and aeroplanes, and the whole of the advanced technology of the era of financial capital which the USSR has borrowed from the West.

Before rejecting our own, Soviet, constructivism, it must be proved that it really does constitute one of those moribund elements of the capitalist order against which we are fighting, as opposed to those elements, which, originating and developing within capitalism as its dialectical opposite, represent the elements of socialist organization. For example, we reject capitalist exploitation, but preserve for future society the collective principle of the organization of production, created by capitalism.

VOPRA did not make this point clear in its wholesale repudiation of constructivism. Obviously not everyone finds dialectics easy.

We think that constructivism—for the time being—is the only true way of developing our architecture, because, without dismissing what there is in the West (Corbusier, Gropius, etc.), it considers as the basis of its work the formulation and resolution of the problems presented by Soviet reality, i.e. it poses questions about social types in present-day architecture (i.e. it does not limit itself to the mere transposition of Western architecture on to our own soil, as our comrades from VOPRA would think).

Further on, the declaration considers as 'irrelevant and nihilistic the position of the constructivists, who deny art any part in the design of an architectural organism'. In the first place, the constructivists have never made a wholesale repudiation of any rôle for art. They have always investigated what sort of rôle it has in the construction of architectural form, but if in the majority of cases this rôle has appeared not positive but negative, it still cannot be inferred that in repudiating the negative rôle of art in the construction of form, the constructivists are falling into irrelevant nihilism; it cannot because in return for it they find more socially-conscious and scientific methods in their work on architectural form.

Secondly, even if for the constructivists architectural form is not entirely based on a given medium (art), this does not constitute unfounded nihilism. A more accurate formulation is needed here, namely: the constructivists, when working on the form of an architectural structure, consider art irrelevant, in the majority of cases, as a means in the construction of a given architectural form, and the logical conclusion from this is that the reason lies not within the constructivists, but in modern art, which cannot play a serious role in the design of an architectural organism; in short, it is not our position, but modern art, which is irrelevant. Our Comrades from VOPRA attack the constructivists only because they do not understand this. Or again, they write: 'we repudiate constructivism, which on the one hand lapses into an aesthetic relish for constructions, and the imitation of the external forms of industrial technology, and on the other departs into a self-indulgent preoccupation with technique, and machine fetishism'. Here we have a false (formal) conception of constructivism, which we also repudiate; but the

fundamental difference is that we repudiate not constructivism, but 'constructivists' who lapse into an aesthetic relish for anything and into the imitation of anything, and we repudiate them for the simple reason that architects who enter these blind alleys logically depart from that tendency in architecture which is called constructivism, and which is not characterized by aestheticism, imitation and narrow-mindedness. But when it is stated that 'we repudiate constructivism with its blind imitation of Western techniques and mechanical transposition of that technique onto our own soil without consideration for local conditions, real possibilities, the availability of materials, and economic factors' then this is worse than 'vulgar' materialism. This is some kind of reactionary desire to smear a great part of the constructivists' work—the journal of OSA, the pioneer and propagandist periodical concerning the application of new constructions, new materials and new constructional techniques. If OSA were called dreamers, and imitators of the West, on account of their flat roofs, the analysis of brick walls (Prokhorov), the presentation of projects in reinforced concrete by the Vesnin brothers in the Stone Age of our architecture, if it was said that all this is fine, but somewhere else, not on our soil, not within our range of real possibilities and available materials, and if those who said it were none other than the most eclectic, the most reactionary section of architects and engineers, then today, in 1929 the VOPRA declaration wishes to take the lead in this disgraceful chorus. True, VOPRA declares that architecture is unthinkable unless technique is raised to a higher level. VOPRA is even in favour of the utilization of European and American technique, but all these 'modern' phrases are far from convincing. What is the meaning of those sections in the declaration where they speak about the utilization of Western technique 'within the range of real possibilities' and about constructivism's 'excessive anticipation in the resolution of social-existential problems'? Rightist deviation, comrades! For example, only a philistine could assert that skyscrapers are not being built because real possibilities do not exist for them; we are convinced that they are not being built only because at the present *it is not necessary* to build them, and that if skyscrapers need to be built for the development of socialism, then we shall build them; for our real possibilities, achieved by the October Revolution, are greater than the possibilities of any capitalist country. What is needed is not to become fragmented by different 'possibilities' but to approach current problems along the path outlined by the party and the state—by overtaking and surpassing the West. And if the technical basis of the building of socialist architecture must not only catch up, but also surpass the West, then not only is it really possible, but it is only on that condition that we shall have progress and the elements of a socialist architecture. According to

VOPRA, it follows that if OSA were making propaganda for the flat roof, then this was 'blind imitation', but if now the VSNKh SSSR[1] has a standard for flat roofs, then they can be built, and it can be said that they are really possible. VOPRA is sliding towards dull narrow-mindedness and over-emphasis on practice. True, there are many correct principles in the declaration. These are: the application to architecture of the dialectical method, the principle of economy, standardization, mechanization—principles which the constructivists put forward three years ago, and in accordance with which they have proceeded to this day in their work. But, obviously, our comrades from VOPRA wish to cede priority in all this to America in their declaration, stating that constructivism 'was, however, unable in its own theory and practice to go further than a leftist phrase and a revolutionary posture'. Let us for a moment suppose that everything said and done by the Association of Contemporary Architects [OSA] amounts to a 'leftist phrase' and 'revolutionary posture'. But really anyone who is at least to some extent familiar with OSA's work would not make such a supposition, because only a fool believes everything he is told. We assert that the root of VOPRA's divergence from the constructivists lies not in the fact that VOPRA is in favour of a class-based architecture and the constructivists are also in favour of this, or the fact that the constructivists are in favour of the application of dialectical materialism to architecture, and VOPRA is also in favour of this. The principle difference between the present associations consists in their very aim, i.e. for the constructivists the social rôle of architecture is essentially as one of the instruments for the building of socialism by means of the collectivization of life, by means of the rationalization of labour, by means of the utilization of scientific data and so on, whereas for VOPRA the social rôle 'acquires special significance', and the essence of this 'special significance' is that you make architecture an art, not contemplative but 'active', which 'must become a means' for the liberation of the masses, a powerful lever in the building of socialism and a new collectivist way of life, organizing the psyche and actively educating the will and feeling of the masses towards the struggle for communism. 'We are in favour of a proletarian art, whose content expresses the profoundest intentions and aspirations of the working class and embraces the whole sphere of sensations, the entire complex of man's emotions and thoughts,'[2] i.e. on the one side architecture is the concrete organization of working and living productive processes into a blueprint for the socialist reconstruction of society on the basis of the latest achievements of science and technology, and on the other, architecture is an art for the expression of intentions, and for the organization of man's will, thoughts, feelings, emotions, and sensations. (We give an example: for the one group, ration books are understood as a means for the distribution of bread, but the others look at them for what they express, and for what kind of emotions or sensations they evoke within a person.) This is the fundamental difference between the associations, and if the principal aims of the constructivists are leftist phrases to our comrades from VOPRA, then to the former their pathetic ejaculations about art are reminiscent of antediluvian searchings for a god; for we believe that what is needed now is not the invention of an art, which should become something, but work on the organization of architecture, proceeding from the essence of the proletarian revolution, proceeding from the concrete problems of the building of socialism, proceeding from the data of economics, science and technology. It is to this great work that we call all the architects of our [Soviet] Union.

F. Yalovkin

3.3 Architectural Thought since the Revolution by Berthold Lubetkin

Note.—The statements in this article are based on memory quotations from Sovietskaya Arkhitektura, *Professor Miliutin's works, and* Sovremmenaya Arkhitektura.

It is a principle of the Cartesian school of philosophy to determine the precise limits of a subject before considering the problem presented by it. The subject with which we are here concerned is the evolution of architectural thought in Russia from the outbreak of the Revolution up to the present moment.

Under a socialist system—a system, that is, which presumes the existence of a guiding plan for the evolution of society, and allows no social activity to develop chaotically or anarchically—the theory becomes 'a sketch which is one day destined to assume the proportions of a vast general programme for humanity'.

'In a capitalistic society the proletariat cannot achieve equality or social liberty. As a consequence it ought to assume a hostile attitude towards the existing state of society, and to be bent on the reorganization of society as a whole. In other words it is bound to be revolutionary. It is for this reason that the proletariat demands a complete and definite theory of human society so that it may determine how to reorganize every social institution. The necessity to base oneself on the authority of a theory—a necessity which has disappeared among the *bourgeoisie*

---

[1] The Supreme Soviet for the National Economy of the USSR. (ed.)

[2] As Grossman-Roshchin puts it: 'Would it be such a sin to ask the question "how does our architecture embody the purpose of the new class not before, but after the victory of October?" ' See 'An ignoramus's observations'—SA No. 3, 1926. SA No. 5, 1929.

ever since the *bourgeoisie* became reactionary—is affirming itself more and more strongly among the proletariat as a direct consequence of the proletariat's special position as the revolutionary class' (Kautsky).

Soviet architecture lives in an atmosphere that is tense with the continuous struggle of conflicting ideological tendencies. These tendencies are the despair of Western Europeans, who pretend they 'got over that sort of thing while they were still at school'.

But theory in Russia is never understood as something mechanically adjusted to the content of a subject, it always remains a fragmentary part of the general plan of the social structure.

It is not astonishing, therefore, that Soviet architects feel no animosity towards theories (as do their colleagues in capitalistic countries) because their ambition is not simply to build architecturally, but to build socialistically as well. The exhortation to struggle against blind chance is inscribed in gigantic letters on the pediment of socialism.

But what about 'absolute truth', 'eternal beauty', etc.? it may be asked.

When Napoleon asked Laplace why there was no mention of the Creator throughout the whole of his great scientific work, *La Mécanique Céleste*, the latter replied with dignity: 'I had no need of that hypothesis.'

The Situation before the Overthrow of the Old Regime

From the earliest days of the Revolution, the Soviet community set itself to face the problems presented by the necessity for fostering proletarian art and culture.

Public interest in them was daily stimulated by the discussion of the conflicting principles and slogans. The ideology of proletarian art gradually crystallized in an atmosphere heavily charged with political and economic struggles.

At one moment this intellectual agitation reached such a degree of intensity that the 'ideologists' of art ran the danger of isolating themselves from realities in the cloud castles of abstract and speculative theorism.

This was clearly impossible from the point of view of Marxian philosophy: an embodiment of materialistic doctrines which condemns all idealistic deviations from its basic principles. On several occasions the Soviet community took the initiative in counteracting this tendency. In the course of a special series of lectures, the Communist Party laid down the theses for an ideology of proletarian art adapted to the transitional period of the dictatorship of the proletariat.

There was no parallel activity as regards architecture. The architects continued in the traditional manner, without bothering their heads about an ideological basis for their work; and ignored the special demands of the present historical moment.

Immersed in an artificial tradition, and engrossed with the sacrosanct forms of the past, the architects refused to tackle the problems presented by the creation of a new social order. Their work remained for some time completely aloof from the masses.

The pre-war period had bequeathed Russia an unfortunate architectural heritage. The form of barbarism known as *art nouveau*, which swept across Europe at the beginning of the century, acclimatized itself effortlessly enough in the picturesque landscape of commercial Moscow. Its opulent forms even penetrated into the Academy, and debased the appearance of the streets and squares of the large towns. Once these *art-nouveau* houses fell into disrepair their ugliness became more unendurable than ever. Government and municipal offices slumbered in complete inactivity, paralysed by the corruption and indifference of their staffs.

On the theoretical side, the eclecticism of the Academies vied with the sentimental and literary opportunism of the protagonists of local colour and folk-lore.

Such was the situation when the proletariat came into power. A complete stocktaking and a wholesale reorganization were essential. Here, as elsewhere, the Revolution began by destroying old fetishes.

The period immediately following the Revolution was entirely devoted to economic reconstruction. All the active forces of the country were concentrated on the reorganization of production, and the creation of a new political framework. Yet a certain activity was shown from the outset by the younger generation of artists, who turned their attention to remodelling the forms and conceptions inherited from the old regime, since these no longer corresponded with the actualities of the new social order.

The streets and squares of Moscow and the provincial cities were filled with makeshift monuments of papier mâché, wood, or plaster. Tribunes and pulpits for orators, and kiosks and stands for posters arose on all sides. The streets began to look like the wings of a theatre. The Revolution was consolidated amid the greatest difficulties, and to the accompaniment of an extraordinary intellectual ferment. The steel ring of the blockade continued to tighten alarmingly round an exhausted country. Further misfortunes soon followed. All constructional activity became impossible in face of the great dearth of food and fuel. In a truly pathetic nostalgia for order, the trees of the public squares were decked with strands of cotton materials to create monumental perspectives for the government buildings in which beat the pulse of the nation.

But as soon as the country started to recover from famine and exhaustion, culture began to assert its rights once more. The faculties of the universities resumed their courses, and the architectural schools were thronged with a new type of student, eager to learn and to analyse.

Constructivism

The hitherto unquestioned authority of eclectic professors and bourgeois specialists, whose knowledge was based on studies of the opportunist past, was swept away by the burning enthusiasm of the young revolutionary architects. Project followed project, and a nucleus was gradually developed. 'Cells' were organized, and an attempt was made to map out the general lines of the new architecture. Each phase of this work was accompanied by the most burning discussions, and the struggles of groups, personalities, and tendencies. Brigades and collective organizations of students were created in rapid succession. Autodidactic cliques were formed and plastered the walls of the schools with proclamations and posters. Revolutionary dynamism blew the bottom out of forms and principles that were historically obsolete. Tatlin constructed the model of his spiral steel tower, with its cubes of glass actuated by a rotary movement. It was intended that the congresses of the Third International should be held in these cubic cells. The model, which for lack of proper materials was constructed of bits of old tins and cigar-boxes, was publicly exhibited; and attracted attention to the new constructivist architecture.

The dynamism of spiral architectural forms, the worship of construction which relied solely on such plastic qualities as answered to a certain canon of industrial forms, that was based on the precepts of a new, and vaguely defined, aesthetic, were taken into serious consideration, and founded a school. The red ribbon which hung above the model, and bore the inscription, 'Engineers, create new forms!', was carried by a band of enthusiastic students, and placed in the corner of honour above the portrait of Lenin.

Once the initial impetus had been given, projects for 'new objects' were produced wholesale. The young architects set to work to devise new types of kitchen-ranges and crockery, and even things for which they were wholly without the technical qualifications, like miners' safety lamps, cranes, transporter-bridges for dry docks, motor-car head-lamps, and field-glasses. This romantic 'engineerism' could not hope to conceal its ignorance of the objects it was applied to for long. The fetishism of 'real objects' and 'useful things' soon broke down, and the movement quickly degenerated into a kind of formal decoration based on a sentimental mechanistic aesthetic.

If we analyse this mania for utilitarianism, this desire to impose engineering solutions at all cost, we shall have little difficulty in discovering that it was based on the psychology of the radical intelligentsia, which had accepted the October Revolution, but was obsessed by a craving for the material comforts now lacking in everyday life. Herded together in overcrowded flats, with rain driving through the decaying roofs, and deprived of all the things they had formerly been accustomed to, they dreamt of glass and concrete palaces, skyscrapers, with batteries of lifts and moving staircases.

Formalism

But the 'constructivist' movement was not the only expression of the new architectural thought. Symbolism was busily elaborating principles of its own. The *atelier* of Professors N. Golosov and Ladovsky launched new doctrines (1920–22) based on the study of forms. The adherents of this school envisaged an 'objective', absolute, and universal system, based on the reactions of the perceptive organism of the spectator. They carried out laboratory investigations into the study of scale, modulism, the relations of rhythm, proportion and mass, statics and dynamics regarded as functions of volume, etc. But in spite of all their endeavours, they remained purely abstract, idealistic and emotional. In a short time a whole series of expressive forms had been created, which could be grouped together in compositions to give the 'idea' of a building. This new symbolism, with its cubes suggesting the conception of integrity, its spheres and balls expressive of the ideas of tranquillity and equilibrium, and its transposition of geometric forms to serve as attributes of dynamism and impulse, soon created an aesthetic canon, imprisoned within its own strait-jacket, that was inhuman and incomprehensible for the non-initiated: a sort of universalism of the Larousse type, but a universalism in which everything became subjective and conventional.

It is interesting that the same ideas which were then gaining adherents in Russia were simultaneously reflected in foreign tendencies. In proof of this it is only necessary to cite the German paper *Freiheit* (1922): 'The capitalistic individualist, when trying to express his personality, prefers the horizontal line or an immobile column. The socialist, on the other hand, prefers the climbing horizontal line (spiral), which embraces his fellow men in its course and soars upwards to embrace the heavens. Collectivist buildings ought to be constructed in a circular form in a spirit of opposition to the limitations of rectangles.'

In Russia a quantity of projects for spherical mausoleums and record offices in the shape of pyramids began to be elaborated. Numerous buildings, intended for various purposes, had spiral planes, so as to embody what was claimed to be a curve expressive of revolutionary dynamism. 'The spiral', one critic of this period wrote, 'is a line of liberation for humanity. With one extremity resting on the ground, it flees the earth with the other; and thereby becomes a symbol of disinterestedness, and of the converse of earthly pettiness.' (Punin, 1922.)

All this romantic symbolism, all these *petit bourgeois* metaphysics, could not hope to survive for long in the atmosphere of Soviet realities; and we soon witnessed the first materialistic reactions to this phase within the same schools as had engendered it. As early as 1928, Ladovsky,

Figure 14   The elevation of Tatlin's project, reproduced as a poster because of the popularity of his design

Figure 15   A plan of a Restaurant in the Boulevard Moscow, 1922. A 'spiral obsession'

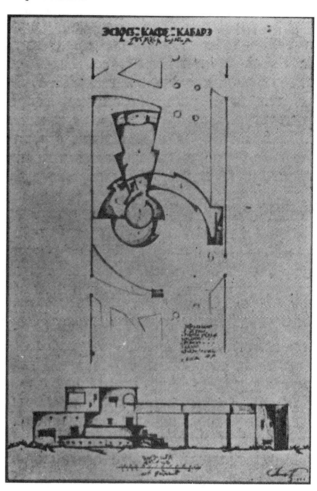

Figure 16   A design for the Svoboda Club for chemical workers by Melnikov. The drawing shows clearly the formalistic aesthetic of the ASNOVA group

Figure 17   The Electro-technical institute at Moscow. Architect, Kosnyetsov. A characteristic example of the aesthetic of the SASS group

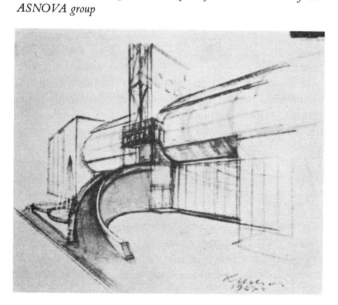

Note: The captions to Figures 14–21 are taken from the original article.

while still continuing his abstract researches into 'the expression of form', tried to break with formal symbolism by introducing 'biopsychological and psychotechnical criteria'. These investigations, though still strongly influenced by aesthetic and abstract researches into what was vaguely defined as 'form in general', none the less mark a decidedly rationalistic tendency. Other groups, though gradually liberating themselves from metaphysical symbolism, speedily fell back into mechanistic symbolism. We saw projects elaborated for theatres in the form of electric dynamos, clubs in the shape of water turbines, and Palaces of the People serrated with toothed cogwheels; to say nothing of public libraries modelled on oil-fired boilers.

Happily for Soviet architecture none of these projects got beyond the paper stage, and consequently they were powerless to prejudice its early development. All the same it would be unjust to deny the great educative influence they exerted on large circles of students, and public opinion generally. At the base of the ideology of the various existing architectural groups we shall find reminiscences of the doctrines which were the battle cries of the moment during their members' student days. It is only by taking this initial period of theoretic researches into account that we can hope to attempt an analysis of the actual ideological bases of the Soviet architecture of today.

The Need of Revaluation of Architectural Values in the Face of Concrete Problems

After the end of the civil war, when the country had recovered from its exhaustion, and was beginning to enter the period of reconstruction—the task of consolidating the foundations of a Socialist State—the architectural manpower of the nation, by then almost entirely the younger generation of architects just emerging from the schools, was confronted with grim reality. These young men were sent to occupy positions among the constructors of the new society.

Here for the first time they were made to realize the gulf which separated the subjective researches of the schools from the imperative demands of the moment, and the lack of proper theoretic and practical training which rendered them impotent in face of the immediate problems raised by the basic changes in economic and political life. Reality caught these young architects at a considerable disadvantage. They had to reorganize their technical equipment and change their point of view with the utmost rapidity.

As a result of the vast programme of construction, large masses of the population began to interest themselves in architectural problems. The various architectural theses were discussed at public meetings and in the Press. The courses of architecture attracted students from ever wider

sections of the community; and as a result, the necessity for the creation of a social-architectural organization became an objective one.

ASNOVA and its Formalism

In 1923 the first association of the new type of architects was founded under the title of ASNOVA. This group also included young painters and sculptors, most of whom came from Ladovsky's *atelier*. It began with works that were wholly in the symbolical and aesthetical tradition. But in proportion as the problems of the moment became more concrete and urgent, this group modified its principles. In recognizing that architecture is a plastic art, the supreme *raison d'être* of which is to rouse the enthusiasm of the masses, it began to approach tangibly nearer to reality.

In the declaration which it addressed to the Soviet Community in *Sovietskaya Arkhitektura*, ASNOVA declared that the creation of new revolutionary forms can only be based on the latest scientific and technical achievements; and that proletarian architecture must co-operate with other social-economic factors in co-ordinating industrial and social functions. In this way it can express its socialist content, and actively mould the ideology of the masses in a revolutionary sense.

Granted such an attitude to architecture, the concrete problems of socialist building construction ought not to be limited to the mere planning of industrial and social processes in terms of space and material; forms ought not to be allowed to fulfil their functions merely passively. They should, on the contrary, create a powerful impression on the ideology of the masses by every plastic means which the imagination can command. In solving problems connected with industrial and social reconstruction, proletarian architecture must present a dialectic synthesis of economic, technical, plastic, and ideological factors. It must also fully respond to the needs of the moment, and at the same time emphasize its socialist elements in a dialectical sense; since its solutions will be plastic as well as technical.

It is clear that on this point the doctrines of the old aestheticizing symbolists, so carefully elaborated in the schools, come into conflict with the Marxian thesis. The definition of the 'plastic factor' as being the same thing as technique, economics, and ideology, explains the idealist and formalist standpoint of the ASNOVA group. Marxian philosophy ignores this 'factor', and pitilessly unmasks the vague criteria of 'universalism', 'abstract humanitarianism', and 'eternal values' as figments of the idealist philosophy of the *bourgeois* world. None the less it is undeniable that ASNOVA has since evolved towards a nearer and nearer approach to the materialistic point of view. Its latest manifestoes, and its more recent work, prove that this group has been gradually liberating itself from 'objective' plasticism, and that it is now definitely beginning to adopt proletarian—that is to say dialectic—methods.

Many members of ASNOVA occupy important positions in the architectural schools, where they are engaged in training the new classes of architects. Among the works of this group mention should be made of the Red International Stadium at Moscow, the Soviet Pavilions at the Paris Exposition des Arts Décoratifs in 1925 (where a Grand Prix was obtained), and the exhibitions at Strasbourg (Grand Prix Hors Concours) in 1929, Bordeaux, Marseilles, etc. This group organizes public discussions and lectures, arranges exhibitions, takes part in competitions, and executes orders on a collective and collaborative basis. Other examples of its work include the House of Industry, the Vzik School, the White-Russian Academy of Sciences, the Palace of Labour, the Palace of the Soviets, and many town-planning schemes (such as those for the towns of Autostroy, Magnitogorsk, and Tchardjui), and the laying-out of squares in Moscow, besides schemes for new parks.

ARU and its Town-Planning Theory

In 1929, Ladovsky, one of the original founders of ASNOVA, detached himself from it, and started a new group called ARU (the Association of Town-Planning Architects). The ideas of this group do not differ a great deal from those of ASNOVA so far as its 'methodological' principles are concerned. We find the same approach to architecture as a medium of formal expression. But the ARU group applies itself to the study of architecture as one of the functions of town-planning, and not as a separate entity, or a thing in itself.

ARU declares that in the complex of questions which the architect is called upon to examine with some degree of consecutiveness, the most important is the consideration of man as a social being in relation to his class environment. They say that it is possible to approach the sum of the problems with which the architect is faced both in terms of space organization and space composition; but these two aspects must be considered jointly, not separately. This method of arriving at a solution of the problem is the only one which can hope to deal adequately with the more general question of architectural organization and planning. It is necessary when examining the relation of these to a given building to refer back to the principles which are involved in solving the general problem: that is to say, to the architectural planning and co-ordination of the town itself.

In contrast to the capitalist system, which precludes the possibility of submitting the whole of a given urban area to a scheme of planning and co-ordination, the socialist system creates objective conditions for its architecture. It is only through scientific investigation of the problems of town-planning that an effective solution can be found for the larger problems connected with the redistribution of population.

In analysing the practical work and ideology of this group, the critic of *Sovietskaya Arkhitektura* has pointed out the metaphysical and anti-dialectic character of the opposition of 'deductivism' (from the general to the particular) to 'inductivism' (from the particular to the general).

In proposing a part of the totality as its principle, ARU offers no dialectic solutions for planning problems, because it is just as necessary to envisage the function of the town as a whole, as the particular functions of its separate zones, buildings, and cells—since these are units complete in themselves within the wider orbit of proletarian political and social economy. On the other hand the principles of town-planning, on which the whole of ARU's work is based, are incompatible with those tendencies in Soviet architecture that aim at suppressing the differences between towns and villages by means of a more rational distribution of the agricultural and industrial population.

It should be observed that, like ASNOVA, ARU often bases its methods of work on an abstract symbolism by giving expressive forms to plans for towns. All the same, in proportion as its guiding principles become more definite, and the socialist programme of construction requires more immediate and concrete solutions, ARU is adopting an attitude which approximates more and more to that of Marxian dialectic.

The practical work of ARU is chiefly concentrated on problems connected with the building of new towns, villages, agricultural colonies, and the laying out of squares and streets. At the same time it is engaged in teaching inside the schools of architecture. Its students participate in the work of the group, which has the effect of stimulating young architects, and results in bold projects with plenty of initiative. Among the other merits of ARU mention must be made of the fact that this group was the first to apply the cinematograph method to town-planning projects. This method—which was adopted in drawing up the plans for the towns of Autostroy, Magnitogorsk, etc.—undoubtedly offers immense advantages for the study of such interdependent problems as traffic circulation, street lighting, orientation, etc.

SASS and its Functionalism

The third group, OSA, which has since changed its name to SASS (Section of Architects of Socialist Construction), arose through the defection of a certain number of architects from ASNOVA in 1928. This is certainly the most radical group among the various Soviet architectural organizations. It is also that which has to meet the most criticisms, and has to defend itself most desperately against a flood of articles attacking its ideology. Analysis of its principles reveals the roots of 'Engineerism', technical fetishism, and the usual utilitarian talk of 'Constructivism', that date from the communism of the civil war period which has already been described. On the other hand its old pupils have learnt much in the schools, and in the years of practical work, which, together with the speeding up of construction, has brought them into closer contact with real problems.

'The architecture of the past,' say the functionalists of the SASS, 'and more particularly the architecture of the end of the nineteenth century, suffered from a basic dualism. In proportion as "art work" differentiates itself from architectural integrity, the architect becomes more and more a "master decorator"; and his methods of work become more and more those of a plastic artist. All notions of aesthetics are lost; or rather a pure cult of aestheticism appears.' This state of affairs has not always existed. There were moments in the history of architecture when the methods of the architect were very close to those of the 'inventor'.

When the cultural and economic life of Ancient Greece was crystallizing, a whole series of architectural forms had to be invented to meet new economic and political conditions. It was thus that the Greek temple, the theatre, and the stadium came into being. These were 'inventions' in the widest possible sense of the word, since the underlying motive in their general conception, as well as of all their details, was a purely utilitarian necessity. But when once these inventions had been made, and the relations of society had been stabilized, the Greek architect began to differentiate his *artistic work* more and more, simply because he had no longer anything to invent.

In the same way the Romans, during the constructive period of their history, invented baths, aqueducts, triumphal arches, amphitheatres and circuses. Christianity invented the basilica; the builders of the Gothic style, the stone and glass cathedral; the Middle Ages, the castle; and the Renaissance builders, the palace, the country house, etc.

The new Soviet architecture having formed its methods of work during the period of the establishment of new social relations, and in that of the achievement of socialism, demands from the architect before all else the invention of new types of architecture, of 'new condensers' of social life, which shall crystallize the new social and productive relations of the new collectivist society. 'We declare that in the epoch of the construction of socialism the architect's rôle is before all else the invention of new types of architecture, of new condensers of the social life.'

SASS's methods of planning resemble those of the engineer-designer. The architect and the engineer have, in fact, identical resources and qualifications: a feeling for space, knowledge of materials, and professional traditions. Indeed, the engineer-designer possesses no other resources,

because even technology cannot be considered an exact science since it is entirely based on empirical hypotheses of the resistance of materials. In the new architecture everything must be changed, including the old systems of classification. Is a communal dwelling a habitation or a public building? Is the cinema, with its clockwork alternation of sessions, a public building or a factory? In a socialist society, is the factory itself a public building or a workshop?

The content of a building is replaced by its function. All the functional ramifications served by architecture can be deduced from simple principles of physico-mathematics and the technique of production. The ideological value of proletarian architecture does not lie in the exterior forms which act on organs of perception, nor yet in rousing the enthusiasm of the masses, training their faculties, and giving them 'emotional recharging'. Its rôle consists of the scientific functioning, and the spatial organization of the concrete problems involved in the practical realization of socialism.

Starting with the principle that form is a function of different variables, the theorists of the SASS are even able to arrive at the view that content is equivalent to the organization of individual, collective, and productive existence. From this the repudiation of architecture's claim to be ranked as a branch of the Fine Arts follows as a matter of course. All attempts to influence the spectator by means of the composition of forms address themselves, not to the productivist psychology of the proletariat engaged in building up a life of its own, but to a class-enemy mentality, a consumer's psychology, based on idealist and religious premises.

The SASS group is certainly the most numerous of the various associations of architects, and its theories influence very wide circles of students. It takes a very active part in social life, participates in nearly all competitions and town-planning schemes, and carries out numerous commissions (such as the Narkomfin employees' house, the administrative buildings of the Turksib Railway, the Theatre of the Populace at Kharkov, etc.). In the field of town-planning, this group has adopted Ochitovitch's idea for the disurbanization of Russia by the creation of a system of roads bordered by houses, with civic centres for victualling, culture, primary education, and medical relief at stated intervals. These roads would unite the centres of industrial production, which would themselves be surrounded by agricultural zones. SASS demands the abolition of the contradictions between urban and agricultural life, by synthesizing the two into a form of socialistic life based on the relations of collectivist man to nature and production. Up till 1930 SASS edited a review under the title of *SA* (or *Contemporary Architecture*) in which, while attacking their critics, the theoretical and practical exponents of this group tried to justify their ideology.

VOPRA and its criticism based on the Dialectic Method

In 1929 the VOPRA group (All-Russian Society of Proletarian Architects) was formed. This organization, which according to its own declaration is the only one that consists of exclusively proletarian elements, proclaimed its monopoly of orthodox proletarian ideology. The ideology of VOPRA, which is based on Marxian dialectic, is in opposition to the theses of all the other groups because it undertakes to unmask the deviations of the right and left wings alike, and to denounce *petit bourgeois* opportunism and 'idealist tautology' just as much as the doctrines of mechanists.

VOPRA's criticism of ASNOVA and ARU is directed against their aestheticizing symbolism, though it admits that the work of both these groups is approximating more and more closely to the spirit of proletarian ideology. It asserts that ASNOVA's formalism, with its 'spatial logic', its 'psychic economics', and its 'objective laws' of visual perception, is clearly influenced by the doctrines of class-enemies. VOPRA asserts that it is only too easy to deduce that the methods of ASNOVA, like the structure of its ideology, are derived not from Marxianism but from Kant's aesthetic, and the theories of Hilderbrandt, Fiedler, and Wölfflin.

ASNOVA declares that 'a high degree of *formal skill*, founded on a profoundly objective basis, ought to be applied to the content of proletarian architecture'; to which VOPRA objects: 'We know what this objective method is. It is based on the laws of visual perception, biology and psychotechnics; and is derived from the study of the composition of forms.'

The forms elaborated by this objective method serve to clothe the content of Soviet architecture mechanically.

Figure 18   A 'Commune' house in Yerevan, Armenia, by K. Alabyan of the VOPRA group. The centre building contains communal services. In the centre of the foreground is the building for infant welfare, containing crèches, kindergarten, etc.

Yet the Soviet architect knows perfectly well that there are no 'eternal laws' for the composition of forms; that the different styles of the various historic periods had different laws of formal composition; and that these were closely connected with the demands of the subject, class, and social content concerned. We know that in reality the fetishes of 'absolute and eternal beauty' are only used to cloak the mediocrity of *bourgeois* art. Thus in the theses of ASNOVA the specifically proletarian content is replaced to some extent by vague universalism and abstract idealism.

But the VOPRA group also attacks the left wing of Soviet architecture, while admitting that it is relatively speaking the nearest to the ideal of proletarian architecture; and that it is more deserving than any other architectural group of the title 'Fellow-Wayfarers of the Proletariat'. Its attack on the left wing is directed simultaneously against its ideological, methodological, and technical bases.

SASS's ideology, which is characterized by the denial that architecture is a fine art, and an obstinate refusal to envisage in architecture 'a means of inflaming the enthusiasm of the masses by forms', calls forth severe criticism from VOPRA. VOPRA does not hesitate to describe these conceptions as counter-revolutionary, firstly, because if they prevailed, the proletariat would find itself deprived of one of its most incontestably efficacious weapons, namely, the emotional influence of art; and secondly, because in advancing these doctrines SASS puts itself into open opposition to the theses of the Vzik (the Central Executive Committee of the Communist Party), which postulate that it is essential to 'inflame the masses with a pathos for industrialization by means of art'.

In the domain of method VOPRA insists that the left wing has substituted function for content; or in other words the functional method for the approach from historical genesis; just as it has replaced dialectic by mechanistic methods. Marxism in no way identifies form with function, but conceives of it as a law of construction, or a manner of exteriorizing the content of an object.

Form is determined by content, but content is not identical with function. The same content may have several functions, etc.

'As long as one seeks to replace content by function, and by the element of organization, one will be unable to grasp the significance of the content as an objective thing having its own genesis and historic motivation. From which it follows that ideology will always be understood as a value mechanically added to form and content.'

This essentially anti-Marxian and anti-proletarian attitude likewise tends to replace concrete class demands by abstract mechanistic logic. According to VOPRA, if ASNOVA can be described as idealistic in a *petit bourgeois* sense SASS, which is undeniably on a plane of vulgar materialism, is just as much influenced by capitalistic philosophy.

Rarely can one find an architectural competition in the USSR in which the VOPRA group is not represented. The designs are generally rather heavy and of rather doubtful monumentalism, but always ingenuous and realistic. Their designs for the Palace of Soviets have created a great deal of interest, although they were not awarded the first prize.

Epilogue

I have tried, in quoting from memory several Soviet authors, to trace briefly the general direction in which the Soviet architectural mind works. Faced with a big social responsibility in the spending of many millions of pounds on the construction of new buildings, the USSR would not trust themselves to any *maestro* who proposes with one stroke of his pen to solve all the problems of proletarian architecture.

The problem, indeed, surpasses individual capacity. What is wanted is the creation of a new style in accordance with the demands of the historical moment. The Marxian materialism has definitely swept away the slogans of 'absolute beauty', 'art for art' and 'apolitic art'. It has shown all the subjectivism which constitutes their fundament, and which expresses itself in a pure aestheticism. Aestheticism, the admiration of abstractly beautiful things, is characteristic of the *bourgeois* aesthetic, and obviously represents a particular ideology. The application of the criterion 'beauty', independently of the hidden contents, is impossible to admit in the system of proletarian aesthetic, and if it is true that 'the object we have created imposes, in the future, its influence on us, it is necessary that this influence, at least, should be ideologically true'.

3.4   Recent developments of Town-Planning in the USSR
by Berthold Lubetkin

(*Note.—The statements in this article are based on memory quotations from* Sovietskaya Arkhitektura, *Professor Miliutin's works, and* Sovremmenaya Arkhitektura)

At the present moment Soviet Russia is persevering in the rapid development of industry and the collectivization of agriculture. This implies a radical change in the technical basis of the economy of the old backward Russia of pre-Soviet days, and the transformation of the country into a powerfully-equipped agro-industrial system.

This great impetus of industrialization has no parallel in history; one result of it is that new centres of production are constantly being created. Their location is determined by such factors as the proximity of raw materials, transport facilities, and to some extent by strategic and climatic considerations.

The change in the social structure of the nation has resulted not only in the growth of new towns, but also in the extension of many existing ones; a state of affairs which brings town-planning problems more and more to the fore.

Karl Marx in his Communist manifesto, F. Engels in his writings on housing problems, and Lenin in his investigation of the agrarian question, have pointed out in many places the importance of the changes which must be made in the distribution of population as a result of the socialist revolution. The gradual disappearance of the great cities, the more rational distribution of the new humanity, the unification of industrial and agricultural production, the transference of education and specialized instruction into immediate proximity with centres of production, the emancipation of women from domestic slavery, and the abolition of the differences between manual and intellectual work, are among the essential basic principles of Soviet town-planning. Each fresh realization in that direction must be considered as a further step in this order of ideas.

In the study of many technical problems Soviet Russia is often obliged to have recourse to the experience of capitalistic nations that are at present in a higher plane of technical development than herself. But owing to the difference of their social systems foreign solutions can never be applied literally. This is particularly true of town-planning, where technical principles have to be submitted to a very critical examination before they can be adopted in the construction of the new socialist towns. In fact, as the structure of society is entirely different in Russia, Soviet solutions are likewise quite different as far as methods are concerned. We shall attempt, therefore, to examine the actual objective conditions and methods of town-planning that have been adopted in the present phase of building up socialism in Russia.

There is one factor of such primordial importance that it must be considered the basis of Soviet urban development. This is the industrialization of the country by means of electrification.

The importance of electrification was recognized by the Communist Party even in the earliest days of the Revolution. Lenin himself said: 'We need electrification as a first sketch of the great economic plan necessary for the establishment of communism.'

These words were a whole programme in themselves; and today, after a lapse of thirteen years, the country is beginning to see the results of it. Electrification is making

Figure 19   The Great Dam at Dnieperstroi

Figure 21

Plan of Magnitogorsk. The principal main road unites the big industrial centre with the collective farms and is about 20 miles long. The houses are along this road. Sets of wooden houses are in chessboard formation. Each group contains eight houses for thirty-two people each. Between the road and the houses are the service houses, clubs, theatres, etc., and between the groups of houses, crèches, schools, etc.

Figure 20a

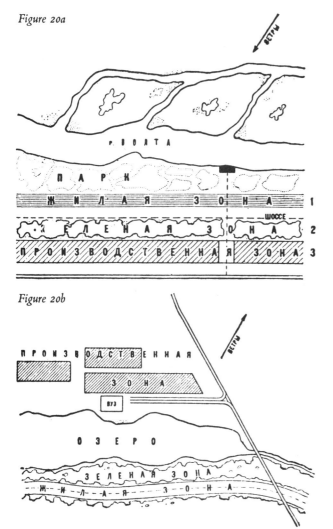

Figure 20b

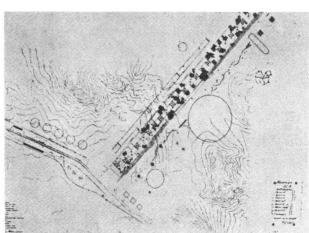

Plan of Magnitogorsk, which is a typical 'ribbon' town. The new scheme, which is designed by May, spreads on to other territory, as the first site was too small

(Left) A scheme for a socialist town, for the tractor factory in Stalingrad, by Professor Miliutin. (1) Housing area; (2) green area, containing the main road; (3) industrial area and railway. The town is separated from the river by a park. The arrow shows the direction of the wind. (Below) Plan of Magnitogorsk, by Professor Miliutin. On the north side of the lake is the industrial area, on the south the 'green' area and the housing district. This is a typical example of the change necessary in a precedent scheme when the housing area cannot adjoin the industrial district. A main road had to be made to join the two parts. At the end of the branch of this road stands the University

astonishing progress in Soviet Russia. A whole series of power stations have been built under the provisions of the Five-Year Plan, and the country is now being covered with a dense network of distributing lines. In the Moscow district several thermal power stations have been built— such as those at Chatourki, Kachyr, Bobriki, Khamovniki, etc.—run on peat and lignite. In the provinces the number of stations is already considerable. Amongst them should be mentioned the huge Volhvostroi and Dnieperstroi hydro-electric plants.[1] But Soviet electrical development is far from being complete. On the contrary the Plan envisages a continuous future extension of electrification, and a corresponding increase in the density of the distributing system, in order that at some far distant date it will be possible to make up for the ultimate exhaustion of certain existing centres of thermal and hydraulic energy.[2]

The existing towns were for the most part built at points of intersection on the lines for the transport of raw materials and the distribution of fuel. This was the result of the differentiation between the processes of extraction and subsequent working up of raw materials required in industry. The progress of electrification assures a more rational distribution of motive power and at the same time strikes at the roots of the distribution of manufacturing towns up and down the country. It also does away with the uneconomic transport of raw materials containing scrap, and eases the transport of manufactured and semi-manufactured goods. In future, cotton will no longer be produced in the South of Russia to be spun and woven in the industrial regions of the north, and then in part returned to the districts where the raw cotton was originally grown in the form of finished products—(a procedure which needlessly increases cost of production and is an added burden to transport). The electrification of the regions in which cotton is grown will enable cotton goods to be manufactured and processed on the spot.

The Adopted Policy of Zoning

We see, then, that owing to the rapid electrifying of the country, the question of transport of power no longer predominates in choosing the sites of new towns, because only the raw-materials centres are determinating.

The problems connected with the actual planning of the socialist town, as well as with the extension of the existing towns, have been widely discussed during the last few years. Schemes have been published in the daily and professional Press, and have been examined at meetings and special exhibitions. As a result of all this theoretical work, a section of the Communist Academy, which deals with the problem of socialist distribution of the population, has evolved a concrete programme of town-planning, which takes into account all technical and social factors characteristic in the present period of building.

The system can be compared with what is known as 'zoning', but it differs strongly from similar schemes in the capitalist country, the differences being easy to understand considering the specific social economic structure of USSR. In the following we shall try to describe the principal points of this system, which lie at the root of town-planning realization in Russia.[3]

The incoherent chaos of capitalist towns—with their anarchical juxtaposition of different quarters, their complete absence of social plan, and their opportunist distribution of population which is the direct reflection of class oppression—must give place to the logical and rational zoning of the socialist town, which assures the best conditions of production and existence. The expansion of the old towns must be arrested at all costs. No new industry must henceforth be allowed to spring up in these centres. Where there are still unexploited reserves of raw materials, satellite towns must be created which have an independent character of their own.

The Central Executive Committee of the Communist Party has accordingly decided not only to refrain from constructing new centres of production in Moscow, but gradually to demolish such existing buildings there as have reached the end of their economic utility, and to lay out parks and squares on their sites at some future date.

The organization of work inside the new towns is entirely subordinated to the needs of production. In this it is diametrically opposed to capitalistic conceptions where markets or business centres are the governing factor. Industrial production is the most important branch of the national economy around which the whole life of a social country groups and organizes itself. Therefore the industrial zone determines the extent and siting of the other zones; and also the lay-out of housing estates and of main subsidiary roads.

Henceforth scientific institutions and the organizations of special instruction will be placed in immediate proximity to the zones of production. By juxtaposition of the centres of work and study a much more immediate contact can be established between the technicians and the workers, and very considerable economy in space can be obtained; thus certain parts of the factories, such as their laboratories, forges and store-rooms, can be utilized for scientific research.

The industrial zone must be separated from the other zones by a belt of verdure at least 500 metres wide. The object of this is not only to safeguard the housing zone from the emanation of dangerous gases, etc., and to create better hygienic and sanitary conditions; but also to facilitate transport, and protect machinery from the dust

---

[1] The construction of the barrage for the latter, on which more than 15,000 workmen are employed, has necessitated the submersion of 16,000 hectares of inhabited area. A dyke of a kilometre in length had to be built to raise the level of the waters of the Dnieper by 37 metres. This has rendered the river navigable for the first time in history.

[2] In the second Five-Year Plan now in the process of preparation, much attention is to be paid to Central Asia. The electrifying of this region will be used for irrigation, chemical industry and cotton industry. In Occidental and Oriental Siberia two new power-stations are to be built, one in Angara and the other in Enissei. These will have about 40 million horse-power, which is equal to approximately twenty times the power of Dnieperstroi. It has been decided that at the end of the second Five-Year Plan, USSR will have 60 to 70 million kilowatts of energy, while America has only 35 million.

[3] There are several organizations of architects and engineers dealing with town-planning problems in Russia, but the most important is the Giprogor

of the city. This green belt will accommodate an arterial road, clubs, restaurants, etc.; and may only be built over to the extent of 10 per cent. of its superficial area. Infant welfare institutions, such as crèches and kindergartens, must be placed in the housing zone, where they will be surrounded by large open spaces adapted for recreation and sport.

The agricultural zone, with its farms and market-gardens, must be placed behind either the housing or the industrial zone; and likewise cut off by a green belt. In planning these zones it is essential that the whole lay-out should be based on what is one of the capital principles of the socialist state: the abolition of the specific differences between the urban and rural proletariats. For this reason it is necessary to envisage the possibility of the factory workers living together with the labourers on the *kolkhozes* (or collectivist farms) so as to pave the way for the ultimate unification of industrial and agricultural production.

The dispensaries, clinics, and surgeries ought to be distributed partly in the housing zone, and partly in the industrial zone. The hospitals, while remaining within the confines of the towns, would be surrounded by a sufficient expanse of verdure. Incidentally, these hospitals will be of the 'poly-medical' type; that is to say, they will combine the functions of a clinic, a medical school, and various medico-scientific institutions.

The most favourable conditions for production, transport, social life, education, and instruction can be created by this kind of zoning, as well as the necessary environment for the reconstruction of social relations on the basis of the new collectivist culture.

A lay-out of this type would also appear to be the most economical as regards contour-planning, main-drainage provisions, etc.

Professor Miliutin has proposed the following scheme for planning a city based on the decisions of the Communist Academy:

(1)   An industrial zone served by railway which permits of its future extension.
(2)   A green strip with an arterial roadway in the middle of it.
(3)   A housing zone containing the public and administrative buildings, blocks of flats, infant-welfare centre, and primary schools, etc.
(4)   A zone of parks providing facilities for sport, rest and culture.
(5)   The agricultural zone of the *kolkhozes*.

This type of scheme has been adopted for the new towns during the transitional period. When local topographical, hydrographical or meteorological conditions do not allow such a scheme to be carried out in its entirety, the necessity for communication with the industrial zone by transverse main roads has to be taken into consideration. A very flexible legislation indicates the best solution in each particular case.

This programme, though based on a dialectical study of the problems and possibilities of the moment, is opposed by the Right and Left Wing alike. We must, therefore, try to analyse their respective points of view.

The Right Wing Theory

The ideology of the Right Wing reflects, to quote Stalin's words at the Sixteenth Congress of the Communist Party, 'the resistance of classes which have seen their day'. They try to justify their opportunism by the slogan of 'maximal economy'. In insisting on the material difficulties involved in the realization of this 'Maximal Programme', the Right Wing proposes palliatives that are based simply on the errors of capitalistic planning; and excuses itself with vague promises to review its attitude in the future 'when objective conditions permit it', etc. In practical terms, what it proposes is the extension and regulation of the existing towns on the assumption that culture is only possible in the old historic centres; and the establishment of new industries in immediate contact with the old (for which the pretext is the greater facilities offered for provisioning them).

In opposition to the resolutions of the Central Executive Committee—which discourages the construction of new industrial quarters in or around the existing towns, particularly in or around Moscow and Leningrad after 1932, the Right Wing maintains that this principle of 'the extinction of the existing towns' is a dangerous one. It considers that the old towns ought to be allowed to develop, and that it is too early to try and define their extent on the basis of prevailing economic conditions. The limits of their development, it insists, will be fixed in the distant future by 'the events of history'. It regards the new towns as a phenomenon of secondary importance, and has done its best to discredit them from the first by dubbing them 'provincial' and 'temporary'. For the Right the 'quarter' is the primordial element of the town-planner's activity, just as in housing it is obsessed by flats of the *immeuble de rapport* type with their private homes, separate kitchens, etc. (in so far, that is, as the survival of such things is still possible under the collectivist regime). It is only to be expected that the representatives of these counter-revolutionary tendencies should try to justify their reactionary point of view by crocodile tears over the innumerable material difficulties, the need for economy in the present situation. All the same, their arguments remain entirely anti-Marxian, and, consequently, anti-proletarian.

The Left Wing Proposals

The Left Wing of the Soviet town-planners goes to the opposite extreme, and in so doing leave all sense of realities behind them. Immersed in speculative and abstract logic, they demand the immediate realization of the 'Maximal Programme' of socialism. This tendency is chiefly represented by the SASS group, with Okhitovitch

(State Institute of Town Planning). Many foreign experts are working on the same problem, one of these being Ernst May, the well-known German specialist, with twenty-five German architects assisting him.

as its principal spokesman. They have proposed a scheme for the new towns that resembles the longitudinal, or ribbon development. Their argument is as follows:

The growth of socialist economy is closely connected with the continually increasing importance of transport. This implies the possibility of effecting delivery of materials both to and from certain hitherto inaccessible districts; a possibility which allows new industries to develop in them.

On the assumption that the basis of the regional planning of a given economic territorial unit is a system of nodal agricultural and industrial centres, linked together by main avenues of communication and channels of electrical distribution, it follows that the proper socialistic basis for the distribution of the population ought to be its 'attenuation' along their routes. These arterial roads are destined to be the rays of a great cultural and economic development in the near future, because they will facilitate all public services, and more particularly provisioning. The creation of a comprehensive network of roads bordered by houses to cover the whole country will furnish the principal means of abolishing existing differences between the urban and agricultural proletariats. They will also be instrumental in creating the closest possible contact between the workers of the different centres spaced along their routes.

Urban 'quarters' are simply the obsolete survivals of capitalistic principles of planning. They represent class and caste prejudices (ghettoes, international concessions, West and East Ends, brothel districts), or now superannuated ideas of strategic defence, etc. The side streets in the old towns are unnecessarily long. They were designed solely for the needs of consumption, and are off from the main roads that serve the economic unit constituted by the region as a whole.

The conception of the 'quarter' is entirely alien to the socialist mentality.

According to the SASS Group, the Ribbon Town is the only logical means of redistributing the rural population. The abolition of small individual rural properties, and the creation of enormous industrialized agricultural domains, make the building of lines of habitations bordering the limits of the collectivized farms an imperative necessity. In this way alone it is possible to overcome the obstacle of distance separating the worker's home from his place of work.

It is also untrue to pretend that the development of culture is only possible in the great cities. Lenin had already formulated this problem when he said that contemporary technical progress allows the latest 'achievements' of science and art to be enjoyed by the most distant inhabitants of our country. This is only another way of saying that we ought to concentrate our efforts on the creation of new systems of 'cultural revictualling', so as to be able to assure a uniform distribution of the benefits of culture to all the workers of Soviet Russia.

If we take into account that in future industry will be a system which synthesizes manual and intellectual work it follows that the centres of production will also be centres of science, education, and polytechnic culture as well.

In this way all the different nodal points associated with the technical development of a certain industry will also be centres of specific scientific and cultural activities. These centres will be more or less uniformly distributed throughout the country, and will ensure the abolition of the historic pre-eminence of the great cities.

The rational distribution of parks, open spaces for rest and recreation, sports grounds, cinemas, theatres, etc., throughout the different sectors of the housing zones will bring the consumer into closer contact with cultural institutions.

But the principal advantage of the Ribbon Towns, which entitles this system to be called a truly socialistic one, is the abolition of domestic economy, and, as a logical consequence, the consistent furtherance of the collectivization of the population.

The adherents of this longitudinal disurbanization are ready to concede that the temporary survival of the individual home can be dialectically justified for the transitional period but they insist that it is impossible to tolerate the continuance of individual households in the new towns.

The cardinal principle of collective services is its regional, 'anti-home' character as regards everything connected with consumption and provisioning. The 'basic points' of its system of distribution to the consumer are placed at rational intervals (though these are different for each of the different types of public service) with due regard to the particular local requirements of the region concerned. The system consists of: (1) Points of production, where products are prepared for consumption; (2) stores and distributing centres for these products; (3) centres of consumption.

The positions of the centres of production are fixed in accordance with the general laws governing the production of the country as a whole in so far as such questions as location, output and supply of raw materials are concerned. On the other hand, the centres of consumption are placed as close as possible to the various groups of consumers they are intended to supply, so as ultimately to permit distribution to the collective dwellings themselves.

The main roads will act as arteries for the provisioning of the whole region. This eminently flexible system guarantees the possibility of future extensions, and this is equally adaptable for all regions, irrespective of their present level of economic and technical development. It must be regarded as presenting a comprehensive complex of all the economic and cultural services of society, since it provides for:

A system of roads, and other forms of transport.

A system of communications (postal, telegraphic, telephonic, etc.).

A system of housing.

A system of provisioning.

A system of hygienic and sanitary services.

A system of distribution for articles of general consumption.

A system of elementary socialist education (infant welfare).

A system of polytechnical education.

A system of cultural and politico-social services.

A system of physical culture, including tourism.

A system of medical services (dispensaries, clinics, hospitals and sanatoriums).

According to the SASS group the whole problem of the socialist distribution of the population can be considered, thanks to this solution, as a dialectic process of disurbanization; a process based on the idea of a perpetually changing Ribbon Town which will promote the growth of a socialist sector, and thereby accelerate the disappearance of the remains of individualist economy and culture.

Criticism of the Ideas of the 'Opposition'

In the course of innumerable discussions it was recognized that the plan put forward by the SASS group contained very interesting suggestions, and went a long way towards the solution of problems involved. All the same the system of longitudinal distribution was officially characterized as uneconomic in its application to circulation of traffic, provision for the needs of transport, and main drainage; and unrealizable as a whole under the conditions likely to prevail during the transitional period. In proposing these decidedly radical solutions, the SASS group failed to take into account the material difficulties that have to be contended with at the present moment, such as the still inadequate technical equipment of the country and the stage of the social development of the workers.

The family has almost entirely disappeared in Soviet Russia as a productive unit; but it still exists as a unit of consumption, although its separate economic existence is in gradual process of liquidation. This is a fact which it would be both absurd and dangerous to deny. The decision registered by Vzik, the Central Executive Committee of the Communist Party, in 1930, defined the standpoint of the Government. While condemning Utopian attempts inspired by the desire to realize 'complete and immediate socialization', they say: 'It is impossible to overcome centuries-old impediments which are the result of the cultural and economic backwardness of society at one bound. Yet this is precisely the policy implied in these (anyhow at present) unrealizable and Utopian plans for the construction at the expense of the State of new communist towns embodying the complete collectivization of existence—including collective provisioning, infant education, and the legal prohibition of family cooking. The precipitous realization of such Utopian and doctrinaire schemes—which take no heed of the material resources of the country, or to what extent the population, with its existing habits and preferences, may be prepared for them—might easily result in substantial losses, and even discredit the fundamental principles of the socialistic reconstruction of society. Architects must avoid the danger of remaining in the domain of the fantastic, because an adequate solution of the problem can only be forthcoming from an architect who understands the life and social conditions of the masses.'

All that is necessary is that during the transitional period a means should be found to enable the family to transform its existence on a collectivist basis. But merely mechanical solutions, such as those proposed by administrative decree, will endanger the success of this movement. The development of the socialist sector can be encouraged and protected by a proper organization of the collectivist services, such as communal kitchens, laundries, crèches, infant schools, etc. The advantages which will accrue in future from the liquidation of the family as a unit of domestic economy will be indeed immense:

(1)   An increase in the well-being of the worker owing to the fact that female labour will be better employed and better paid.

(2)   An increase in the numbers of industrial and agricultural labourers.

(3)   A decrease in the population of the towns, owing to the fact that there will be a decline in the number of women not engaged in productive work of nearly 50 per cent.

(4)   A reduction in the cost of construction of dwellings owing to the suppression of separate kitchens, and other domestic services hitherto provided for in every home.

But this process must be allowed to take its course gradually, according to dialectic laws. It must be borne in mind that socialist town-planning, unlike capitalistic, is free to adopt measures spread over a long period of time, without being constrained, as in countries where an anarchical social system prevails, to have recourse to temporary and not co-ordinated solutions of a ridiculous and purely makeshift character.

All the same it would be unjust to conclude from this, as the opportunists of the Right Wing seek to do, that the programme of Maximal Propagation for the collectivization of the new towns within the limits of possibility is one that ought to be abandoned.

On the contrary, Soviet town-planners ought to keep this objective consistently in sight in all their efforts. The policy of the collectivization of all services, including housing, in the new towns, ought to be pursued methodically. This can be done by intensifying the socialist sector of production and existence in every way possible, and by including in it ever larger and larger sections of the population, who will willingly join the new communist sector attracted by the numerous advantages which it has to offer. But at the same time it is equally necessary to recognize the possibility that during the transitional period certain groups of workers can, if necessary, continue to live in separate dwellings on the basis of individual domestic economy.

Part 4   Aspects of Town Planning

4.1

A comparison between Le Corbusier's and Ludwig Hilberseimer's approach to town-planning. Häring brings out the salient features of both architects' work, but is critical of both.

4.2

These extracts came from Platz's compendious picture-book of the new architecture, *Die Baukunst der neuesten Zeit*, published in 1927. They show Platz's concern with the need to counteract, by rational and ordered planning, the disastrous social effects of nineteenth and early twentieth century speculative building in German cities. These particular extracts do not show Platz's emphasis on the possibilities of mechanized building to achieve these results, but they do hint—with his emphasis on the need

for a variety in the overall form of cities, his strictures on recent Dutch housing, and his acknowledgement of German individualism—at some of the difficulties such rationalization poses.

4.3

CIAM's fourth congress was due to be held in Moscow in 1932, but was cancelled as a result of the outcome of the Palace of Soviets competition (see Unit 14). The congress—with 'The Functional City' as its theme—was subsequently held in July–August 1933, aboard the S.S. *Patris*, and in Athens and Marseilles. The following is the draft statement issued at the end of the Congress. It was subsequently published in English in J. L. Sert's *Can our Cities Survive?* (from which this version is taken).

4.1   Two Cities by Hugo Häring

I

Both for Le Corbusier and for L. Hilberseimer, the problem of the big city is how those things that millions of people need for their homes, their lives, their work, their entertainment, their education, their relaxation—how all these things can be organized so as to fit in with the highest level of order that meets all the accepted requirements of the individual for space, air, hygiene and comfort, so that the course of life through these various factors is smooth and orderly, perhaps even pleasant and beneficial, and so that all this can be brought into harmony with the individual's economic efficiency. To both of them the solution of this task of organization, packing, supply and management, points to *concentration* of the masses in the most limited space by the development of the city upwards, for the primary reason that traffic decreases when the need to build long streets is eliminated (**Fig. 22**). (If television, improved forms of radio and so on ultimately reduce the need for traffic to a minimum, then we get nearer to the breaking-up of the cities, which brings us closer to Bruno Taut.)[1] The average worker in Berlin spends fifty-nine minutes twice a day in some form of transport simply

to get to and from his work. In Hilberseimer's and Corbusier's cities he walks for five minutes or goes up to the 37th floor in a lift in a fifth of that time. Hilberseimer accommodates five million people in one-fifth of the space they occupy in Berlin today. Even so they will still have more light and more air. If the traffic were also reduced to one-fifth or even less at the same time, the effect would really be very tempting.

The separate blocks in these cities become business units as big as a small town of, say, 8,000 inhabitants. Giant hotels, ocean liners—but on dry land. Undoubtedly an economical business proposition for all concerned. Both architects take for granted the highest technological perfection, generosity of scale and an ultimate pleasure in all that and in the fantastic.

The aesthetics? For Hilberseimer, the by-product of an achievement of thought and will, bright and clear, neither

Figure 22b   L. Hilbersheimer, Scheme for a high-rise city

Figure 22a   Le Corbusier, Scheme for a large city

[1] A reference to Taut's *Die Auflösung der Stadte oder die Erde*, Hagen, 1920. (ed.)

deliberate nor essential; for Corbusier, the effulgence of a cleaned-up world of geometrical culture, enhanced by the attraction of technical things. Not without a salute to the monumental, the majestic pathos of the Latins. But how could he be so crazy as to drive cars through triumphal arches? Is that really necessary?

II

Their idea of a city, then, is an opportunity for organization in the interests of economy, routine, business. Fordism.[1] What are such cities for?

III

Disadvantages:

(a) *The human being.* In so far as, outside his spiritual convictions, outside his interest in the general run of development, outside his personal position in the economy, in business and in progress, he is still a man he will do better to live somewhere else. The human being is completely excluded from Hilberseimer's city, while in Corbusier's he is just there on a visit, just passing through. Of course both Hilberseimer and Corbusier do postulate a new society of the future—Hilberseimer clearly looks for this in the direction of socialism, while Corbusier has in mind rather the 'good society'—but all the same they subordinate man to the geometric principle of a mechanistic world, thus putting the principle of mechanistic order above the demands of human beings. In other words, their planning leaves no room for real life; it is just organization for its own sake, degrading man to the level of a thing. No doubt the superior orders of the right angle and the square block do contain some democratic principle, but they base this principle only on the separate individual, not on the individual as a cell in the composition of society. The cell-individual stands outside the application of democratic conceptions, he even repudiates them, for what he wants is life, development, achievement. That leads to race-consciousness, aristocracy. That is why we cannot speak, as Spengler does, of the social value of a military world like the Prussian, for the subordination of the individual in that society is antisocial. What is genuinely social can only be what the individual demands. A socialism that leaves no room for the aristocratic nature of the individual soul is no socialism. Thus the view that communal life leads inevitably to uniformity and standardization is wrong; exactly the opposite is true. What we want is to free the individual being from uniformity and standardization; we want to give him room to live while we observe and encourage his individual development as a prerequisite of the development of the whole. That means that we have to subordinate the guiding principles of a mechanistic world to the development of the human being, and not the other way round. Unfortunately we have

already almost become a sacrifice on the altar of administration, especially in the cities; but we don't want to go so far as to make a principle of it. Are we not carrying on the struggle against the big cities precisely on the principle that enables the living to defend itself against mechanization? It is in the new creation of an organic, i.e. a *non-geometric*, conception of planning that the heart of the problem lies.

(b) *The Countryside.* For Hilberseimer's big city it just doesn't exist. It is outside, beyond the city limits. If you feel a need for it you can go out and find it. You're better off without it. Even the existence of the sun only forces a concession to orientation. The city lies in the clean air of its intellectual order; the flat plane, the drawing-board takes the place of the landscape, so that it contains no hills, nor woods, nor rivers, nor lakes. Such things are not only disruptive, they would actually be foreign bodies, elements of the anti-city. Away from the soil to the city *per se*.

Corbusier's attitude to scenery is a bit more considerate. He lets a few hills remain on the horizon, he makes you enter the city from flat country, rush straight through it and out into flat country again. The speeding motor-car is the quickening element of the city, and the country is chiefly there to make this speeding possible and to connect one city with another. While life in Hilberseimer's city has nothing to do with space and goes on like the teeming activity of an ant-hill, everything in Corbusier's city is full of this space. Tension and space are the elements which are generally needed for the vitality of its inhabitants and effectively regenerate the joy and vigour of living. The sun not only reinforces this work of regeneration, it actually enhances it to splendid effect. This city with its gigantic hotels in gardens and parks looks like a watering-place which takes for granted that all its guests will enjoy nearly the same standard of living, i.e. the standard of hotel guests. Thus even the social problem is instantly and simply solved by abolishing the differential between kings and proletariat so that they all meet on a pleasant middle ground. But even in Corbusier's big city the scenery is not essential; it is important only to the extent that it is important to have something more sociable, more festive than what this city, with its triumphal arches, has to offer.

IV

Another concept of the city

Cities are 'form-discoveries' on our way to incarnation. It is certain that men are not there because of the cities, but the cities because of men. But aren't the cities the fruit of a landscape, and men the masters of its destiny? Without the demonic forces bound up with a given landscape, no object, no city even, can be comprehended. You only

---

[1] 'Fordismus' in the original; a reference to the automated methods of the Ford Motor Co. in the USA. (ed.)

have to look at the cities of this earth, those of the past as well as of the present, to understand how closely cities and the landscape are connected, how much the destiny of the one is also the destiny of the other, how completely the cities realize the destiny of the landscape.

It may be that, after all we have already discovered, we are still discovering nature. But the form of a city is created by its countryside (site) it draws its life from it and in it; thus every city is different. One city resembles others only in outward things, not in character and content. It is wrong to think that the contents of different cities are alike; it is an error to assimilate them. Berlin, Cologne, Hamburg, Munich, Breslau [Wroclaw] are cities of completely different character. Paris, New York, Peking have nothing in common. Cities are living things, born of the landscape, with their own racial peculiarities. Their peoples grow like them, change with them. All that grows within them lives in them, develops in them, absorbs the inherent characteristics of the soil. The power of this soil shapes the city together with its inhabitants. Cities are individualities; there is no such thing as a city in the abstract. There is no norm for a city. Cities, like individuals, are active intellectually as well as economically. Their economic problems and cares, moreover, are only worries about their material existence and prosperity, they have no sort of creative, constructive forces in them. Such forces arise only in the spiritually motivated and creative individual they arise from his physical circumstances, that is to say, from the constitution of the landscape. The form of cities is the work of non-material forces; economic problems bear the same relation to it as the problems of the individual man's existence bear to his actual character. The problems of spiritual things are thus immeasurably more important than economic problems (which the economists will surely deny, but then the economists are bankrupt; they have lost the only thing on which they depended and which gave them power and esteem—money. Who will take them seriously now? So long as we don't make a start on the breakthrough to immaterial ends, even they, the 'creators' of our prosperity, will never make a come-back.) The making of men comes before the making of cities, before the valuing of property, before the economy, before business, before Fordism, before prosperity. It is tempting indeed to think that the luxurious life of the watering-place, which we can afford for a few weeks in the year at best, could be made a permanent factor of our city life. Such living conditions are not only in accord with the true spirit of the ever-restless townsman, they not only lead to real freedom for the independent person to move from town to town carrying no more than a suit-case, unhampered by the removal-van; they are also in accord with economic ideas of getting away from the individual household (there are a million one-person households in Berlin—what economic madness). The hotel suits a lot of people at times. But it does not always suit them, and it does not suit everybody. Another man likes a particular spot, he likes peace and quiet, hearth and home and family, he is as it were in tune with the time. He needs rest, time to think, stability. He looks to his house as a workshop to meet his personal requirements. He needs nature, scenery, to nourish his psyche. He needs a counter-weight to state mechanization. He also needs psychic regeneration. None the less he is a real townsman, not just because he works in the town but because he too shares the townsman's nature, because he likes the busy-ness of the town life, its tempo, its scale, and other things about it. What he requires from the town is quite different from the requirement of the hotel guest. And against these needs of a second man we can oppose those of a third, a fourth, a tenth, all different from one another in important matters. For the moment we will only draw the conclusion, the challenge, that we cannot elevate the requirements of one individual to be a rule for the whole city, that all the people of a city cannot be lumped together in one category. But if we ever managed to do that, if we could ever find a formula for mankind, then we would certainly be able to build cities for them on Hilberseimer's lines; though if the future permitted great affluence to everyone, then Corbusier's lay-outs would be preferable. Since we don't rule out either of these possibilities completely, Hilberseimer and Corbusier have done a great service in making us conversant with the future. It is clear moreover that we have already partly realized these city-concepts (especially in America) and that Hilberseimer and Corbusier have only taken the trouble to work out these concepts clearly. If we are a bit shocked at Hilberseimer's conclusions, that is not his fault.

4.2   Municipal Architecture by G. A. Platz

1   Economic and Technical Basis

The economic elements in modern municipal architecture are so extensive that we can only discuss them briefly. The manner of life and growth in a town should be examined by measurement and observation before commencing any general plan of house-building. Traffic flow, railways, waterways, stations for passengers and goods and for marshalling, ports, tramways, suburban express ways, car and lorry routes must be planned ahead for many years of development along with the zoning of areas for industry, trade, warehousing, housing estates, public buildings, parks, playgrounds and sports fields. The height and density of building must decrease towards the outlying districts for healthy growth. Town planning can obviously only lay down the overall guide lines and the plan should remain 'elastic' so that new possibilities can be accommodated. If a large community wishes to keep control of its affairs, it must have at its disposal considerable amounts of its own property in the area. Studies on dwelling habits in England, northern France, Belgium and Holland, especially by Eberstadt,[1] have shown that, under conditions of natural land husbandry, and with corresponding general prosperity, the small, single-family house or the rented house for a few families is the normal type. In London the occupation rate is 6–7, whereas in Berlin there are 76 persons per house. These dreadful living conditions in the state capital arise from a single, architectural calamity: from 1860 the building plan for Berlin allowed tenement houses with five storeys and corresponding street widths for the whole area. It is clear that under these circumstances unscrupulous house and land speculation, combined with foolish building regulations, was bound to lead to a lemming-like influx of human masses in complete disorder to the city in the second half of the 19th century. The building regulations of the large provincial towns were copied for decades by those of the state capital in a disastrous misunderstanding of local living conditions. Progressive industrialization encouraged, even demanded, the massing of crowds of people into narrow quarters and no one with a sense of responsibility attempted to stop it. Respect for private property, even for that dishonestly acquired, was too deep rooted, too many people had an interest in it, the price of arable land was raised to the limit through speculation, and thus the erection of mass living quarters was 'lucrative'.

Rational men have fought against these ills from the beginning, without, however, being able to break through the wall of egotism and stupidity which opposed itself against a healthy development of dwelling habits. Misfortune had to reach enormous proportions before a larger group of people began to realize that the modern large town, in its present form, signified the beginning of the end of this 'built vice'. (Friedrich Nietzsche.)

The stages on the way to this perception are sketched graphically by Werner Hegemann[2] in his book *Der Städtebau.*[3] The numbers and details in the book tell a shocking tale. Within the Berlin conurbation in 1910 there were 550,000 people in overcrowded dwellings, where every easily heated room was filled with 4–13 people. 220,000 children were found in these dwellings with no playground or recreational space other than the dusty, dangerous street. Intelligent theoreticians, who

were not perhaps brought up in the social Democratic party, pointed out untiringly that it is a nonsense to retain the conditions of a closed fortress (with its consequence of building upwards) on the vast scale of a modern megatown, and that the living conditions of modern London could be made possible in the large towns on the continent by beneficial and steady development.

But, in spite of all warnings, a disastrous combination of unfavourable circumstances favoured the growth of these dreadful monsters which have surrounded the cores of the old towns and these have poisoned themselves. If today one wants to lay blame on anyone, one must hold responsible the stupid administration, the time when the opinion of the masses was ignored, just as much as the exploiting instincts and money grabbing of the ruling classes and finally the indifference or inadequacy of the authorities.[4] The rigidity of some laws, the clumsiness and dependence on party moderates of the legislation, the proliferation of administrative departments and the scarcity of responsible leaders with corresponding power, all these have contributed to the making of a monster out of modern large town.

In view of this fact there remains for us, today and in the future, only one possibility: to deepen understanding and strengthen our will to thwart this chaotic disfigurement and to lead the future development of towns in a healthy direction.

After the catastrophe of the war and the revolution all the elements of town planning were investigated, including government, economic and business affairs, as theoreticians had already done before. What transpired was what Rudolf Eberstadt, lecturer in habitation-styles, and Raymond Unwin, the urban architectural theorist and creator of Hampstead garden suburb in London, had already recommended before the war: the checking of the further spread of large towns by the formation of satellite towns—this now received general acknowledgement. An examination of traffic problems (Blum-Hanover) and sanitation showed that the large conurbation could not be allowed to expand without severe detriment to the population, that suburbanization must take place, with large, permanent open spaces for parks, gardens, playgrounds and sportsfields interspersed, as 'lungs' for the town. By this time the garden city concept, which was formulated at the beginning of the century by Ebenezer Howard, had already taken root in a large percentage of the population.

The admirable dwelling pattern in England, where the one family house predominates, gradually became the ideal in Germany. In spite of the profitability calculations of the enthusiasts for blocks of flats, low level building began to take over as the ideal concept. A decisive influence was the advancement of the land reform idea, which proclaimed land as publicly-owned and aimed

---

[1] R. Eberstadt, German social reformer. (ed.)

[2] Editor of *Wasmuths Monatshefte.* (ed.)

[3] Ed. W. Hegemann: *Der Städtebau nach den Ergebnissen der Allgemeinen Städtebau-Ausstellung in Berlin, 1910,* 2 vols. Berlin, 1911–13. (ed.)

[4] The jurisdiction of the police until recently only included order and safety. Cultural requirements were first introduced in the present century and the laws against disfigurement are scarcely 20 years old. Policing and care of buildings are still in most places separated from each other in different branches of the administration.

to halt ruinous speculation. Everyone today knows the beneficial influence exerted on the health of people by life in individual houses with gardens. On a knowledge of the best mode of dwelling hangs the distinction between welfare and misery for future generations. For those to whom an individual house is not a necessary requirement, regulations should allow small and medium-sized blocks of flats with limited numbers of storeys and a rational layout for human habitation; grouping repetitive units around communal gardens removes the fatal image of the barracks[1] from blocks of flats. The most recent consequences of this aware, socially orientated town planning, which has no parallel in history, is the present day area plan which maps out traffic arteries, agricultural areas, forests, mines and industrial areas so that they can become well-integrated and the individual communities work together; it also eliminates urban sprawl.[2] Only such an overall plan can ensure beneficial architectural development from our fragmentation. The new town will develop from a rational overall plan which will be determined before the scientific and technical details are worked out. It will be the work of well-informed urban administrators, who will take account of the growing cultural ethos and, through continuous collaboration amongst all the administrative departments concerned, predetermine the future lot of their communities in the full knowledge of their responsibility.

2   The problem of Form

The artistic aspects of town planning depend on the whole character of the landscape and the particular situation of the town. The task of artistic town planning is to lay out the squares and streets in space under an open sky, to insert monumental buildings into the space, ideally: the spatial arrangement of the entire system of the town. The first theoretician of the new principle of town planning, Camillo Sitte[3] in Vienna, was already demanding the organization of public spaces (breaking up the *Ringstrasse* in Vienna into *fora*, in the style of the Roman Caesar-*fora*) in 1899.

A. E. Brinckmann[4] in his fundamental books has researched into and formulated the basic laws of formal town planning (especially of the Italian Renaissance and Baroque). Obviously we can learn something from this approach to the ideal, but only by synthesis and by adaptation to the individual case. Who today would copy Napoleon's straight street plans in rough or mountainous country? In Rothenburg, Nuremberg, Heidelberg, Baden-Baden, Marburg am Lahn, or Meissen the twisting street is a convenience which is there just as acceptable as it is to be avoided, on the other hand, in flat country in order to present least hindrance to fast through-traffic. Thus,

the rules of beauty for a town in the mountains are different from those for a town on a plain. Spatial effects, on which the beauty of the town depends, are not limited by twisting streets. Regularity and order in a town plan soothes and satisfies, picturesque disorder stimulates and creates excitement.

The style of beauty one chooses depends on one's nature. Romantics and women love town planning in the 'Rothenburg style'; earnest business men treat it with greater circumspection, though they do not always reject it. By all possible means we must try to counteract the tendency towards monotony of a townscape, especially through the regulation of building heights. This is as true for the skyline as for the plan. In past centuries the sculptural appearance of the town would be modulated by the irregularity of the buildings and articulated through the dominant symbols of religious and secular power (towers and dominant groups of buildings). Churches, fortifications, townhalls and warehouses enliven the mass of a town and give rhythm to it. Today other forces are at work. Moreover, townscape is secularized—one may praise or deplore that. The landmarks of our time, watertowers, gasometers, factories and chimneys, are added as new annual rings to the city form, on the periphery of the old monuments as enriching (or disfiguring) constituents. Until now we have unwillingly accepted these structures, for they appear crude and vulgarly functional. We need not be ashamed for they contribute and proclaim the same strength and life as the old secular buildings. But neither do the modern, multi-storeyed administrative and office buildings bow to them, for in them reigns the spirit of our time, the spirit of organized, creative economy. They serve a similar purpose to the old department stores, in uniting people and regions.

If a new life and a new beauty blossoms in modern towns out of these structures then they have gained an absolute right to existence. They are indispensable to a modern townscape, since it becomes monotonous through enforced regularity. Anyone who has seen the view of Berlin from Kreuzberg cannot shut his eyes to the perception that this vast stone desert is punctuated only by (isolated) skyscrapers.

The artistic unity of the overall townscape was a foregone conclusion in times of a completely civic culture—today it is, as yet, only wishful thinking or a desired dream. Is it possible that such a diversified culture as that of the present be moulded into a type of construction which bears a uniform character?

This bitter knowledge should not mislead us in our search for artistic unity. Nowhere is the difference between intention and accomplishment as great as in architecture. Nowhere should one seek size in order to attain this

---

[1] The attempt by some large towns (e.g. Vienna) to solve the pressing housing problem caused by poverty through the mass building of tiny dwellings illustrates the complexity of the situation. Already fresh conditions have appeared in the form of social advancement, whose unfortunate consequences the next generation must bear.

[2] The form of Prussian town building regulations from 1926 draws together concepts of modern architecture and prepares the way for systematic colonization in the best sense.

[3] Camillo Sitte (1843–1903), Austrian architect and author of the influential volume of essays *Der Städtebau nach seinen künstlerischen Grundsätzen* ('City Planning according to Artistic Principles') Vienna, 1889. (ed.)

[4] Albert Brinckmann (1881–1958); writer on art history and town-planning and a critic of Sitte's theory and methods. (ed.)

possibility.

The artistic unity of a whole town has grown over a century; it is the most beautiful fruit of a universal contemporary architectural conviction. The strongest will, which attempts to create it, shatters itself against reality: limits on ownership, shortage of money, the individuality of builders, architects and tendering. In spite of all this only a town which makes its vocation clear, creating space between massed buildings, combining its architectural forms in a sculptural and spatial unity, only such a town can claim cultural value.

For a while an ideal, stimulated by baroque townscapes, appeared in the image of the 'Unified façade' (W. C. Behrendt). In fact the Danes (in Copenhagen) in peacetime and the Dutch on a large scale after the war (in Rotterdam and Amsterdam) illustrated the effect inherent in blocks of housing designed by a single architect. So far, however, the fact that other possibilities may be dormant in a conglomeration of blocks of housing has been overlooked; awakening these will be the job of the next generation of architects. The unified block of houses is a primitive, doubtless very beautiful, space form, but surely not the only one to be considered. In any case, some order must link together the parts of the block into a whole.

Different types of roof (saddle-roof, garret and flat roof) near each other disturb the overall picture just as much as different levels of roof, gables and towers, which break through the dominant lines. An extravagant variety of shapes in massed buildings mirrors the disunited and confused circumstances in which we live, an expression of the one-sided individuality of our times.

Only a despotic sense of art, bestowed on appropriate authorities, could today force a marriage amongst the forms of construction within a block or within a group of country houses, which have grown up gradually under the influence of a thousand individual wishes. In the near future only energetically applied and artistically sympathetic building laws and the growing insight of the architectural profession can help here. The unity of the collective shape of a street side is best preserved where the house shapes are consistent. Yet even here unthinking application is dangerous, sensitive and decisively shaped exceptions, graduations, accents are welcome as 'dynamic' means of expression.

Undoubtedly there are dormant, in the massed buildings of a large town, possibilities of constructional variations of enormous effect, as one can see convincingly in rough brickwork, which expresses the essence most clearly. These could be brought to life beautifully by a strong artistic personality, if constructed by sympathetic builders. But even the boldest will always find its limits in reality in the inadequacy of human strength. At times aesthetic culture was provided solely as a result of the art of town planning which had attained a high level of perfection. But almost always it originated in a 'perfect whole'. Is it possible in the future to achieve that unity of artistic culture which has made the perfect creation of Italian and oriental towns? The German is still an 'ardent individualist'; and his townscapes still show that spirit which splits up Germany into small states and parties. Higher insight matures only slowly, with isolated works of modern town planning hurrying on in advance.

'No period had greater difficulty than ours in achieving unity, for none had so many threads to combine as ours. We extend ourselves over town, country and European culture and there is coming a world culture. That this will take longer to mature and differentiate itself among the races than did each earlier one cannot be doubted. One thing is sure: it can only mature through the convergence of creative forces. He who seeks unity works the tapestry of life.'

(K. E. Osthaus: *Grundzüge der Stilentwicklung*, Hagen, 1918.)

4.3 Town Planning Chart[1] CIAM (Congrès Internationaux d'Architecture Moderne)

1 Definitions and preliminary statements

Town and country merge into one another and are elements of what may be called a regional unit.

Every city forms part of a geographic, economic, social, cultural and political unit (region), upon which its development depends.

Towns or cities cannot, in consequence, be studied apart from their regions, which constitute their natural limits and environment.

The development of these regional units depends on:
(a) *Their geographical and topographical characteristics*—climate, land and waters, natural communications both within the region and with other regions.
(b) *Their economic potentialities*—natural resources (soil and subsoil, raw materials, sources of energy, flora and fauna); technical resources (industrial and agricultural production), the economic system, and the distribution of wealth.
(c) *Their political and social situation*—the social structure of the population, the political regime, and the administrative system.

Down through history, the character of cities has been determined by special circumstances, such as those having to do with *military defences*, scientific discoveries, admini-

---

[1] As drafted by the CIAM in Athens, August 1933.

strative systems, the progressive development of the *means of production and of locomotion.*

The basic factors governing the development of cities are therefore subject to continual changes.

It is the uncontrolled and disorderly development of the Machine Age which has produced the chaos of our cities.

All these essential factors taken together constitute the only true basis for the scientific planning of any region. They are:

(a) interdependent, the one reacting upon the other;

(b) subject to continuous fluctuations that are due to scientific and technical progress, and to social, political, and economic changes. Whether these fluctuations are forward or backward, from the human viewpoint, depends upon the measure in which man's aspirations toward the improvement of his material and spiritual well-being are able to assert themselves.

2 The four functions of the city

The following statements of the actual conditions of life in cities and what is needed to correct their deficiencies relate to the four functions of the city: dwelling, recreation, work, and transportation.

These four functions constitute a basic classification for the study of modern town-planning problems.

3 Dwelling, the first urban function. General statements on present conditions of housing in cities:

The *density of the population* is too great in central districts; in many cases it exceeds 400 inhabitants to the acre (1,000 to the hectare).

Overcrowding is not only to be found in the central parts of our cities. It also occurs in the vast residential areas which developed as a consequence of the industrial growth of the past century.

In overcrowded districts, living conditions are unhealthful. This is due to the fact that the land surface is overbuilt, open spaces are lacking, and the buildings themselves are in a dilapidated and insanitary state.

This fact is all the more serious in view of the low economic means of the inhabitants of such districts.

The progressive extension of the urban area has destroyed the green open spaces that once surrounded the dwelling districts of the city. This has served to deny many people the opportunity to enjoy the benefits of living near the open country.

Dwelling blocks and individual dwellings *are often badly located,* both in relation to their function and with respect to the sanitary conditions required for healthful housing.

The more densely populated areas are frequently those sites which are least appropriate for dwellings, such as those having northern exposures on hilly ground, lowlands subject to inundations or fog, or sites too close to industrial districts and consequently disturbed by noises, vibrations and smoke.

Districts of a low concentration of population have been developed on the best sites, favoured by good climatological and topographical conditions, sheltered from industry, and easily accessible by roads.

This irrational location of dwellings is still permitted by *legislation* that does not take into consideration the health factors that are thereby jeopardized. Zoning plans, together with zoning legislation capable of enforcing such plans, are wanting. In fact, existing laws seem to ignore the consequences of overcrowding, of the lack of open spaces, of the dilapidated condition of many dwellings, of the want of community services. They also ignore the fact that the application of modern planning and modern technics would create illimitable possibilities for the reconstruction of cities.

Buildings erected on heavily traveled streets and in the neighborhood of corner crossings are made undesirable as dwellings because of noise, dust, and noxious gases.

In residential streets whose façades face each other, the varying circumstances of exposure to sunlight have usually not been taken into account. As a general rule, if one side of the street receives the necessary sunlight in the most desirable hours, sunlight conditions on the opposite side are different and often bad.

Modern suburbs have often developed rapidly, without planning and without control. Consequently their later connection with the metropolitan center (by rail, by roads, or by other means) has met with physical obstacles which might have been avoided if suburban growth had been considered as part of a regional development.

Suburbs have generally been incorporated under city control only when fully developed as independent units.

Their process of growth and decay often escaping all control, frequently these suburbs take on the shape of shack-towns—disorderly groups of hovels constructed of all imaginable kinds of discarded materials. In spite of all, this type of suburb is still openly tolerated in many metropolitan areas.

The distribution of buildings intended for *community services* is of an arbitrary and heedless nature. This is notoriously true of schools, which are often situated on the most congested thoroughfares and too far from the dwellings they serve. The following statement of desiderata is based upon what precedes.

Residential districts ought to occupy the *best sites.* The climatological and topographical conditions of those sites intended for dwelling purposes must be carefully considered, as well as their proximity to existing unbuilt land surfaces suitable for recreation purposes. The possible future location of industry and business in the immediate vicinity should also be considered.

A minimum amount of *exposure to the sun* should be established for residential structures, regardless of their location or class.

Different *density limits* should be fixed for different residential districts, based on the factors influencing the living conditions within each district.

Modern building technics should be employed in constructing high, widely spaced apartment blocks whenever the necessity of housing high densities of population exists. Only such treatment of dwellings will liberate the necessary land surface for recreation purposes, community services, and parking places, and provide dwellings with light, sun, air, and view.

The building of dwellings along *traffic thoroughfares* must be forbidden on grounds of health, since these houses are exposed to noises, dust, and gases emanating from traffic.

4   Recreation. General statement of recreation problems:

Open spaces in cities today are generally insufficient.

Open spaces are often poorly situated and consequently difficult of access to many people.

Since most open spaces are situated in outlying and suburban areas, they do not benefit the inhabitants of the unhealthful central districts.

The few existing playgrounds and fields for sports occupy, as a rule, sites that are destined to be built up in the near future. This accounts for their frequent displacement. As ground prices rise, these open spaces disappear, leaving the playgrounds, and playing fields to be reorganized on new sites, each time further away from the central districts.

It should be required that:

The general sanitation of too densely populated districts be improved by the razing of slums and other buildings, the *cleared sites to be devoted to recreational purposes.*

That open spaces near kindergartens or playgrounds be used as sites for nursery schools, and that certain sites in parks be devoted to general community purposes, with branch public libraries, small neighborhood museums, or auditoriums.

The chaotic development of modern cities has ruthlessly destroyed many sites in the environs of the urban zone which might have been converted into *week-end recreation centers.*

Advantage should be taken of those sites near cities whose natural features (rivers, beaches, forests, lakes) make them favorable for recreation purposes.

5   Work. Statements concerning problems in industrial and business areas:

Places of work (industrial, business, governmental) are not situated in the city structure according to their functions.

The *absence of a planned coordination* of the locations of work-places with those of dwellings creates excessive traveling distances between the two.

Traffic is overtaxed during *rush hours*, on account of disorganized communications.

Owing to high land values, increasing taxation, traffic congestion, and to the rapid and uncontrolled expansion of the city, industry is often forced to move away, bringing about a *decentralization* which is facilitated by modern technics.

Business districts can be expanded only through the costly action of purchasing and razing surrounding dwellings.

Possible ways of solving these problems:

Industries should be classified according to their character and their needs, and should be distributed in special zones throughout the territory comprised of the city and the region it influences. In delimiting these zones, it will be necessary to take into account the relation of the different industries to each other and their relation to zones intended for other functions.

The *distances* between dwellings and work-places should be direct and traversable in a minimum of time.

Industrial districts should be independent of residential districts (indeed, of other districts as well), and should be isolated by means of green bands, or neutral zones.

Certain small industries intimately related to urban life and not the source of any inconvenience or nuisance should remain within the city, serving its different residential districts.

It is necessary that industrial zones of importance should be contiguous to rail-roads, to navigable rivers or harbors, and to the principal transportation routes.

Business districts should enjoy favorable means of communication linking them to residential districts and to industrial zones.

6   Transportation. General statements concerning traffic and street problems:

The *street systems* found in most cities and their suburbs today are a heritage of past eras (the Middle Ages in many European cities, and later periods in America), when they were designed for the use of pedestrians and horse-drawn vehicles. As such, in spite of successive alterations, they no longer fulfill the requirements of modern types of vehicles (automobiles, buses, trucks) or modern traffic volume.

The insufficient width of streets causes congestion.

The *lack of space* in our streets and the *frequency of crossings* make the new possibilities of locomotion almost useless.

Traffic congestion, which is the cause of thousands of accidents, is becoming increasingly hazardous to everyone.

Our present streets fail to exhibit any *differentiation* in terms of their possibile functions, a circumstance which excludes an efficacious approach to the modern traffic problem.

The solution of this problem is unattainable through present corrective measures (street widening, traffic restrictions, or others), and can be reached only by means of new city planning.

A certain type of 'academic' city planning, conceived in 'the grand manner' and striving mainly toward monumental effects in its layout of buildings, avenues, and squares, often complicates the traffic situation.

Railroad lines are often obstacles to urban development. Encircling certain districts, they separate them from other parts of the city with which they should have direct contact and easy communication.

Changes necessary for the solution of the most important transportation problems:

The universal use of *motorized transportation*, bringing speeds unknown only a few years ago, has violently agitated the whole urban structure and fundamentally affected living conditions within it. A new street system, designed for modern means of transportation, is therefore required.

For the purpose of providing a *new street system* corresponding to modern traffic needs, it is necessary that accurate statistics be available for the rational determination of street dimension requirements.

The speeds to be provided for in each street will depend upon the function of the street and upon the nature of the vehicles it carries. *These speeds therefore are also factors of classification*, determining the features of those thoroughfares intended for fast-moving traffic and those intended for trucks and other slow traffic, and differentiating these from tributary or secondary streets.

In the proposed network of restricted streets, provision should be made for *pedestrian lanes*, designed for the convenience of pedestrians and therefore not necessarily following vehicular routes.

Streets ought to be classified according to their functions, as residential streets, business streets, industrial streets, and so on.

Buildings of all kinds, but especially dwellings, should be *isolated* from heavy traffic by green bands.

With these difficulties solved, the new street network would effect other simplifications; for by means of efficient traffic organization and a proper coordination of different urban elements, *traffic could be reduced and concentrated within the great arteries.*

7 Buildings and districts of historical interest[1]

Buildings or groups of buildings that are remnants of past cultures should not be demolished:

(a) When they are really representative of their period and, as such, may be of general interest and serve for the instruction of the public.

(b) When their existence does not affect the health conditions of populations living in the area.

(c) Whenever it is possible to route main thoroughfares so that the presence of these old districts does not increase traffic congestion and so that their location does not affect the organic growth of the city.

All attempts at adapting new districts to these old layouts (which is often done under pretext of preserving local characteristics) have had bad results. Such adaptations to the past should not be tolerated in any case.

By a planned clearance of slum areas, which are frequently to be found in the neighborhood of these monuments of the past, it is possible to improve the living conditions of the residential areas near-by and to safeguard the health of their inhabitants.

8 General requirements; statement and summary of the preceding:

One might summarize the analysis of urban functions, as presented in the preceding pages, by saying that the living conditions found in most cities today do not correspond to the most elementary *biological and psychological needs of great masses of their populations.*

Since the beginning of the Machine Age, these conditions have been an expression of the ceaseless growth of private interests.

The growth of cities has been caused by the increasing use of the machine—the change from the manual labor of artisans to big industry.

There is apparent in most cities a disastrous rupture between the economic resources and the administrative and social responsibility of the municipality.

Although cities are constantly changing, it may be stated as a general fact that changes are not anticipated and that their development suffers because of the absence of control and the failure to apply the principles recognized by contemporary town planning.

The magnitude of the work to be undertaken in the urgently needed reconstruction of cities, on the one hand, and the excessive *division of urban land*, on the other, represent two antagonistic realities.

This sharp contradiction creates a most serious problem in our time:

That of the pressing need to establish the disposition of the land upon a basis that will satisfy the needs of the many as well as those of the individual.

In case of conflict, private interest should be subordinated to public interest.

The city should be examined in the economic ensemble of its region of influence. A plan of the economic unit, the 'city-region' in its totality, must therefore replace the simple city plan of today.

It will be necessary to fix the limits of the plan in accordance with those of the region defined by the scope of the city's economic influence:

---

[1] Section 7 of this chart has been omitted from the general text because it applies only to certain cities. It was introduced by the Italian delegates, who had to deal with these problems frequently.

(a) To produce an *equitable layout*, with respect to location and areas, of the various districts intended for dwellings, for work, or for recreation, as well as to establish traffic networks.

(b) To *establish plans* that will determine the development of different districts according to their needs and their organic laws.

(c) The town planner should also establish the relationship between places of dwelling, work, and recreation, in such a way that the daily cycle of activities going on in these various districts may occur with the greatest economy of time.

This is a constant factor determined by the rotation of the earth on its axis.

In establishing the relations between the different urban functions, the town planner must not forget that dwelling is the first urban function, a primordial element in the city pattern.

The urban unit should be able to *develop organically* in all its different parts. And each phase of its development should assure a state of equilibrium among all its respective functions.

It should therefore assure, on both the spiritual and material planes, individual liberty and the benefits of collective action.

To the architect engaged in town planning, *human needs and the human scale* of values are the key to all the architectural compositions to be made.

The point of departure for all town planning should be the cell represented by a single dwelling, taken together with similar cells to form a neighborhood unit of efficacious size. With this cell as the starting point, dwellings, places of work, and recreation areas should be distributed throughout the urban area in the most favorable relationship possible.

To solve this tremendous problem, it is necessary to utilize the resources put at our disposal by *modern technics* and to procure the *collaboration of specialists.*

The course to be taken in all town-planning projects will be influenced basically by the *political, social and economic factors* of the time and not, in the last resort, by *the spirit of modern architecture.*

The dimensions of the component parts of the functional city should be estimated on the human scale and in relation to human needs.

Town planning is a science based on *three dimensions*, not two. It is in admitting the *element of height* that efficacious provision can be made for traffic needs and for the creation of open spaces for recreation or other purposes.

It is of the most urgent necessity that *each city should provide itself with a town-planning program*, coordinated with the programs of its region and of the nation as a whole. The execution of these programs on a national, regional, or urban scale must be guaranteed by the necessary legal arrangements.

Every town-planning program must be based upon *accurate researches* made by specialists. It must foresee the different stages of urban *development in time and space*. It must *coordinate the natural, sociological, economic, and cultural factors that exist in each case.*

Part 5   Industrial Architecture

5.1 and 5.2

The following two items give detailed first hand accounts, by the engineer Karl Bernhardt (who was one of the major German engineers of this period) and the architect Peter Behrens, of the technical and aesthetic problems involved in the design and building of the new Turbine factory for the AEG.

5.3

These extracts are taken from a very influential book of splendid photographs of industrial constructions and buildings. The scope of the work, covering everything from giant cranes to old barns formed part of the appeal, but the text included an interesting attempt to tackle the problem of finding norms of good design which would avoid despoiling the countryside with ugly industrial excrescences.

5.4 and 5.5

These are two of a series of articles written in the 1930s by this most intriguing of architectural critics. 'Architecture and Engineering' examines the relative roles of the architect and the engineer. The original version of 'Concrete' was full of facts about the origins of the process and its implications for modern architects. We have picked out only the more general parts of the article, in which Shand tries to awaken British architects to the possibilities, formal and constructional, of reinforced concrete, instead of relying on steel frames which were usually completely concealed.

5.1   The New Turbine Hall for AEG by Karl Bernhardt

. . . Whereas the previous factory, which was hardly sufficient for present-day demands, had a span of 18 metres and moving gantries with a lifting capacity of 25 tons, the new one is 25 metres wide and its gantries can carry loads of up to 100 tons. The new building had to be erected in the shortest possible time, both because of the increased size of individual units—no less than 8 turbo-dynamos of 20,000 horsepower each are now in production, and propeller turbines of 14,000 horsepower each have also been delivered—and because of the large number of orders.

According to Herr Lasche, the factory's director, who specified the technical and operational requirements for the new installation, the contents of the factory's order book in 1901 amounted to only a few thousand horsepower, while by the beginning of October 1905, i.e. after scarcely five years' progress, deliveries had already exceeded a million horsepower. Although the current commercial situation is only moderately favourable, 2,600 men are at present employed at the factory. The turbo-dynamos and ship's turbines built by AEG are notable for their economical use of steam and safety of operation.

The new hall was designed by the author of this article in collaboration with Professor Peter Behrens, who was responsible for its aesthetic aspects. It has a length of 207 metres on the Berlichingenstrasse and a width of 39·3 metres on the Huttenstrasse.

The internal volume totals 151,500 cubic metres. The building consists of a main hall spanning 25·60 metres and a two-storey secondary hall at the side with a basement. . . . The main hall had to project above this for artistic reasons, and this was also an advantage from a technical point of view, since the rails of the gantries in this part of the building had to be 15·3 metres above the floor level so that the heavy machine parts and components, etc., could be moved freely to and fro above the machines being assembled on the factory floor. In addition, the main hall had to be equipped with a large number of swivelling cranes which had to be able to function without hindrance from the gantries moving overhead. For these reasons, the cornice level of the building on the Berlichingenstrasse was situated at a height of 18·64 metres, in compliance with the building authorities' provisions for maximum building height.

The structural principles are governed by the unusual structural stresses created by the particular manufacturing operation. The moving gantries in the main hall had to have a lifting capacity of 50 tons at a speed of 2 metres per second, so that the thrust on the four operative wheels of the gantries is 40 tons in each case. The upper storey of the side hall is equipped with moving gantries of 10 tons lifting capacity; its normal floor loading capacity was required to be 2,000 kilogrammes per square metre, which increases in places to 3,000 kilogrammes per square metre. The lower storey has moving gantries with a lifting capacity of 40 tons and the floor loading is 10,000 kilogrammes per square metre.

The structural framework of the main hall, which carries the most powerful external stresses, is composed of 22 steel girder frames, which are arranged at intervals of 9·22 metres; their position is dictated by the layout of the railway tracks running into the hall. For artistic reasons, the apex of the barrel-vaulted roof, which is formed by a series of flat planes, rises 25 metres above the floor. . . .

The roof girders are stiffened by adjustable steel tie-rods, which run between the extremities of the arched roof girders directly above the open space left for the

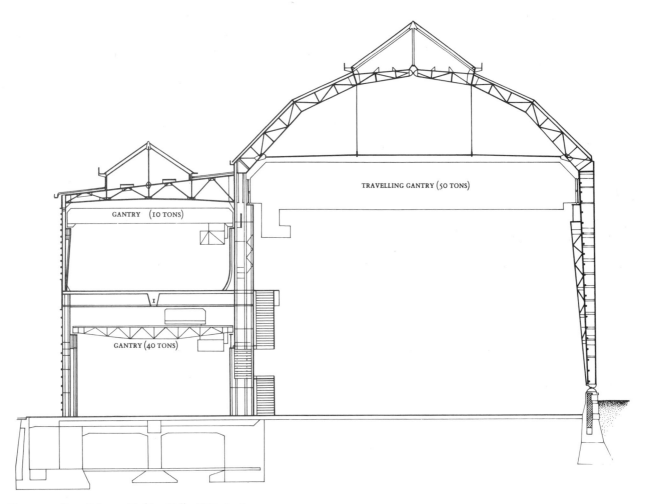

TRAVELLING GANTRY (50 TONS)

GANTRY (10 TONS)

I

GANTRY (40 TONS)

Figure 23   Peter Behrens, Turbine Hall, AEG. Section

gantries. The tapering of the main stanchions on the Berlichingenstrasse side is particularly noteworthy, both for its aesthetic effect and for the amount of space which is saved thereby, for the stanchions project like pillars some 30 centimetres over the building line. . . .

The appearance of the end walls was dictated by artistic considerations, and the method of construction has to conform to these. The walls consist of steel uprights and cross-pieces which are clothed partly in glass and partly with a concrete filling. . . .

For artistic reasons put forward by Professor Peter Behrens, the main hall was emphasized by setting the side hall back from it slightly. The same consideration confirmed the author's desire to bring the masses of steel together so as to avoid the confusing network of normal girder construction. The intention was, in particular, to have the interior space closed off on all sides by flat planes, so as to display the formality of the architectonic proportions and the cathedral-like spaciousness of the interior to best advantage. The solid-webbed construction of the

main stanchions contributes substantially to the favourable appearance of the exterior.

One essential feature was that the interior should have as much light as possible, which meant that large areas of glass had to be used. Thus the side walls consist almost entirely of steel and glass, concrete being used only at the base. Moreover the concrete is used here as a filling and not as a load-bearing medium. The windows on the Berlichingenstrasse are canted flush with the inner edges of the vertical steel stanchions, so that the horizontal linking girder running lengthwise above the windows casts a deep shadow on to them. This horizontal beam has the effect of a steel cornice and together with the pediment at the front end makes the roof appear as a solid mass resting on the main stanchions and on the window frame of the façade. The rounded corners are made of concrete divided by steel bands so that they appear merely as a filling, as against the vertical structural members of the side wall. In contrast to the flank on the Berlichingenstrasse, the large window on the Huttenstrasse stands vertical, and the glass is laid flush with the steel framework, which is reinforced against wind pressures on the inside by a gallery at the same level as the upper floor of the side hall. The front end of the side hall is constructed entirely of concrete, so as to emphasize the internal character of the two halls as seen from the side. On the yard side of the secondary hall, the supporting beams of the upper floor are revealed between the steel uprights; these are 2·1 metres high and reach approximately to the level of the window sills. Here again the windows form a continuous surface with the structural steel members. The use of glass and steel as a continuous medium is adopted as a general principle, so as to strengthen the overall impression of the building. All sculptural and ornamental decoration was omitted, since the function and character of a factory building demands simplicity of form, and also because the impression of solidity desired by the architect, and the proportions contributing to this impression, would only have been diminished by its use.

The reinforced concrete construction of the building, which was initially built to a length of 123 metres, was carried out by the firm of Czarnikow and Company in Berlin, while the structural steel frame was built by Union of Dortmund. The building was completed in five months, a prodigious performance when one considers that over 2,000 tons of steel alone were used. In this respect the hall is the biggest steel building in Berlin.

5.2   The Turbine Hall of the AEG by Peter Behrens

The new turbine building recently completed for the AEG was erected from my design on the corner site bounded by the Huttenstrasse and Berlichingenstrasse in north Berlin. The ground plan was arranged so as to take into account the existing railway tracks and at the same time to make the maximum use of the site within the limitations of the building line. It was nevertheless possible to emphasize the main hall by pulling the secondary hall back from it slightly. In the construction of the main hall the overriding architectonic idea was to make the steel supports more massive rather than spreading them out as is customary with the normal lattice construction. In this way the interior space would be closed off by flat planes on all sides, so as to allow a clear view of the architectonic proportions, such as can only be afforded by a very large internal area. For similar reasons, as far as the external appearance was concerned, it was decided to make the structural girders extend to the full thickness of the wall. This seemed all the more desirable as the original intention was to construct the whole building as far as possible from glass and steel. Where these two materials were not sufficient, only well finished concrete walls were to be used as filling, since unlike stone, which gives the impression of a load-bearing material, the former leaves the load-bearing entirely to the steel framework. Following the same principle, the windows on the Berlichingenstrasse are slanted parallel with the inside edges of the heavy vertical steel stanchions, so that the horizontal linking member running lengthwise above the windows casts a deep shadow on to them.

This linking member has the effect of a steel cornice, and together with the pediment at the front end, makes the roof appear as a discrete mass resting on the stanchions and on the window frames of the façade. The rounded corners of the building are made of concrete, divided by horizontal steel bands so that they appear merely as a filling in contrast to the vertical structural members of the side wall. The supporting framework is given aesthetic expression at the front end by the large steel window, which for this reason consists of a steel frame with all its members of the same thickness. In order to express its identity with the load-bearing parts of the building, the window is made flush with the front of the pediment, and to reinforce this impression the glass is laid flush with the steel frame.

The front end of the smaller adjoining hall is constructed entirely of concrete and this is continued for the first 4 metres on the yard side (up to the first of the main hall supports), so as to emphasize the steel framework of the two halls as seen from the side. The yard side of the secondary hall displays a row of steel supports between wide horizontal connecting girders of the same material. The windows form a continuous surface with the steel framework. This use of glass and steel as a continuous medium is intentionally extended throughout the whole building; since the structure consists largely of these two materials, the intention is to make it appear as solid as possible. Both steel and glass lack the solid appearance of stone facings. The impression of spindliness and fragility can only be avoided by setting both materials in the same plane, so that they give an appearance of solidity and homogeneity. The result is an aesthetic expression of the stability and strength which steel can be proved to have by calculation, but which the human eye, bound to outward appearances, would otherwise be unable to perceive. All forms of sculptural and ornamental decoration were omitted, firstly because the function of a factory building demands simplicity of form, but more especially because the desired impression of solidity, and the proportions contributing to this impression, could only have been diminished rather than enhanced by it.

I was commissioned by the AEG to design both the external architectonic framework and the arrangement of the interior, and in so far as the internal use of space is governed by the structural concept, this was carried out according to my specifications. The structural execution of this concept was in the hands of the well-known engin-eer, Bernhardt. Thus in all structural aspects, the building is the fruit of the most up-to-date technical knowledge and ability. Bernhardt produced the technical drawings and carried out all the necessary calculations with the utmost understanding for artistic considerations, solving all the problems which this presented with commendable technical ingenuity.

5.3   Engineering and Aesthetics by W. Lindner and G. Steinmetz

Together with its other feats, the buildings which have issued from modern engineering tend to inspire a sense of amazement in us, more than perhaps any other work of man. They are the product of a technological skill developed to a degree which has been hitherto unattainable. Their diversity, and their manifold and sustained effect on the world of commerce, no less than on man's existence taken as a whole, qualifies them as a remarkably conspicuous expression of our civilization. Some, and in certain cases whole series, of these buildings are or appear to be without precedent in our history; others have developed brick for brick, from the time when artisans and guilds prevailed, in an unadulterated form. But in both instances they are closely allied to the cultural problems of the present day, and pose specific puzzles to building designers, all of whom are sensitive to the extraordinary and the finely conceived. In their outward manifestations, our times are directly and decisively influenced by them. The more or less constant and durable conformity of these edifices, visibly expressed in terms of purpose, rhythm and energy as well as in totally new construction materials and structural methods, can in fact point to the right direction which progress should take more aptly than all our other creative energies, which have been convulsed, exploited and often bewildered by the forces of the time. But for a long time now not every functional product of civil engineering has, at the same time, been a thing of beauty although no compelling reason for the reverse stands out. Indeed those involved do, in most cases, concern themselves up to a point with the aesthetic aspect of the matter, and have frequently acknowledged that the crux of the problem is essentially a cultural one. In many cases it even seems in the first analysis as if specific technical perfection not only contradicts a certain natural beauty, but even excludes it *a priori* completely. But the lucid and handsome expression of the qualities inherent in such a construction—at times elevated to the level of art—is indeed tangible proof of the highest degree of perfection conceivable in practical and functional terms too. This is a distilled maturity, resulting from simul-taneous consideration of and compliance with all the requirements at hand, and it represents the highest obtainable excellence of a building or construction.

For decades all our artistic and cultural activity has lacked uniformity both in its principles and in its aims. There has been an overall absence of clarity about the prerequisites of, and laws governing, all artistic and creative design. Thus the impossibility of imposing any restraint on the unconsidered destruction and cheapening of our once so well-endowed cultural stock. In spite of the indisputably salient importance of certain more recent individual artistic achievements, we are therefore faced with a horrifyingly slender overall cultural output amongst all our current activity.

From the aesthetic point of view, not all areas of engineering developed proportionately. In the case of machines —locomotives, for example—automobiles, lathes, and ships, particularly significant and typical solutions were often, but by no means always, found. Little by little, and with tenacity, typical solutions were achieved not only by finding the most perfectly developed functional form conceivable, but also as a result of attentive sensitivity. When it is a question of building, however, the engineer often lacks this inner relationship to his work. The attempts to emphasize the beauty of a construction in its design is often no more than a concession to public opinion. But if one leaves this to the discretion of the architect, one presupposes that he will have the necessary ability in this field too—and this often causes more than a little disappointment. The architect, too, will often make light of such a task. In addition, overall design and the use of space, particularly when related to the environment, require an extraordinary knowledge of and feeling for the essential. A bridge, for example, or a water-tower or a crane, practically and solidly constructed and well executed in all ways, can have an unsatisfactory, worryingly fragile or squat or inorganic effect, if our unconscious sensitivity to status is not convinced by the function, stability or capacity, as the case may be, as expressed in the overall shape and in the details. In this respect a particular, artistic permeation and definition of the functional form is imperative. In a sequence of economically and technically flawless possibilities, it is often the case that only a few of them, or even one alone, will be altogether satisfactory.

Nevertheless the fact that unsuspected forms are produced as it were by themselves in a logical way, is evidenced by the work of engineers who work as technicians with a natural sensibility, and are unencumbered by random conjecture and artistic aestheticizing. Occasionally there are works of such lucid, stirring and convincing impact, that present-day architects can hardly put themselves on the same footing as their authors. Think for a moment, for example, of the beautiful, overwhelmingly grotesque phantasy of some cranes and loading bridges which results from organically developed construction, and, most of all, the functional quality which can be detected at first glance, and which has just as little need of any ornamentation to reinforce the effect as it does any explanation to facilitate comprehension of it. In these forms and lines, which involuntarily summon up some rearing prehistoric monster ready to pounce, there is no contrivance for effect, no esoteric symbolism: they embody strange and primordial examples of creation and man's work. Taken all in all, the products of engineering thus have very different effects on us, whether they are large or small, unusual or typical, emanating considerable or secondary energy, and this depends on the strength of their design and impact. Those solutions which turn out well are still, first and foremost, chance hits, for the most part. Progress hitherto certainly showed quite clearly why no overall satisfactory outcome had been achieved. There was no uniform, thoroughly consistent, organic and harmonious development of the whole and of all its components and details, in layout, construction and form, with simultaneously technical and intuitive fulfilment of all the economic, structural and aesthetic requirements to be considered. These requirements, which, though hard to meet are absolutely essential, are extremely closely interlocked and have the most varied reciprocal relationship with each other. The fulfilment of each single one is a vital prerequisite for complete fulfilment of all the others. Thus, for example, without the correct solution in terms of craftsmanship and construction, for the whole and for the details alike, it is impossible to achieve either any economically viable establishment or any satisfactory, appropriate and pleasing impact from the construction. The vital prerequisite for the latter, as well as for the specialized structural success of it, is, once again, the form which in every respect is simple, obvious and unaffected.

In the current situation of general upheaval and in particular in the case of all utilitarian constructions, there is only room for a sleek, objective type of beauty. It must issue from the fact that, in the choice of the construction, site and materials, in their technical elaboration and in the uniform and functionally relevant execution of the structural conception in both ground plan and elevation with constant attention to the immediate and wider environments, all the legitimate requirements are both technically and tangibly fulfilled in such a way that our natural aesthetic sensitivity is satisfied. To this end, there is no need for any decorative trimmings whatsoever, nor for any other devices which will increase the cost of the plant, execution or use. Rather, it is precisely the strict fulfilment of the economic and technical requirements which constitutes the most reliable basis for good design and impact. Thus the more simply and straightforwardly the whole and the details are developed, and the more conspicuously overall the consistency and functional quality is expressed, the more successful the impact will be.

The striking proof of this, as of the durable effect of this type of sleek, objective beauty, is given by the well designed old buildings, which certainly belong to the progression of modern development, and precisely for this reason have such a convincing effect and harmonize so strongly with everything else around them. Herein, and consequently not in their stylistic aspect and not in gradually developed 'Romantic' effects, lies their durable value as valid examples for all time, which can be used in themselves for new works and differently conceived requirements.

As construction materials, iron and cement, which were not made fully available to us until the Coal Age, and which have emerged triumphant in modern engineering construction, have, as such, a cold effect and appear stark and lifeless as completely uniform and homogeneous masses. In addition, and like other artificial materials such as roofing felt—whose reasonable use in engineering construction is quite legitimate—they appear persistently alien in the landscape. In using them, therefore, all the more consideration must be given as a matter of course to good execution and formation. But this is also far more difficult than with old-fashioned wrought iron. This has a consistent process of manufacture on the construction site. With the new methods of execution, and particularly with steel structures, this is in no way the case, or at least it does not apply to the same extent.

Steel structures are ready-made from preformed material manufactured in heavy industrial units—again almost always with machine work—and transported from workshop to assembly site. What is more, the job entailed is scrupulously divided up and carried out in the most meticulous and mathematically accurate spirit, following the relevant work's specifications right down to the most fastidious calculation. On the construction site itself, in general, only the final assembly of the parts manufactured in the workshop is carried out, forming the uniform whole in a way which has a so-to-speak inevitable aspect to it. Nevertheless, considerable importance attaches (and not just for social reasons) to the enthusiastic, alert collaboration and shared feelings of all those involved, not forgetting the individual and happily often extremely interested skilled worker.

Obviously, concrete structures, like steel structures, require a similar standard of technically trained and experienced workers and entail a certain amount of additional surface work (storeys, supplementary concrete and so on). But the actual work process is, essentially, still a mechanical one, and nothing to do with the craftsman. Likewise, the process of reworking contains the nucleus for the subjective simulation of other materials or mindless systematic treatment.

But as a result of the specific properties of the new construction materials, their arbitrarily plastic mass, extremely hard quality and high load capacity, new construction techniques in house-building—techniques which are in no doubt whatsoever—have been developed. Wide, flat overhangs, the replacement of solid wall structures with frameworks composed of slender pillars and beams and so on have given rise to new forms and effects. But the playful nimbleness and astonishing boldness of these initially contradicted, in many ways, our conditioned sensitivity towards the proven ratios of force and mass of stone and wood construction. A certain readjustment of ideas is called for to absorb the proper aesthetic appreciation of the new structures, although people are undoubtedly convinced by the effective reliability of the minutely calculated techniques used. On the other hand, however, certain concessions here and there have to be made towards our static and aesthetic sensibility, even in these new constructions. The static requirements have to be met not only in real terms, but also in a way which is easily comprehensible and totally convincing to the observing eye. It is thus often necessary to combine the sheer simplicity of the structure with a suitable heightening of the expression of stability, strength and so on. This can be achieved in each individual case by increasing the dimensions beyond what is necessary on the basis of calculation, or else by emphasizing the corresponding effect by special arrangements of the linear planes and the profiles, by introducing definite rhythms in the recurring forms and parts, and the like. In particular, steel structures— in which virtually abstract lines take the place of defined masses—must present an arrangement of these lines which is even more simple, distinct and expressive, and they must be kept uncluttered by any accessory structures. In all structures made up of girder and lattice work, just as in all other types of construction, attention is first focussed on the physical and spatial effect. The eye must learn to grasp these physical and spatial shapes which are often only specified in the framing structure and in the profile.

The major elements of creation (mass and space) are in no way as diverse as is often thought. An overview of the whole pattern of development from way back shows rather that relatively few actual basic shapes recur invariably at any given time in the most different constructions, and the differences only emanate from the constructional materials used. Any changes in the details and in the outward shape correspond to the particular function involved and contemporary taste. Likewise for the overwhelming majority of completely new structures which have emerged as a result of the new propositions and constructional methods of engineering, it is not hard to find forerunners, and even whole series of them, among old constructions. More or less the same thing applies to the individual forms, and to 'functional expression' in construction and art forms.

In her infinite fullness, nature is nevertheless extremely economical in her themes, as is shown by a constant repetition in her basic forms. But these forms appear modified a thousandfold, diminished or extended in parts, fully developed in some parts and only hinted at in others, depending on the stipulations of the various creatures and creations and on different conditions. Just as nature has her own history of development within which the old themes constantly show through despite the various changes, so art is based on just a few standard forms and types which have been handed down from the most ancient tradition. By the same token, these offer an infinite diversity as a result of their constant re-emergence, and like those natural types have their own history. In this process nothing is purely arbitrary; everything is conditioned by circumstances and relationships.

(Gottfried Semper)

In this way good engineering constructions become 'typical solutions' quite by themselves and with compelling urgency. But this claim has turned into an often misunderstood slogan. For such constructions can only result with utter consistency from the all-round complete fulfilment of all the particular economic, structural and aesthetic requirements.

Thus, although engineering constructions, like all constructional building, are subject to immutable laws, to which these achievements insistently refer, fixed rules for the individual case cannot be drawn up. Here the creator himself has the last word. But a sense of what is necessary can and must be refined until, subsequently, a general clarification of the bases of good design is promoted.

5.4   Architecture and Engineering by P. Morton Shand

'Every building that is treated naturally, without disguise or concealment, cannot fail to look well.' A. N. Welby Pugin
'As soon as we know how to use the materials which industry supplies us with we shall be able to create an architecture of our own.' Theophile Gautier in 1850

That the chaos manifested by our urban civilization is the direct result of the unnatural separation of the two branches of architecture is a simple statement of fact. Every year it becomes clearer that its annulment is our only chance of a return to civic order. But the essential preliminary to reunion is the recognition that engineering is as much architecture as architecture is engineering, and an unreserved acceptance of all that this implies. It is necessary to insist on their irrefragable identity because under existing conditions in England it is more and more being lost sight of.

Various explanations have been given for this disastrous schism between architecture considered as one of the fine arts and architecture regarded as an exact science. The most specious, because the most flattering to architects and engineers alike, is the continuous increase in 'specialization': an explanation which confuses cause with effect. But what actually brought it about is sufficiently obvious. During the nineteenth century architecture with a capital 'A' became more and more academic, and proportionately sterile; whereas engineering, called upon to solve industrial problems for which no precedents existed, had freedom thrust upon it, and made amazing progress in consequence. The nineteenth century architect, whose training incapacitated him from keeping abreast with the scientific discoveries which the engineer was turning to practical account, found comfort in the reflection that he was an artist and a gentleman. His structural methods continued to be such as he had been taught: the imitative reproduction of the different traditional styles in the materials traditionally proper to them. Untraditional types of construction and construction in untraditional materials he left to the horny-handed Philistine. The result was that the Philistine prevailed, and drew apart to found an exlusive and untraditional profession of their own. Art could have nothing to do with industry, though it could be patronizingly polite to genteelly amateurish handicrafts; for art meant looking steadfastly backwards, and mirroring the present in the past. Unlike the Lady of Shalott, the Victorian architect was never 'sick of dreams'. In dreams of the 'glory that was Greece and the grandeur that was Rome', high chivalry, or Renaissance splendours he lived, wrought and had his being. Within that ivory tower, the studio,

mechanics could be ignored; and the sacred flame, however dim, had no physical connection with the local gasometer. Architecture was aristocratic and feudal; engineering irredeemably plebeian or blatantly plutocratic. A formal letter of introduction, an engraved card and correct calling clothes might allow a prospective client to be received by Messrs Gargoyle, Palladianissimo, and Wrenkin; a knock at an office door, enabled business to be done with young Mr Fitz-Archimedes.

In the course of the last decade architects have become more and more dependent on engineers, and engineers less and less dependent on architects. The only occasions on which engineers still have to call in architects is when public opinion demands that some new bridge, considered of more than local importance, or likely to jeopardize 'existing amenities', shall be suitably architecturalized 'so as to harmonize with its surroundings'. In plain language this means that after appointing an engineer to be *responsible for the design*—that is to determine the type of construction to be adopted, and the material most appropriate for its execution—an 'eminent architect' has to be found willing to fill the somewhat humiliating *rôle* of adding 'architectural' trimmings to a design already structurally complete in itself.

Thus two men are paid for what is really the work of one. Doubtless many qualified English architects could design a light stone or brick bridge single-handed; but there is hardly a single one living, however eminent, who could design an ordinary steel or concrete bridge unaided. Were one invited to do so he would probably answer rather indignantly that it was not his job; but that he was quite ready to 'collaborate' with an engineer. Now the word 'collaborate' implies joint, but approximately equal, participation. We do not speak of a dresser 'collaborating' with a surgeon, because the surgeon could, if necessary, do his own dressing, whereas the dresser is a subordinate who could not be trusted to perform an operation single-handed. Put bluntly, the architect acts as a dresser to the engineer, covering up the engineer's work as soon as it is finished. Since he no longer commands the necessary technical knowledge or experience to co-operate in the essentials of the design, his 'collaboration' is confined to supplementing them with non-essentials, and masking certain conventional 'objectionable' structural features by impeccably conventional ornament. Even as the engineer's professional decorator the architect's share in the design is being progressively restricted by economic circumstances. Sir Reginald Blomfield's original elevations for Lambeth Bridge envisaged a complete stone veneer of the steelwork. As a result of revised

Reprinted by kind permission of the *Architectural Press* from the *Architectural Review*, November 1932, pp. 169–171.

estimates the use of stone was regulated to the piers and approaches. Though not very many people regard this bridge as an outstandingly successful monument of collective thinking, the design has undoubtedly gained in sincerity and simplicity in consequence.

We often hear the complaint that architects are too much preoccupied with form, and engineers too exclusively concerned with materials. How should this be otherwise when the training of each virutally ignores what is the life-study of the other?

But whereas profound knowledge of a material sometimes enables those unversed in the laws of formal design to mould it into magnificently expressive forms the profoundest knowledge of abstract form cannot achieve significant, or even economical, expression in an unfamiliar material. As long as building materials were confined to brick, stone and timber, engineers and architects were working on common ground with a common fund of experience. The introduction of new materials, cast iron, steel, reinforced concrete, changed all that. The engineers were quick to exploit them successfully; the architects took their stand on tradition, confined themselves to the old materials, and refused to study the formal possibilities of the new. So science monopolized one field, 'art' another. Unfortunately art (especially reproductive art) has more need of science than science has of art. As one of our wittiest anonymous critics has put it: 'The engineers carried off the swag, but the architects were left with the swags.' Willy-nilly the architect has been forced to use the new materials, but he uses them without understanding their structural and formal potentialities. He can clothe these materials but he cannot wield them. Every time he adopts steel or concrete the engineer has to be consulted; and the engineer speaks a language the architect has never learnt to understand.

The remedy for this state of affairs seems a simple one. An architect's training should proceed from a study of materials to that of form, and not, as at present, inversely. Then, and only then, will he be of real use to the engineer, and able to 'collaborate' with him in big things. And he will also be of far more use to himself because in his ordinary routine work he will need the engineer far less; an independence that will save both his own and his client's pocket. It may be objected that this reversal of the established order of things in the curriculum of our architectural schools will inevitably increase the term of the young architect's already long and expensive training.

This need not be so. English architectural education is still hopelessly encumbered, not to say obscured, by a pedantic insistence on what, under modern conditions, has become archaeological lumber. Its elimination would stimulate a sense of architectural realities, and leave time for an adequate instruction in subjects more germane to them.

In England the dual qualification of architect-engineer or engineer-architect is almost unknown, although no one has ever disputed the right of marine engineers to call themselves 'naval architects'. There are very few FRIBA's who are MICE's as well, or MICE's who are also FRIBA's—perhaps on account of the embarrassment of having to decide which of these hieratic groups of initials to give precedence to on notepaper headings. Even the Institution of Structural Engineers, which is exclusively concerned with building, cannot boast many members who are incidentally either A or L RIBA's. Not being 'artists', the engineers must humbly submit to the deprivation of that ennobling 'R' which even veterinary surgeons are entitled to. The only 'Royal' engineers are pucka *ubique* sahibs who have graduated from 'The Shop'. With such persistent snubbing it is little wonder that engineers are popularly supposed to lack the finer artistic sensibilities which scholarly concentration on 'the Orders' imparts. Just think of the difference it would make if they could be 'finished' at the AA! On the Continent, particularly in Germany, the architect who has thought it worth his while to become a qualified engineer and the engineer who has acquired a recognized architectural qualification are almost as common as permanent working partnerships of architects and engineers. These joint capacities and collaborations are reflected in industrial landscapes that are infinitely more seemly than our own, and in towns in which order is steadily vanquishing disorder instead of the reverse.

Rennie and Telford and Eiffel were great architects for all that they were 'only engineers'; just as engineers like Freyssinet, Dischinger and Maillart have been among the truest architects of our own age. The Brothers Perret were Beaux-Arts-trained, but they have designed buildings which, like the pit-head structures of that gifted architect, the late Adolf Meyer, Poelzig's gasworks, and Gropius's and Mendelsohn's factories, engineers enthusiastically acclaim as superb engineering. None of these men found it necessary to 'collaborate with specialists', whether formal or structural. They were sufficient unto themselves.

Across the Channel the divorce never became anything like as absolute as over here. The result is that foreign architects are rather better engineers, foreign engineers rather better architects, than their English colleagues. On the mainland they have been quicker to see that since building in the near future is bound to approximate far more to what we have hitherto called structural engineering than to what was till yesterday architecture (but is already only architecture in an obsolescent sense), the rift must be closed if the architect is not to be squeezed out altogether.

The mutual antagonism of two French institutes, the

Ecole Polytechnique, founded during the Revolution in 1794, and the Ecole des Beaux-Arts, founded by Napoleon in 1806, is usually supposed to have been the immediate cause of the emergence of engineering as a separate profession. The spirit of the first was realistic, speculative and scientific; while that of the second was romantic, and traditional and reactionary from the outset.

In the Polytechnique men were trained in applied mechanics and technical processes. In the Beaux-Arts, which promoted architecture to academic parity with painting and sculpture, budding artists were constrained into the fossilizing formulas of reproductive classicism. The former prepared the world for the advent of the modern spirit; the latter led it firmly backwards along the trodden path of the *ancien régime*. The first known instance of an architect and an engineer being employed on the same 'job' was in the rebuilding of the Paris Halle au Blé in 1811. Their names were Belanger and Brunet. It is significant that the old corn-market, which was erected in 1783 and burned down in 1802, had a wooden roof, and that the new had a complicated copper and iron dome. It was nearly half a century later before architects began to feel that their position was seriously threatened, and to insist with almost morbid emphasis on their special status as art-workers. In 1864 we find the Beaux-Arts-trained Anatole de Baudot, who was far freer from aestheticism than either Ruskin or Corbusier, writing:

We see how frequently the public prefers engineers to architects, and day after day we have to listen to its complaints about the latter. The reason is that the engineers do not assume a chilling attitude of academic correctness, but are ready to confine themselves scrupulously to fulfilling the programme set them; whereas architects only too often act at variance to their clients' reasonable demands on 'aesthetic' pretexts.

And again, addressing the International Congress of Architects in 1889, he said:

For long the influence of the architect has been waning and the engineer, *l'homme moderne par excellence*, is beginning to take his place.

Were the latter in the position to replace the architect altogether, the former could doubtless disappear without art being extinguished as a result. Form will no longer be the basis of the new architecture. It will find its expression in the laying-out of the plan, and in the structural system which it necessitates: a general expression from which individual expression will proceed. But,

it may be objected, the method you suggest is the engineer's method. I do not deny it, for it is the right one.

César Daly, in the *Revue Générale de l'Architecture* of 1867, was no less outspoken:

Is architecture destined to yield its place to civil engineering? Will the engineer absorb the architect? We speak of the organic art of the future, and yet we affect to have no illusions as to the present state of affairs. Where is this eclecticism, which fogs the whole modern world, leading us to? We breathe it in with our lungs; it mixes with our blood, and affects both our hearts and brains.

Davioud, the joint architect of the Trocadéro, won a prize offered by the *Institut* in 1877 for the best dissertation on, 'Ought the architect and the engineer to be one and the same person, or ought they to be members of two separate professions?' Davioud maintained that:

We shall only succeed in arriving at proper solutions when architect and engineer, artist and scientist, are united in one person. For too long we have been living in the fond belief that the nature of art differentiates it from all other forms of human intelligence; and that being wholly separate and apart from other activities its only source is in the capricious imagination of the artistic temperament.

Where does architecture begin or end? Was the man who in 1772 built the purely functional double-armed iron crane in Würzburg, and the lovely Baroque stone pediment it stands on beside the River Main, an architect or an engineer? And would he have minded very much which he was called, having an equal proficiency as each? The conception of architecture has grown too narrow, or, put in another way, too many new forms are arising which have nothing to do with the old formalizations in brick and stone. Each new model of the same type of machine is a new example of architecture. Every new class of machine represents the emergence of a new architectural 'style'. The machine has come to stay, but the conventional forms which stone evolved so long ago are passing away. Modern quarries furnish raw material for concrete, not cornices. Architecture has ceased to be exclusively, or even predominantly a question of 'building' in the old primary, site-and-scaffolding sense of the word. In the past it has constantly changed its skin. Now, like a chrysalis, it is changing its body; and with its body the nature of its being.

5.5   **Concrete** by P. Morton Shand

In 1855 Portland cement concrete could withstand a pressure of 157 lbs per square in. after 7 days.

In 1880 Portland cement concrete could withstand a pressure of 222 lbs per square in. after the same interval.

In 1930 concrete made with Super-Portland cement could withstand a pressure of 5,000–6,000 lbs per square in. after 4 days.

In 1930 aluminous cement concrete could withstand a pressure of 8,000 lbs per square in. after 24 hours.

Comparative figures for St Peter's in Rome, the 'Jahrhunderthalle' at Breslau, and the Leipzig Markets will help to explain the revolution in the science of building brought about by reinforced concrete.

In St Peter's (1506–1526) 10,000 tons of material were required to cover a superficial area of 1,600 sq metres with a masonry barrel dome 40 metres in diameter.

In the 'Jahrhunderthalle' (1914) 6,340 tons of material were required to cover a superficial area of 4,200 sq metres with a massively-ribbed reinforced-concrete dome 65 metres in diameter. In each of the three continuous halls of the Leipzig Markets (1929) 2,160 tons of material were required to cover a superficial area of 5,700 sq metres with a 'Dywidag' reinforced-concrete dome 75 metres in diameter; or 4/5 less material than in St Peter's to enclose $3\frac{1}{2}$ times St Peter's area.

When the average educated Englishman wants to know something about a fairly weighty or technical subject he turns, not to text-books, but to the *Encyclopaedia Britannica*. If he takes down the Sixth Volume of its current (Fourteenth) edition, and looks up 'Concrete', he will find a sketchy sort of article, neither very readable nor very informative, that tells him little or nothing about the history and development of the type of construction with which the word has become synonymous. Apart from the way it is written, the reason why it is not very helpful is because it is almost entirely based on American practice; and Americans have had comparatively little to do with the evolution of this branch of structural engineering— far less, anyway, than Frenchmen or Germans. The *Encyclopaedia Britannica* boasts that it is not merely up to date, but that it employs all the best-known international specialists to write on their own pet subjects. When reinforced concrete engineers as eminent as Herr von Emperger, Monsieur Freyssinet, and Sir Owen Williams were presumably available it is somewhat disconcerting to find that the article referred to was entrusted to nobody in particular.

The eleven columns (less diagrams) to which it runs are supplemented by a single page of photographic reproductions almost worthy of the daily picture press.

Into it are dovetailed ten very small illustrations of (exclusively American) uses of concrete, of which only one typifies (and that indifferently) a form of construction peculiar to that material. The centre and cynosure of this extraordinary scrap-album selection is a 'monument' at the entrance of Valhalla Park, Burbank, California; an example of Neo-Spanish-Mission exhibition architecture which ought never to have been built of anything more durable than lath and plaster, but was for some quite unaccountable reason carried out in solid concrete. A naïve, though illuminating, caption explains that 'the intricate outer decoration was made of precast architectural concrete' and not, as it appears, of icing sugar. It is only fair to add, that if it was necessary for this *British* publication to confine itself to the United States, a wide choice of infinitely worthier and more interesting examples could easily have been obtained from that country.

What follows is an attempt to piece together such information about concrete as one might have hoped to find in the latest edition of the *Encyclopaedia Britannica*. Sir Owen Williams has pointed out that reinforced concrete was 'mentally born in the brains of mathematicians and physicists long before it became a substantial fact', while Sigfried Giedion calls it 'a laboratory product which has made the architect with his sketch-book look rather ridiculous'. Why ridiculous? Because reinforced concrete has changed the optical impression of buildings to an even greater extent than steel. To those brought up in string-course constructional methods the entirely new equilibrium it establishes between support and load seems a wilful architectonic anachronism.

The riddle reinforced concrete is apt to present to all except the engineer trained in its use (and sometimes even to him) is 'Where does technique end and form begin?' A good example of the way in which it deranges all pre-existing architectural values was furnished by Sir Owen William's scheme for a new structure in this material to replace Rennie's Waterloo Bridge. The writer sent the drawings when they were published to M Robert Maillart —a famous Swiss engineer who has probably had wider experience in designing reinforced-concrete bridges than any man living—and invited his comments. M Maillart replied that he very much admired the 'elegance' of the design, but was rather doubtful about certain of its structural features—which meant that he fully shared what we might call Sir Owen William's 'concrete aesthetics'. Now the almost universal 'architectural' criticism of this design, whether 'professional' or amateur, was that, ingenious as it might be as engineering it was very bad as architecture because the spans were quite flat, and the piers, instead of being at least as wide as the platform, were simply cylindrical stanchions propping up the middle of it. In other words, our eyes have grown accustomed to arched spans because brick and stone bridges can only be built in this manner. When, therefore, we are brought face to face with a design in another material that is able to ignore the arch convention, we upbraid the author's choice of medium, his lack of 'taste' or his inexcusable disregard for the aesthetic susceptibilities of others. This, if we only knew it, is equivalent to lauding reminiscence over resource, approximate over precise design, amateur capacity over technical proficiency, and waste of space and material over exact calculation of how much of each is required. Thus are passions aroused under democracy in defence of that higher *bonum publicum* which transcends reason. Yet when no calls to arms to succour outraged 'art' are sounded the British public is as willing to become interested in the 'marvellous' potentialities of reinforced concrete as in any other of the manifestations of material progress which fill it with such a pleasantly personal pride. This was demonstrated clearly enough on what was probably the first occasion for the daily press to draw attention to the subject.

Towards the end of the war two 'mystery ships' were under construction on slips in Shoreham Harbour. Actually they were huge reinforced concrete caissons intended for anchoring the ends of a great submarine net that was to be stretched across the Straits of Dover. The Armistice found them still under construction; and the only one to be completed was eventually towed to Portsmouth, and sunk on a predetermined site, where its superstructure was afterwards adapted to replace one of the old Spithead forts. For days the papers devoted nearly as many photographs to this operation as to the rumps of Southsea bathing belles snapped as 'interested spectators'. Some even printed columns of descriptive 'copy'. . . .

Concrete: Reinforced-concrete versus steel

Steel and concrete, the materials which have allowed the function of support to be separated from the function of containing space, are largely interdependent in use. Owing to its high conductivity, steel, when attacked by flames, soon attains a temperature that causes it to twist, and eventually collapse. That is why steel girders in buildings are almost invariably squared off with a solid layer of concrete, or encased in a sheathing of some other fire-proof material. Concrete being really reconstituted stone, is a poor conductor of heat and an excellent insulator. The outstanding quality of steel is high tensile strength. That is to say it excels in resisting tearing and splitting strains. The outstanding quality of concrete is great compressive strength. That is to say it excels in resisting the crushing stress, or pressure, of heavy weights. And just as, economically, the compressive strength of steel is insufficient to

make it a serious rival to concrete in this respect, so the tensile strength of unreinforced-concrete is too low to enable it to compete with that of steel. Reinforced-concrete unites the merits peculiar to steel and stone construction and to a very large extent overcomes the intrinsic defects of each. Though quantitively unequal, and unevenly distributed, the steel rods and rubble and cement amalgam which constitute this composite material form a compact and coherent mass. But if concrete that is reinforced combines most of the advantages of masonry and metal, it does not combine them all. It is true that in ordinary buildings the cost of carrying a given load is 150–200 per cent more with steel girders than reinforced-concrete beams and stanchions, and that the latter need not be more numerous than the former. There remains the important question of speed in construction. The rate of progress on a building is in direct ratio to the number of men who can work on it simultaneously without impeding one another.

In the case of a reinforced-concrete structure virtually the whole work has to be done on the site itself. That means the raw materials for its elements are assembled there instead of finished fabricated sections embodying these elements. Carpenters are engaged in sawing up and bolting together the lengths of timber shuttering required for each successive pour, and unbolting and striking those in which other pours have already set; artificers in bending and interlocking the metal rods, and cross-tieing them with wire at intervals according to the engineers' drawings; labourers in mixing aggregate, sand and cement with water in specific proportions, shovelling the liquid concrete into fresh sections of shuttering waiting to be filled, and tamping it home round the naked bones of the articulated reinforcement. Though rapid-hardening cements allow fresh pours to be made about every 24 hours, the difficulty is to have the new lengths of reinforcement connected up, and the new forms completed round them within that period, with men continually moving backwards and forwards across a generally cramped working space.

With steel construction the work proceeds on two sites simultaneously; the building site proper and the fabricating shops. At the former soil is being dug away from between supporting points that may be already fixed in position; girders are being encased in concrete and hollow-slab floors laid between them; walls are being bricked in and tile partitions run up; stone facing is being hitched on to the outside of the rising skeleton; finished beams and stanchions are being hoisted out of lorries and swung into their appointed places by cranes and shears perched high aloft on tripod gantries; while those already lowered on to their sole-plates, or fitted into their spans, are being bolted together and rivetted into the frame-work. At the steel shops, perhaps some hundreds of miles away, the various fabricated sections are being rolled, built up, painted and numbered according to specification; and then despatched to the site on a time schedule, so that delivery is neither earlier nor later than the particular day, or even hour, when they are wanted. The result is the minimum encumbrance on the building, and the minimum of involuntary interference between the different gangs of skilled and unskilled workmen. These are the outstanding advantages of construction based on the progressive assembly of ready-made parts, or, as it is called on the Continent, *montage*. The drawbacks of *montage* are continuous dependence on transport (which is very expensive for heavy out-of-gauge girders that have to be sent by rail) and the employment of a much higher proportion of skilled labour. Moreover, when deliveries are behind-hand, substantial losses in wages are apt to be incurred. With reinforced-concrete construction the whole of the materials required are grouped ready to hand before the ground is broken, and drawn on as required.

The advantages of *montage* are not, however necessarily confined to fabricated steel; but it must be admitted that in practice steel has hitherto enjoyed a monopoly of them; a monopoly which is pretty certain to be challenged before long. Concrete beams are just as suitable for mass-production as steel girders. As early as 1914 the dome of a big circus in Copenhagen was roofed with pre-cast concave segments, though a better known and more recent example of *montage* in concrete is the ribbed cupola of the Gebrüder Einmal Garage at Aix-la-Chapelle. Factories in Brazil (a country where steel is expensive) have been erected with precast stanchions and roof-trusses, almost identical in form with light standard steel-frame sections, in which the reinforcement was only partially encased so as to leave about a tenth of it protruding at one or either end. As soon as a couple of these had been hoisted into position by windlasses, the main crank-up rods were inter-locked and cross-wired in the usual manner, shuttered together, and then poured so as to form a monolithic weld with the rest of the framework. The French *Ponts et Chaussées* have employed standardized precast members in bridge-building for several years; while Corbusier, Gropius, and others have experimented with standardized precast sections for small dwellings. Examples of the latter can be seen in Pessac, near Bordeaux, the Törten suburb of Dessau, in Germany, and at least one LCC building estate (where elements of this type are rather grotesquely combined with timber rafters and tiled gable roofs).

A poured concrete structure has the advantages and disadvantages of being a monolith, while for all their homogeneity the parts of a steel-frame structure remain separate and separable entities.

The rivets and bolts of steel construction might be compared to the mortar joints of masonry. In both the multiplication of imperfect articulations is a source of structural weakness. Autogenous welding, which is still in its infancy, promises to make a steel skeleton as mono-ferric as a concrete one is monolithic. Yet even so, concrete will still have the advantage of plasticity and requiring much simpler and less expensive plant. It is easier and cheaper to pour and mould than to hammer and bend. Once set, a complex of monolithic elements can withstand an earthquake in which, as experience in San Francisco, Tokio and New Zealand has proved, a steel frame crumples up like a wicker basket. The worst enemy of concrete is the magnesium sulphate present in sea water; but this can be successfully kept at bay by very rich 1:1:2 mixes made with aluminous cement. Though more resistant to weak acid solution than ordinary steel, it is liable to be attacked by stronger ones, liquids containing alkaline salts, and certain vegetable oils that unite with its lime content.

The point at which work on a concrete building is really as good as finished is the point at which half the work still remains to be done in a steel-framed one. Ultimately, no doubt, rustless steel will become an economic material for both structural and facing uses. Ordinary steel, however, rusts when exposed to air, earth, or water; and therefore requires regular painting, or encasing in another material, to preserve it from erosion. The fact that steel is a rigid material, pieced and not poured together, makes it less flexible for 'out-shapes'; and entails a waste of space, and, above all, surface. Ideal for rapid handling, the I girder presents no less than eight corrodible surfaces; whereas a concrete beam, which presents no cavities requiring subsequent filling, and is impermeable to erosion, can be moulded into any section, angular or round, *in situ*. The only waste with concrete is in the sizing of the shuttering. At present it seldom pays contractors to stock standardized steel forms.

One of the admitted (though considerably exaggerated) drawbacks of a monolithic building is the difficulty and expense of altering, or adding to it subsequently; though, if it comes to that, steel is only easy and cheap to replace where, as in station roofs or bridges, the elements remain exposed. Loose strands of reinforcement can be curled up and hidden away under tidy circular bosses of mortar, so that when the structure is to be built on to, all that need be done is to uncover the spare ends, straighten them out, and link them up with the armature of the new connecting elements. An important road bridge over the River Ruhr at Mülheim provides a good illustration of how easily future requirements can be provided for in reinforced-concrete construction. This bridge, which crosses a wide expanse of water meadows subject to periodic flooding besides the river itself, at present consists of twelve elliptical arches. Ultimately these twelve spans are to be increased to seventeen; and the existing pavements, which are 1·50 metres wide, will be taken into the roadway and replaced by others double their width, cantilevered out from the parapets. It will be just as simple to make these extensions (for which provision has been duly made in the design of the reinforcement) as it would be to bolt on fresh sections of girders in the case of a steel bridge.

It is no doubt perfectly true, as Dr Oscar Faber says, that the steel frame of a relatively 'plain' building represents only one-tenth to one-fifteenth of its total cost; and that though concrete (or rather shuttering) is 50 per cent dearer since the war, the price of structural steel has remained practically stationary. (His figures, of course, only apply to Great Britain, where steel is artificially cheap in relation to reinforced-concrete construction.) We all deplore the decay of British shipbuilding, but the very natural desire of our steel mill-owners to roll more structural girders, to compensate them for a continually decreasing demand for ships' plates and bulkheads, is not a valid reason in itself for cold-shouldering a form of construction which has proved essential to the industrial expansion and economic re-equipment of other nations. Steel and concrete have their separate spheres, where each is admittedly either economically or structually supreme. But there is also a sort of neutral no-man's-land between them—where either is theoretically equally suitable, and local conditions, or individual requirements, may happen to make now one and now the other the more advantageous —in which they inevitably compete. On the Continent— even in countries like France and Germany which have just as important and well-organized steel industries as our own—the economic factor decides the choice. In England it is no exaggeration to say that steel is frequently employed where on logical, economic, engineering, or aesthetic grounds (or a combination of any or all of them) concrete ought to have been adopted. That it so seldom is, need occasion no surprise. Many of our local authorities (to say nothing of the Ministry of Health) insist that in cases where concrete beams are used instead of steel girders, they must be of equal, or even greater, thickness. The London Building Act—which dates from 1909, and is only now in process of modernization—allows reinforced-concrete to be stressed to a maximum of 600 lbs per sq in, when modern cements enable it to be safely stressed to as many thousands. It is true that steel construction is also made needlessly solid and extravagant by superannuated regulations, but steel is not penalized to anything like the same extent as concrete, and never to its profit.

6.1–6.3

These articles are taken from a series of radio discussions broadcast by the B.B.C. between April and June 1933 under the title *Design in Modern Life*. The titles of all the programmes are listed below, with the names of those taking part. Dates and page numbers in brackets refer to the printed publication of the talks in *The Listener*.

Design in Modern Life

6.4

Quite apart from the intrinsic interest of an item like this which enlarges the scope of the debate on Modern Architecture by removing it from the grip of the specialist press and bringing it into the more public columns of *The Listener*, this questionnaire is of particular interest for the range of positions represented by the participating architects. They run from the arch-traditionalism of Blomfield, through the middle-of-the-road-modern of Holden, to the 'new architecture' of Fry and Coates.

6.5

This is fascinating confrontation between one of the grand old men of academic architecture (Blomfield) and one of the chief exponents of the International Style in England (Connell, of Connell, Ward and Lucas). Blomfield pursues the line already set out in his reply to 'Is Modern Architecture on the Right Track?' (6.4) and developed in *Modernismus* (see *Form and Function*, no. 91). Although many of his criticisms of the Modern Movement are justifiable he tends to vitiate them by his rabid anti-internationalism, his bizarre ability to equate the International Style with both Bolshevism *and* Hitlerism and easy jibes at 'modernismists'. Connell's response almost seems to vindicate Blomfield, partly because it invokes such an orthodox litany of Modern Movement responses, but also because it lacks either the agility and persuasiveness of a polemicist like Le Corbusier or the committed social view of the central European International Stylists.

6.6

Besides offering an interesting contrast with Lubetkin's earlier articles on architecture in the USSR (3.3 and 3.4) this article also provides an illuminating commentary on the background against which 6.4 and 6.5 should be seen and on the practical obstacles faced by modern architects in England in the thirties. Lubetkin's observation on the architectural press is one which should be borne in mind in any examination of the periodical literature of the time (and, moreover, it is a comment which still applies to the architectural press of the present day).

6.7a and b

These two items are essential reading for radiovision programmes 23 and 24. It is worth noting Walford's statements about his role in the design of his house since the architects have given a rather different picture of the evolution of the design.

6.1   The Living Room and Furniture by Edward Halliday and Gordon Russell

Edward Halliday: Let us discover what it is we mean when we talk of the 'living-room'. Don't we live in every room in the house? What is particularly distinctive about a living-room?

Gordon Russell: In most houses the living-room is that room in which we spend our leisure time, entertain our guests, read, write, play the piano or listen to the gramophone or wireless.

E.H.: That is a good deal to ask of one room, isn't it?
G.R.: Yes. It is really a return of the mediaeval hall, which was the communal room used for all activities of the house in the fifteenth century. From the sixteenth to the nineteenth centuries, the number of rooms increased and the hall decreased in size. The dining-room, sitting-room, parlour, drawing-room, morning-room, study, library, ballroom and others arrived.

E.H.: I suppose of all those, the only ones left are the dining-room and a kaleidoscope of all the others into what is termed living-room.

G.R.: Yes. Lack of space, economy and difficulties of domestic help have reversed the whole position, and it is now quite common to find a sitting- or living-room with a dining space in an alcove.

E.H.: Can you give a reason for this simplification of the house? You say that entertaining, reading, writing and so on are now, generally speaking, carried on in one room. Surely it was more civilised—more spacious—to have a separate room for each function?

G.R.: I agree with you. I am all for the separate room, but you are forgetting two very important things, Halliday—developments of modern life which have changed our conditions of living enormously; namely, the spread of sport and games, and, of course, the motor-car. Much less time is spent in the house than formerly—our sitting-room is spreading outwards to the loggia, sun-porch, garden and even to our golf links and open road. Our cars have indeed become our sitting-rooms for quite a long period each year. Take another example; the large plate-glass windows which wind down into the walls in some modern German rooms emphasise this connection between the living-room and the open-air. They frame up a piece of country as if it were a picture on the wall, thus bringing it into the room when the window is closed: open it and the room goes out to meet the countryside. Social customs are changing too: entertaining is difficult and expensive. Dining out is being succeeded by 'taking coffee out'. It is, therefore, easier to merge the dining-room in the living-room, and the extra space enables a bridge party or dance to be arranged at short notice. You must remember that the small house and cottage have more rooms than they used to have. It is the large house which has shrunk. And the size of families is much smaller.

E.H.: I see. Still, I think there is something to be said for the idea of a room of one's own—to work in; and surely this concentration of functions means an equal concentration of furniture, doesn't it? With so many activities going on, how can such a room contain all the necessary pieces of furniture?

G.R.: Of course there is a demand for less and smaller furniture: it is one way of getting more space at a time when rooms are shrinking. And then the use of the dual purpose piece of furniture will be seen—the table-bookcase, table-stool, even bed-settee, which converts the living-room into a bedroom for the unexpected guest, thus taking us a full cycle back to mediaeval times. A further way of saving space is to get built-in furniture, and this is being done to a much larger extent than formerly—its disadvantage in the rented house is obvious, but even there it is gaining ground. Many houses and flats are now fitted as a matter of course with kitchen cabinets and refrigerators,

hanging cupboards for clothes and so on. Besides saving space usually taken up by the back and sometimes the sides, fitted furniture is very easy to keep clean: it has no spaces for dirt to lodge in. A still further way of saving space is to plan each piece of furniture so as to fit into it exactly what is required. This may sound obvious, but in very many cases it has only recently been done. Adjustable shelves in bookcases occur to mind: in bedrooms most people are now familiar with the fitted wardrobe; in the kitchen, the kitchen cabinet; and in the living-room, the writing desk, cocktail cabinet, perhaps canteen for silver. Remember that low furniture makes a room appear large. In some cases unit furniture—furniture that is made to a unit of size so as to be interchangeable—may prove more useful than fitted furniture. The unit bookcase is familiar to most people, and the principle ought to be extended—in fact it has been extended. Someone thought of making a writing desk which, on its base, would take up exactly the same space as two unit bookcases. It is a very convenient arrangement to be able to write within easy reach of one's books of reference.

E.H.: But if that sort of thing becomes widespread, won't it mean that all rooms will become alike; if everyone furnishes with standardised furniture?

G.R.: I think not, Halliday. The infinite variety of arrangement to meet varying shapes of room makes this unlikely. Think what a vast number of variations you could have with only six patterns—cupboards, with and without doors, writing desk, chest of drawers, bookcase in two sizes, one double as large as the other, deeper for larger books. And again why not combine fitted and unit furniture? Book-shelves are cheap to fix and one can think of many pleasant arrangements. Interesting pictures, pieces of sculpture, pottery, curtains will give intimacy and individuality to such a room. No, I don't believe people will become standardised. Mass production will supply our everyday needs, but it must also raise the standard of living and education and give us more leisure. I believe also that it will lead to a much greater demand for fine individual things made by hand.

E.H.: That's most interesting. I suppose all essential pieces—bookcases, radio cabinets, desks, etc.—should be fitted, that is, part of the fabric. And I can see an additional advantage in this—it does away to a large extent with 'tops' which, as you say, collect dust, but usually collect a lot of unnecessary junk as well—bits of china, photo-frames and what-not.

G.R.: Yes, Halliday, I'm afraid many people look upon their living-room as a sort of museum—full of bits and pieces of no earthly use except to fill space, and only adding to the labour of cleaning and sometimes making the room a veritable trap for the unwary.

E.H.: Of course, Russell, you're now touching on a fundamental problem of design in the living-room.

While I agree with you that junk should be swept away and all unnecessary things strictly barred, I must say I sympathise with those who like collecting things—souvenirs of holidays, and so on, and naturally I am more than sympathetic with those who collect pictures—what about heirlooms, for example? Why shouldn't we have an affection for the past if we want to? As Gloag said the other night, some things have been invented and perfected in the past, and to discard them would be to throw overboard all sorts of civilised legacies. Is not the modern trend of design in the living-room towards a severity and uniformity which will make it little better than a machine to live in? Many of us don't look forward to that.

G.R.: Well, Halliday, let us see what we have a right to expect of our living-room. It should be as spacious as may be. In some houses it may prove a good thing to take down the partition between dining and living-room. It should be well lit, sunny, the walls covered with a light and cheerful material. Many light colours in distemper or paper are fast and washable, so are curtain materials. Electric light will be carefully arranged to give adequate lighting for reading in several places in the room. This will not be as easy as it sounds, for many electric fittings are not designed to light a room. If the room is centrally heated it will probably have an electric or gas fire, which is needed as a focal point in the room rather than for heat.

E.H.: Excuse me, Russell, do you really think with centrally heated rooms a focus *is* necessary? It is not just tradition which makes us sit round an electric radiator? Even if it is disguised to look like a coal fire?

G.R.: Yes, it is curious that some people like to have things disguised to look like something else. I suppose they understand the enormous ingenuity of the designer. At the Paris Exhibition of 1900, a piano was shown carved to look like a tree. The child in us applauded such a crystallising of the fairy story. I can't help feeling that it is merely childish. As to your question, we do need a point of main interest and a fire does supply this. It may be just tradition, as you say. But to return to our living-room there will be no more furniture in the room than is necessary for comfort. The increasing complexity of life leads us to demand simplicity in our surroundings. It is so much more restful than the over-loaded rooms of fifty years ago; it is also, as I have said, much easier, to clean a room of this kind. The bric-à-brac and curios will no longer be littered over the tops of all furniture; these tops will be useful for the things we use every day, or think we do—papers, pipes, cigarettes, books, things which make a room look lived in. The chairs will be really 'easy'; this is a characteristic of our times. We no longer sit upright on hard seats, and some of us have even given our living-rooms the undistinguished title of lounge! Just as the complexity of life today leads to simplicity in surroundings, so the pace at which life is lived makes comfort at home essential. Few of us fail to

demand, and some of us achieve, physical comfort, but the lack of mental comfort is not perhaps so obvious to everyone.

E.H.: That's very true. That is why so many well-designed easy chairs, for example, are ruined by a garish upholstery that sets the nerves a-jangle. It is also to my mind the great weakness in the argument for pure functionalism in design. Why can't designers realise that we all have minds as well as bodies?

G.R.: You seem to lay the blame at the door of the designer, Halliday, and I am not sure that you are quite fair in that. There are competent designers in Great Britain today, there are enlightened manufacturers, there are shops which try to set a standard in the things they sell, there are members of the public who care about these things. But they are in a minority. I am certain there is a very large public which is vaguely uneasy. It feels it is missing something. It is. It is missing beauty in the things it uses every day. I maintain that ugliness does affect everyone. It is so common today as to be taken for granted by most people. To start the planning of better towns we may as well look round our own living-rooms. As with towns, so with living-rooms, there are very few which would not be improved by throwing things out of them. There is no better exercise than to go round one's rooms at intervals—it is a fine game on a wet afternoon—and try to look at everything in the room separately as if one had not seen it before. William Morris, the poet, said: 'Do not have anything in your house which you do not either know to be useful or believe to be beautiful.' This is a good standard to go on. Don't imagine this is a game which only experts or art critics can play. Appreciation of good design can be taught, and there is no better way of learning than by looking at things which informed opinion has approved over several generations; things which may be seen in plenty in our great museums. To be able to form an opinion of any value on the work of today, it is essential that we should study the best work of yesterday.

E.H.: I agree entirely over that, but the trouble is that many of us never seem to associate what we see in an exhibition with our own everyday lives. All we can afford is the stuff in the less expensive stores—furniture we know to be sham—but what can we do? As long as the machine is made to turn out this kind of thing, there is nothing else for us to buy. What are we to do about it?

G.R.: There again, Halliday, you are blaming the manufacturer. I am saying that the taste of the consumer should be educated so that there will be a larger demand for well-designed things, and the machine will then be used as it should be—to turn out cheaply and by tens of thousands examples within the reach of the slenderest purse. After all, the much maligned machine is already doing this where it is controlled by men who understand its peculiar limitations and scope. The exhibition of British Industrial Art in June will show this quite clearly.

E.H.: Yes, that's going to be really fine—the best contemporary work—but, you know it is to consist of what the public terms 'modern' design. And you must admit there is a prejudice in some people's minds against the 'modern'.

G.R.: Possibly; but most *young* people are not ashamed of their own period. In many ways it is a great age. Isn't any prejudice there may be really against 'modernistic' design rather than 'modern'? Just as designers without either culture or originality have borrowed the more superficial decoration of various periods of the past, so today they content themselves with taking the superficial motifs of good contemporary design, and thinking they have 'mastered the tricks of this modern stuff', they produce the horrible 'modernistic' carpets, lights, fabrics and furniture which are seen everywhere today.

E.H.: But how can the ordinary man tell the difference between 'modernistic' and 'modern', especially if he hasn't had much chance of seeing the modern?

G.R.: I think it is a very healthy sign that it is disliked by so many people, but I am afraid the same people go in for what are in fact equally deplorable imitations of the past. Good design will please you after seeing it continually for years. Meretricious work soon palls.

E.H.: Then how, in your opinion, should one judge these things? Is there a standard of good design which applies equally to, say, a Sheraton table and one by a good contemporary designer?

G.R.: Yes, emphatically there is. There is furniture which is good, furniture which is fashionable and sometimes furniture which is good and fashionable. Let us start criticising from the point of view of whether a certain table is fitly designed for its job. Does it stand level? Is the top smooth and without cracks? Is it a convenient height? If it is an occasional table, is it light enough to be moved? If a dining-table, does the raise bark our shins or the frieze damage our knees? Is it strong enough to sit on, for few pieces of furniture are used solely for the purpose for which they were designed? All this is sheer commonsense, and if we had more of it and less talk of periods and styles we should get much better furniture. It is time we made an end of this tyranny of imposed taste, or rather snobbery which passes as taste. Everyone can decide to think for himself. He will soon see that things are as badly designed as they are, not because the makers think they look better like that, but because they haven't thought at all. Just laziness—the same laziness which induces the customer to buy the article which is put before him when he knows it to be bad, rather than search for something better. The public is becoming steadily more critical and will certainly get what it demands. It is annoying to be considered a crank because one criticises the design of an article. Especially as design should start from the very beginning, and if it is good the completed article will be more efficient—design is not something added at the end.

E.H.: I agree that we all should be more critical. There is a sort of moral laxity abroad on questions of taste. Not enough righteous indignation at things pretentious and vulgar. Today pots and pans and other things in common use, are sensibly, if not beautifully, designed; in fact, it is often the kitchen which is the most pleasing room in the house on that account.

G.R.: Yes, Halliday, and yet the housewife will move from her kitchen, where she wouldn't for one moment tolerate a saucepan which was not at once easy to clean and conveniently designed for pouring, to her living-room with its accumulation of knobs and mouldings neither useful nor beautiful. You see, the general standard of design in housing is lamentably low, but certainly improving. This is perhaps responsible to quite a large extent for much of the poor furniture, curtain materials, carpets and other things. Jerry-built, jerry-designed houses naturally contain things that match.

E.H.: That's the old question—which came first, the egg or the chicken? I mean—do poorly designed houses breed bad taste in their tenants, or is it the low standard of taste which demands such ghastly villas and things we see today—what Lethaby so aptly described as Tea-shop Tudor, furnished by what he called the Cocked Hat and Candlestick school of designers?

G.R.: The builder and furniture designer supply a demand: they can't afford to do otherwise.

E.H.: But the trouble is that people whose sensibility is more developed and want a house or a piece of furniture to be more contemporary and efficient can't get what they want. They've got to accept what they can get, and if 'Tea-shop Tudor' is all there is on the market, they must buy it or go without altogether.

G.R.: No, they must demand good stuff. As I said, it's just laziness to take things as they are when you know they aren't good enough. Shopkeepers pride themselves on knowing what the public wants, but does the public itself know what it wants?

E.H.: But if we go into a shop for, say, a table to fit a certain purpose—to write at, or to hold needlework—that is, knowing more or less exactly what we *do* want, we often have a long search among a lot of rubbish, and if our need is pressing enough we accept in the end what the shopkeeper has, which very rarely is exactly what we wanted.

G.R.: You can hardly expect a shopkeeper to stock things to fit every individual taste, but what we ought to expect is that each piece is good of its kind and for its price.

E.H.: I expect to find things designed by men who are experts, and, therefore, have produced something which exceeds my demands, which are, naturally, only formed in a vague and amateurish way. There are many ways of doing most things, and I expect the expert designer to have chosen one of the best ways.

G.R.: Yes: I think the aim of designers for mass production should be to produce furniture which is functionally perfect and pleasant to look at in as small a range as will meet most requirements. It would be possible to spend quite a lot on the designs in the first place. The manufacturer should get the very best designer he could; the cost of design would add very little to each piece, as so many would be made. The problem of the specially designed piece of furniture is the same as the made-to-measure suit—mass production offers us the suit or the furniture ready to wear. I should like to suggest that if you are going to furnish a living-room, you should write down your requirements. This clarifies your ideas. It will be necessary to make a plan of the room, showing which way the windows face. Be sure to sit in the room—to walk through a room gives such a different impression. Don't buy anything until you know what you want, and then buy the absolute minimum, but buy it good. As in cooking, it costs so little more to buy the best materials, but avoid waste like the plague.

E.H.: What of the man who really likes pictures in themselves, and collects them as he does books? Is not this bound to result in overcrowding and spottiness on his walls?

G.R.: He cannot read more than one book at a time, neither can he look at more than one picture at once. Let him collect his pictures, but put them, as he does his books, in a library. In the same way it may prove useful to have one or two beautifully designed and hand-made pieces of furniture in a room which is otherwise furnished with things made by the machine—a great deal of the work in cabinet-making, for instance, is still more efficiently done by the hand than by the machine. It must of necessity be expensive, and few people appreciate the niceties of cabinet-making sufficiently to judge between first-rate and poor stuff. What is very important is that we should not look upon machine-made furniture as an inferior substitute for handwork, or imitation of handwork. Both have their own characteristics, and real advance will be made when we realise this fully, as we are beginning to do. I think all designers worth their salt want the public to be much more critical of their efforts. To say that the English are not good at designing things is wrong. At one time we built houses and made furniture which have hardly ever been surpassed. We are essentially a home-loving people. There is a great stirring of the public conscience about slum clearance, bad housing, poverty, disease, spoiling the countryside. Ugliness is always the enemy—bad design is one form of ugliness. It's up to public opinion to fight ugliness in all its forms.

6.2   Modern Dwellings for Modern Needs by Geoffrey Boumphrey and Wells Coates

Geoffrey Boumphrey: I think, Coates, the best way to lead up to the questions I want to put to you is to quote a statement made the other day by a well-known architect on this subject of the design of dwellings. He said, or rather, he wrote:

'Our small houses today look much like they did a hundred years ago—as a matter of fact they often look much worse—but is there any real reason why they should not? Houses, unlike most other buildings, are still used in much the same way as they always were. In them we eat (sometimes), sleep (usually), bring up our families (if any), and keep our household goods.' That seems to me about as wrong as it could be. What have you to say about it?

Wells Coates: I should say, Boumphrey, that your well-known architect would be the last person to appear in the streets of London dressed in the clothes of a century ago. And yet, the reasons for wearing clothes are much the same as they have always been: to keep us warm (sometimes), to be comfortable in (usually) and, nearly always, to hide our nakedness. Good design in clothes, as in houses, follows the purpose and the intention of the life of the day pretty closely. When society as a whole wants to do a lot of things that have not been done in the past—or merely do the same old things quicker, or more often—then the form of each individual's life is changed. The form of his clothes, their appearance and what they are made of, changes too. And eventually, everything we use and live with must change.

G.B.: You mean everybody accepts the change in costume that has taken place, even in the last twenty years: but very few people realise that the form and appearance of our homes is almost as ridiculous?

W.C.: Yes, that is probably true. Anyhow, it's a good start for a discussion.

G.B.: Why do people cling to the same old forms in their homes—or what seems still more curious, go even further back than a century ago, to Tudor, or some other 'period'—while at the same time they are very careful indeed not to be behind the times in the matter of clothes?

W.C.: I think there's one important reason, and that is we wear our clothes out, we use them up. This makes it economically possible for us to accept as necessary the changes in the design of clothes. But when it comes to the much larger question, the much more expensive question, of buying a house and furnishing it, we want to be sure we are doing the right thing, doing the thing that *lasts*.

And the right thing for an Englishman is, of course, to have a castle all to himself—or at the least what they call in the advertisements a 'baronial hall'—to give him the feeling of stability, security and individuality. It is amazing how many discomforts he will put up with to secure this.

G.B.: Then do you suggest that we ought to wear our houses out every other year, and buy a new house in the latest fashion?

W.C.: It would be a very good thing for the building industry I'm sure, but I'm afraid it can't be done—not for a long time to come, anyhow. No, I'm not going to suggest that. But I'm going to suggest that for the purpose of this discussion we might think of dwellings as buildings for a certain purpose, not as designs in this style or that, or constructed in this material or another. I think we might try to tackle the question of what changes in our mode of life really affect the design of dwellings. We shall find there are a great many points to talk about before we can begin to discuss design?

G.B.: I'm glad to hear you say that. We hear a lot of talk these days about the countryside being spoiled by ill-planned jerry-built housing schemes . . . a few refined shocked voices lamenting that they don't like modern buildings—betraying our glorious English heritage and all that—but practically nothing about the real conditions which produce designs of both sorts. That is why I am not going to start by asking you a lot of fatuous questions like—do you prefer bricks or concrete?—or, do you think that flat-roofed houses clash with the English country-side? I shall ask you first of all, what do you consider are the changes in the conditions of life today which call for a change in the design of dwellings?

W.C.: Right. In the first place, I think we could say that very few people have a permanent family home now—I mean a home which was their father's and their grand-father's before them. We don't *possess* our homes in the old, permanent, settled sense, we move from place to place, to find work, or to find new surroundings. We do this much more than we used to, and the chief reason is that we can travel easily, quickly and cheaply. Time and space are being measured in a new way.

G.B.: And for the most part, we rather like it.

W.C.: Yes, we leave the old home and family, we get rid of our belongings, if we can, and make for a new, an exciting kind of freedom. Our freedom as workers—and still more as holiday-makers and week-enders—very greatly alters our attitude to our dwellings. We want to make flexible arrangements about our homes. We may—who knows?—get a new job in another part of the country, or even in another country, next year, and we don't want to feel tied down. We don't want to spend as much as we used to on our homes. So the first thing is that our dwellings have got to be much smaller than they used to be.

G.B.: There are other reasons for that: for instance, only

a few people can afford servants to keep up the big family mansions; and those who haven't servants, or don't want them, need fewer rooms and things to clean, and so forth.

W.C.: Yes, that means we architects have to plan the new houses more conveniently, compactly and economically.

G.B.: In a way that is bringing the homes of the different classes more into the same class.

W.C.: Exactly. There is a levelling up taking place; we must remember that there are hundreds of thousands of people who really haven't enough rooms to live in. The next point that occurs to me is that the hurry and bustle of modern life outside the home, at work or at play, make the real comfort, quiet, and convenience required in our dwellings during the short periods we spend in them, an essential purpose of our design.

G.B.: Convenience is an important point. The pace at which life is lived today makes it essential for us to spend as little time as possible on the routine of existence—washing, dressing, writing letters, and so forth. But go on.

W.C.: The next thing is that the family-unit is becoming much smaller. The rate of increase of population is slowly dropping—some say it will be stationary by about 1938—but the old family groups are being split up into smaller units, and actually there is a greater increase of families requiring separate shelter than ever before. By a family I mean any group of people living in the same house, flat, or apartment. So that there is a demand for many more small dwellings than are being built. That is one of the big problems of today: to provide the new dwelling-unit that suits the conditions which have produced the new family-unit.

G.B.: Instead of having one large house for a family of eight or even ten, there is a call for three or four dwellings containing families of two, three or four persons?

W.C.: Yes. Attempts have been made, and are still being made, to overcome this shortage by the conversion of large houses into so-called flats or maisonettes; or—and this is worse—you find that several families are being overcrowded into one house, with only a room or two for each, and more often than not, one bathroom and one little backyard for the lot.

G.B.: But that is only a makeshift, and an expensive makeshift at that—expensive for the tenants, and expensive, eventually, for society as a whole.

W.C.: Urged on by these new conditions, architects are inventing new plan-forms and new groupings of these plan-forms, which distinctly alter their shape and size and their situation. I think it will be useful if we agree to keep to the one word *dwelling*—a good Anglo-Saxon word which originally means a place where one lingers or tarries —to include all types of dwelling-units: houses, flats, tenements.

G.B.: Right you are. Well, that seems to sum up the main changes in social conditions; our dwellings are less permanent; they are smaller, both to suit our pockets and because we are out of them more often; there is a need for them to be more restful and convenient; and, lastly, large families are becoming rarer and small families far more numerous. Now, what new demands are being made by the new conditions?

W.C.: I should say that one of the first demands, since we don't live in one place all our lives, is to get rid of some of the many personal effects we carry about from one place to another. And here it seems there is a distinction to be made between what we possess for show, what is our own, and what we possess for use.

G.B.: You are talking about furniture, I imagine?

W.C.: Yes, furniture, and what we call today equipment. The word 'furniture' means loads of cumbersome articles, many of which should not be personal possessions at all, but should be a part of the actual structure of the dwelling. We cannot burden ourselves with permanent tangible possessions, as well as with our real new possessions of freedom, travel, new experience—in short, what we call 'life'. Of course, we've already gone a certain distance towards what I call the 'ready-to-live-in' dwelling. We take it for granted that a dwelling should have the elementary decencies of a bath, hot water and a lighting system.

G.B.: And it should include a great many other things about which the man in the street knows nothing?

W.C.: Yes, the dwelling of tomorrow must contain as part of its structure nearly all that today is carried about for the purpose of furnishing one house after another. Very soon it will be realised that it is as fantastic to move from house to house accompanied by an enormous van, filled with wardrobes, chairs, tables, beds, chests and whatnots, as it would seem today to remove the bath and the heating system complete, including all the pipes.

G.B.: Yet, you don't mean that dwellings will cost more?

W.C.: Most certainly less. And don't forget that in counting the total cost of dwellings today, you must add on the extra cost of the furniture, fittings and furnishings. Take motor-cars. One used to pay for a lot of extras when one bought a car. Nowadays everything is included. You wouldn't think of buying the lighting fittings for your car at a furnishing store, would you? Anyhow, the point is that it now costs you less, because these accessories are designed into the car, and made as part of it. The same thing will eventually apply to the new dwellings.

G.B.: Then that's clearly to the good, not only because it will be easier to move about, but also because built-in furniture is easier to keep clean and generally better in design than the things many people have to buy as 'extras'. The only danger is that people may be afraid of houses all looking alike. What are we to consider as personal possessions?

W.C.: Everything that gives individual character to our homes must always be a personal possession. Let us see what these things really are: not a Jacobean dining-room set, mass-produced like hundreds of thousands of others, nor windows with leaded lights, nor fake oak beams or aspidistras. No. Our *real* possessions—that give personality and character to our dwellings and the life we lead—are, let us say to start off with: good manners; and good taste in clothes; our crockery, glassware and other small objects of personal choice or vanity; our own books, pictures, sculpture, musical instruments, even the quality of our wireless sets. . . .

G.B.: And colours, coverings, curtains and so on. Of course it's perfectly true.

W.C.: Yes, all that I call 'the select value of a personal environment'—or what is personal and individual, as distinct from what is social and universal in the equipment and arrangement of the dwelling.

G.B.: All that is going to allow people to change their methods of life more readily as they develop, which seems to me a very important thing. In the past one was too often born into a household, took on its colour and way of thought, and stuck to it more or less throughout life. Now we have to adapt ourselves and our ways of thought to conditions that change far more rapidly than previous generations thought possible. But before we go any further we ought to show what life in such a house is going to be like. You don't want to frighten people with the suggestion that they will be living like machines in a laboratory.

W.C.: For my part I wouldn't think of designing a dwelling to look even remotely like a laboratory or a dentist's room. The best way to show what I mean would be to talk about the arrangement of the various rooms and spaces, or what we call the *plan* of the dwelling, which determines the final shape of the whole design.

G.B.: You suggest, then, that modern design starts from the interior arrangements and proceeds outwards from those to the final design, not the other way round?

W.C.: Precisely; that is the point of view of the modern architect. He is not concerned with stereotyped shapes and sizes and details. He tries to foresee the type of life that might be lived, and designs directly for it. I used to have a Japanese architect tutor, who put it this way: when you are designing anything, the right principle is 'of the thing itself—never on it'.

G.B.: That's very well put. But let us hear about the plan.

W.C.: The first consideration is the comparative size of the various rooms. All the rooms in which the business of the house is carried on—the kitchen, and the bathroom, and the rooms for dressing in—must be very well equipped with the necessary supplies and fittings. For economy's sake these spaces should be no larger than they need be for use, so as to allow within the total space we can allot for housing our family-unit, one large room, of many purposes, which we in England call the living-room. The dwelling divides itself naturally into three zones—all of them united by the common element of a hall or passage or staircase. The first of these zones is that taken up by the living-room, closely related to the hall and the entrance, and also to the garden, the balcony or terrace. The second zone is that which includes the rooms and spaces for sleeping, dressing, and washing. Let us say that our typical family-unit of four persons requires three bedrooms—that is, one double and two single rooms. I like to think of the principal bedroom as a room for sleeping and resting in primarily—or you might say for living in during the night—and so it should be equipped with only such intimate fittings as are required. It should also be comfortable enough to live in during temporary periods of illness. Then there should be another space, between the bedroom and the bathroom, specially designed and equipped as a dressing-room, where one's clothes are left, and usually left about. The smaller bedrooms would be fitted up as cabins—sometimes with two bunks, one above the other, to save space. It is astonishing how comfortable and cosy a well-designed cabin can be. Then there is the bathroom, which ought to be as large as available money can make it. It should get the morning sun, and give access to a protected balcony or terrace, for athletics and sun-bathing exercises.

G.B.: And sleeping-out accommodation for those who want it?

W.C.: Oh yes. Before leaving this subject of bedrooms, there is another point to make. I think every single person in the family should have a room which he can call his own—a room to be alone in. The only way to provide this is to make the bedrooms serve a double purpose and to include there a small desk and a space for books and writing materials, an easy chair, or a bed which can also be a divan or sofa. The bedrooms should have the morning sun, and should also face the view; a good principle is to design for 'a room with a view' for every individual in the dwelling.

G.B.: Now what about the third zone?

W.C.: The third zone includes all those spaces and fittings where food is stored, prepared, cooked and finally served and eaten in the dining-room, whether this latter is separate or incorporated in the living-room space. The kitchen should not be too hot from direct sunlight, but it should be a cheery place, well-lit and well ventilated. All these three zones—the living-room with balcony, terrace, or garden; the bedroom-dressing-room-bathroom area; and the kitchen-dining-room—though closely inter-communicating, ought to be insulated the one from the other against sound transmission. It should be remembered that this can be done by planning as well as by a suitable choice of materials. In the case of groups of dwellings in one building, insulation is of the first importance.

G.B.: All these considerations you have dealt with determine the size and the disposition as well as the con-venience and comfort required of the dwelling-unit. They are also bound to determine the shape, to a great extent.

W.C.: Yes, indeed they are. The living-room should obviously be arranged to have the maximum amount of daylight and sunlight—and that means the largest possible windows as well as the right aspect. There are also other things which determine both shape and size. I mean economic considerations, and those of not infringing on other people's rights.

G.B.: Let's come to that later. Do you agree with me that, given the requirements and the economic limitations of a dwelling, it does more or less shape itself? So that it is no good expecting, as people do, to start off with a pre-conceived idea of what a house should look like from the outside, and then hope to pack everything into it?

W.C.: We don't begin to think about the actual design until all these things have been carefully worked out. Our dwellings have got to be built in smaller, more compact units, and they have also got to provide for the service of a great many more things and purposes than the old houses did. It is all a question, you might say, of purposes and of purses. Every dwelling has got to have the best lighting, heating and cooking devices, and some form of heating for the general warmth; if it is central heating it should be designed to provide warmth but not hotness or stuffiness, and ought to be amplified at important points in the house by subsidiary heating of the botherless sort, the tap and switch variety; and also refrigerators, telephones, wireless, and, it may soon be, television.

G.B.: And this can only be done, of course, by a much more economical system of grouping than has yet been adopted.

W.C.: Yes, the day of the detached house, with obvious exceptions, is rapidly drawing to a close. There isn't enough of England to provide everybody with that type of life. If you look at p. 16 of the pamphlet *Design in Modern Life*,[1] you will find an illustration of a solid, square, logical English house, of about 1690, which was a self-contained unit, with its own services provided exclusively by and for itself. When we come to more recent designs, typical of English suburban and country development, we find that the principle of the individual or semi-detached house still persists, and that these houses, though linked together by a common system of sanitation, gas, electricity, telephones and other communications, are otherwise planned as individual units, with individual positions, not all equally good from the point of view of aspect, and that they are individually owned, and individually staffed.

G.B.: And it is this phase, Coates, which has almost reached the limits of its development?

W.C.: Yes, what *is* the use of moving out from high rentals near your work if by so doing your travelling costs increase by more than the saving in rent, to say nothing of

---

[1] Published by the BBC, 1933.

wasted time and energy? Or what is the use of moving out of overcrowded towns, merely to overcrowd the country? Every year, larger and larger areas of England are becoming a no-man's land, neither town nor country. No; the next step in the design of dwelling-units must be the block or group of dwellings with every centralised service which the sharing of costs makes economically possible: the provision of large open spaces for social, athletic and other community interests within a stone's throw of one's own dwelling—swimming baths, nursery schools, children's playgrounds, parks and walks—all as an essential element in the main design of the community life. The community structure is the only one that will give us better buildings, more open space, better living facilities, freedom to move and breathe and rest, and cheaper rents and transportation costs.

G.B.: It is difficult to see any alternative to that solution. We clearly want many more of the smaller dwelling units costing much less to build than at present, and each more completely equipped with services than at present.

W.C.: And somehow or other we have got to provide all this at rentals between—let us say—7s. 6d. and 25s. per week.

G.B.: How is it to be done? Are you proposing skyscraper buildings or enormously high towers?

W.C.: Certainly not; such a solution would be only rarely necessary. It would be *economical* only where the extra cost of land very near the centre of the town is balanced by the saving in travelling time and fares to that centre, and then only for hotels and the most expensive type of dwelling. Even then ten, or at most twenty, stories is probably the desirable height limit. The main community blocks would be four or five stories high, and so placed as to give the principal living and sleeping rooms the best aspect—light, sun, and air; these are the rooms, you will remember, which I said ought to be 'rooms with a view'—and the view ought to be across open green spaces, laid out as gardens, parks, and playgrounds, with swimming pools and sun-bathing facilities; well away from the noise and the danger of the main traffic routes.

G.B.: And the building materials?

W.C.: The new plan-forms, developed out of a study of the needs and rights of people today, demand new ways of construction, and, in turn, these new ways of construction and of finish determine the lines, the contours, the colours —the final appearance—of the building. It's no use trying to lay down the law about materials. Everywhere the most economical systems of construction and methods of finish will present themselves, and be used accordingly. The proposed use of concrete and steel, and all the other satellite materials which modern industry and science provide for use in building, makes it possible to create designs in these materials which will provide the shelter and the detailed services we have been enumerating; these materials also provide all the conditions which it is necessary for the architect as artist to work with.

G.B.: Then it seems that if we are to proceed logically it is hardly a question of opinion or taste at all. It is primarily a matter of economics.

W.C.: I think it is useful to take that extreme point of view at the moment. There is already too much talk about style—ancient and modern and 'modernist'—and about specific materials and finishes, and not enough about social and economic conditions which must, in the end, determine the possibility of design of any sort existing— design of dwellings, design of land and amenities, design for modern life. . . .

G.B.: And that brings me to one of the last points: what are the main obstacles in the way of progress?

W.C.: That's a very big question indeed. Let me say that with our system of private property there are too many regulations and petty restrictions of the wrong sort, and not enough laws to give real liberty and freedom. I remember the saying of the old Chinese philosopher Lao Tze: 'where laws and regulations multiply, the world will be full of robbers and thieves'. Whether you enjoy rights of one sort or another today, they are all coming up for question, and the rights over property which we shall enjoy in the future will, I think, be of a different character. You come to a point when individual rights cancel themselves out, and somehow the rights of the community to be a community must be given full expression.

G.B.: And finally there is the question of taste, or aesthetics. How are people to be expected to judge the new dwellings? Not quite as they judged the old?

W.C.: In the first place I think they ought to judge from the point of view of comfort, convenience, freedom to move in the open air and sun, freedom to be alone and to be rested, freedom to play and to be healthy; and in the second place, the right to have these things at a reasonable cost. Everyone knows that we pay too much of our hard-earned incomes in rent nowadays. Today the argument for plan and order and beauty in the arrangement and aspect of life is more than ever an economic one. Twentieth-century economics and technical facility create not only the possibility but the necessity for a new dimension of this order and beauty. Everyone can help by demanding the 'most for the least', and refusing to put up with the shoddy pretences to beauty at second hand. The modern architect starts from human needs and requirements and rights: an intimate study of the human raw materials which he is designing for, and an intimate and detailed knowledge of systems and methods of construction and the uses of materials and finishes. As architects we know that there are a great many different solutions of the purely technical and economical problems of efficiency and organisation, and of assembling and construction: from all these we take those solutions which dispose of such problems and give also the qualities of form and space, fine scale and proportion, cleanliness and service and comfort and convenience, which we call architecture.

6.3 Meaning and Purpose of Design by Frank Pick

A concluding summary by the President of the Design and Industries Association

It is something of an effort to look at the things that are round about us with our minds as well as with our eyes. We so soon accept them unthinkingly. That is one excuse for a good holiday every year. It uproots us and that opens our eyes to see things afresh. On our return home, for a day or two at least, we ask ourselves questions about our surroundings, but habit soon grips us again. So in default of our keeping this questioning spirit in any other way, we must make a business of it. We shall find it an amusing, interesting and instructive business, as I am sure my friends who have spoken in this series will have already convinced you. You cannot have heard Mr Laver, for instance, without finding history written in your clothes, or Mr Meynell without finding craftsmanship manifest in your books.

My friends have been by way of being experts at their subjects, and on that account you may have listened to them with respect and not thought of copying them. I come along, a jack-of-all-trades, and I am boldly going to ask you to copy them, to join their company, becoming missionaries throughout the length and breadth of the land for the conversion of things from bad to good, or from good to better, or from better to best, if that is possible. You must first startle your shopkeeper by asking questions, in the fashion of the dialogues you have heard Tuesday after Tuesday for the last ten weeks, and then he will startle the manufacturer by passing them on, and the manufacturer will be compelled to look about for designers skilled and competent to embody the answers which you want in the things themselves. The movement starts with you, the consumer or user.

Now this matter of design is nothing abstruse at all. By nature we are all designers. It is only a matter of using our brains, of bringing thought to bear upon the making and fashioning of things for everyday use. It is putting as much brains into making a pot or pan as a wireless set. When men were making the first pots and pans they had to think about them, but now we are so clever we can make pots and pans on a mass production basis with scarcely any thought at all. But a frying-pan, to take a definite problem, is not the simple affair we may imagine. It must be of solid metal which will absorb and hold heat. Iron is better than aluminium—or is it the other way about?—and thick is better than thin metal. If we ask for a light frying-pan we are forgetting its main purpose. The handle must be firmly rivetted or welded on, yet the handle must not get hot. It must be of metal, shaped to dissipate heat. Design is applied science at this stage. Those of us who use frying-pans, and on occasion I do myself, know how often we scorch our hands, how often the handle wobbles, and we know how much better a pancake is that is cooked quickly and not slowly. An omelette is another problem. Now, is our experience turned to account so that we cannot go into a shop and get an unsatisfactory frying-pan? Well it is not, but it ought to be. Thought is not always in the frying-pan.

Now I shall try to show you what thought in things means in its simplest terms, so that you may become familiar with design, and not afraid to talk about it.

First, it means order. We all appreciate symmetry. Cut an ordinary ornament down the middle and the halves are alike. Or have a pair of ornaments one on each side of the mantelpiece—to match, as we say. This question of balance starts with simple things like handle and spout on either side of a teapot. There should be a proportion or relationship between them. They should let the teapot look as though it were not being weighed up or down one side or the other. It may also be studied in flower vases which have so narrow a base that when filled with tall flowers they are unstable and with their fall cause us also to fall into hasty and unseemly language. But perhaps the best illustration is found in chairs. The wooden chair that stood firmly on its four legs has given place to the metal chair which looks as though it had no legs at all and yet is just as stable. In some the upholstered seat and back look perilously suspended. Such a chair has the added advantage of using its bent metal tubing to give resiliency which the wooden supports were unable to give, but when not in use the seat is not quite flat but slightly tilted upward. This looks odd, but it is there to counteract the weight of the sitter so that it is level when in use. It may be compared to loading a spring on a motor-car. It shows that the design is adapted to the material, and is incidentally a true application of fitness in design.

Nowadays we find symmetry too obvious, and we deliberately set ourselves more difficult problems of balance. We know that masses, which are far from symmetrically disposed, will yet balance round a central line or point, and so we set ourselves to judge nice and difficult problems of asymmetry, or the opposite to symmetry, and if we are clever enough to judge aright, we get more pleasure out of it than out of the obviously symmetrical. The old balance of symmetry looked at rest. One part definitely offset another part. The new balance looks as though caught at rest just for a moment, as though it would move if the slightest change occurred. It has the attraction of being caught and held just at the right moment. Afternoon tea-tables with shelves at odd levels, or stands for cactus pots with little ledges climbing about, as it were, look balanced, when they are cleverly arranged. Orderliness and use do not enter into our judgment to any extent. Unluckily this taste for asymmetry may lead us astray. It may be fitting for an occasional table to slip things into; it is only foolish for a writing table, for example. There you must sit with all things about you in an orderly fashion, which rules out any playful variety of level or arrangement.

Order is a notion which we all try to put into practice. Look in a cupboard and see the tea-set or the dinner-set packed away. The better it is packed away the better it looks packed away. The cocktail cabinet, essential feature of the modern home, is become a masterpiece of neatness, and so of design in this sense. It holds such a lot with its racked glasses on its doors and its ingenious fitments that economise every bit of its space. It is the same with a fitted wardrobe. If well fitted, it gives a sense of order, confirmed by experience, which is an added grace of design, so that we look back with shame upon large ill-equipped cupboard-like affairs or vast drawers in which things tumble about. This virtue of order in design is the same as the virtue of tidiness which I hope we cherish in ourselves. We all know the bedroom of the untidy man. Socks on this chair; suit thrown over the back of that; here a shirt and there a collar; the drawers not closed; a cigarette left burning on the mantelpiece with the marks of many scorchings which have gone before. I admit all this may make on occasion an attractive human picture, but not a room to live in, and if the outward show is like this, what about the inward, represented by the insides of the drawers which are not seen? We know this tidiness is not designed. Now look at the furniture that fills your room in the same way. Is it arranged in an orderly manner? Loose furniture has given place to fitments on a unit pattern. It is a great advance in room design, giving more space in our smaller houses. All we have to ask is whether it is made up of useful parts to hold things properly? Whether any part is idle or ornamental? If so, what is its value to us? Even the untidy man may blame untidy furniture for his own untidiness.

But let us pass on. Thought next means the fulfilment of purpose. We think out how we can do something, and if we think well, we can do it better. Take our knitting for example. We begin on the plain jobs, 'knit one, purl one', and only later take up the 'knit one, wool forward, knit two together' patterns. We commence with mufflers and finish with pullovers, or even with our bathing costume, but we buy the ornamental flourish and stitch it on, the fish, or flower, or mermaid that identifies it. One day we shall venture on this decoration. Our knitting when done must serve our purpose—or else we give it away as an unkindly present. We know that stage by stage in our progress we must put thought into it. Habit only comes with practice. So we must see that when we buy things thought is put into them. This applies to dinner plates, for example. Dinner plates should hold a generous helping; the rim rising clear of the sauce or gravy, not too steep to hold the salt and mustard without slipping, a trifle hollow for this; a nice colour not to clash with the food. A tone of green or blue does not improve the appearance of the meat. Then we want to know if the plate is clean, which means the pattern or decoration should not sprawl about the centre hiding any marks which there may be, and even at the edge it should be plain and clear. There is a chance for thought in the choice of a dinner plate if it is to fulfil its purpose satisfactorily, which goes beyond the mere pattern on it. Or take an easy chair. I have paid for my experience dearly, for easy chairs are dear to buy. Support for the head is often lacking in these modern, low, box-like chairs. There is too much support for the arms in these box-like chairs too, which pin you in and hinder writing, or that knitting again. I hardly like to think of my uneasiness in easy chairs. And what a lot of patterns there are in the shops! They obviously cannot all be right.

When we come to this test of purpose, all of us are competent forthwith to pronounce judgment. We use these common things and our purpose is served or it is not served. We should be quite outspoken about it. Fitness for purpose, that is the keynote of good design.

If a thing is hard to do, we have to think before we do it; and that is a good job, for then we are not likely to make a mess of it. Consider the wireless set. The chassis is a difficult affair and we can hardly make a bad job of it. If we do the wireless set is cast out as useless. It stands condemned at once. Open the case and see the orderly wiring, the grids and screens, the carefully-finished valves in their container, everything in its place, nothing superfluous or merely decorative. Yet it has a pleasantness of design we can all grasp. Close the case again and what do we see about it? That fret-saw that gave to the mouth of the loudspeaker a rising sun over a billowy sea, or a couple of willows by a stream. It is so easy that thought was wasted on it. Then the handles to lift it by, if it is a portable. Can we get a firm hold of them? Wireless is of the twentieth century if you like, but should it be put in an eighteenth, seventeenth or even sixteenth century case? The period case! Not all wireless cases are bad, of course, and a word of praise is due to those recent designs which have had regard to modern requirements and modern sensibilities, which are fit—the exterior and the interior being in some sort of harmony.

What is to be said upon this point of ease or difficulty in manufacture falls under two heads. First, a respect for material; second, a regard for craftsmanship. We are often afraid to recognise cheap material. It is a form of snobbery, and so we attempt to make it look what it is not. We all know the mock marble that comes from paint, or the deal that apes the oak with graining. Plywood has come to our defence, for it may wear a lovely face honestly enough and modern design must take account of plywood. Even the silver gilt of the rich often seems to me to indicate a lack of real taste. It is only another form of snobbery.

We often fail to recognise the labour of the maker. We have our silver smoothed out and burnished sometimes, even when it is hand-made, so that the work of the hand is entirely lost and hidden. And then by way of contrariety, our brass pots, which are spun on a machine, are filled with steel bullets and shaken hard so that they may look as though they had been beaten out with a hammer. Any respect for craftsmanship would stop all this. Try, therefore, to imagine when you buy how the thing was made and look for the natural and healthy signs of labour.

Watch a blacksmith humouring the hot metal and with heavy strokes now this side and now that giving it the shape he wants. Or a carpenter with a gouge or chisel making sure and certain cuts in the wood so that they have a crispness and sharpness which hold something of beauty always. Then think how different the effect would be if the strokes or cuts were fumbling or tentative. The resultant shape might be the same but all the surface and texture would have been destroyed and spoilt.

Then by way of contrast watch a machine. Take a rotary planing machine. The rough wood goes in on one side and on the other side the boards come out of a regular and even thickness with their faces smoothed and true. If there were any play such as the hand might give, it would mean the machine was out of truth and wanted adjustment. The signs of craftsmanship have altered.

When you buy painted pots where the colour has been added by strokes of a brush, seek those signs of directness and sureness which the hand can give. Appreciate the slight variations in the pattern which flow from them. But when you buy pots where the pattern has been printed on or taken from a transfer seek then the qualities which a machine should give. Be sure the transfer is carefully placed, that its ends join together exactly. You must all have noticed on a plate the break in the pattern where the transfer has not joined exactly. There is a craftsmanship of the hand which is expressed in freedom and there is a craftsmanship of the machine which is expressed in determination, in accuracy.

This brings me to another point. Design is something more than just using material aright, or showing skill in its use to bring out its beauty. It is something more than serving a purpose. It is something more than ensuring tidiness and order. It is also expression. It is the designer saying something for himself. The further we get away from use, the more we must seek expression. Fitness for purpose must transcend the merely practical and serve a moral and spiritual order as well. There is a moral and spiritual fitness to be satisfied. We know it sure enough when we see it. In our charming country cottages the furniture is mainly for use, but the charm depends upon its being also an expression of the life lived in the cottage. So in our homes we should express our lives. I am not at all sure we should not help our friends to guess what our employment is, what our interests are, what are our fancies and ideas, when they come into our house. So often we hide the personal note away and produce what is a conventional room, which is often characterless. There should be no concealment. It is snobbery again in another guise. Into the void that snobbery makes, comes the devils of fashion. So with the things that go into the house. They should have an expressiveness of their own as far as possible. Wherever they are ornamental or decorated we must insist on this expressiveness, for it alone can keep the ornament or decoration within reasonable limits. Textiles demand it. I believe we reveal ourselves most in our curtains and carpets. Certainly we do in our clothes, in spite of convention. The most dangerous things we buy are textiles.

Often I think there is only one right solution of this problem of design. Many of the common things which we use have had their design settled long ago. Take the face of a clock, for instance. The hands go round and so the figures should be arranged in a ring. Yet in these days you get clocks which are triangles, squares and oblongs. The hands at one moment are trying to reach the figures on the margin, the next moment they entirely overlap them. There is only one right answer to the design of the face of a clock, and I often think of the wretched designer forced to improve on the best for the sake of novelty. But it is the consumer's fault. I cannot think the designer is naturally so perverse. If you would not buy them then they would not be made.

Of course, there are things which, luckily, allow of a convenient variety of solution, like the length of a skirt, which may wander from the knee to the ankle, or even down to the floor and trail. But the height of, say, a street bollard is fixed. It is a sign, a warning light, which should always be in the same relative position.

What illustrations I have chosen have been among homely and familiar things that have nothing to do with art or aesthetics, or beauty in itself, and yet they may be artistic or fine or beautiful. When we have to deal with such things we may feel justified in approaching them along easy, recognisable paths. We can ask whether they are orderly or tidy. We can ask whether they are fitted for their purpose. We can ask whether they show respect for the material of which they are made. We can ask whether they show the craftsmanship of hand or machine, as the case may be. We can ask whether they say or disclose anything to us beyond the bare thing itself. All this while we are on fairly safe ground, and if to all these questions we can give anything like a satisfactory answer, then I might safely hazard the conclusion that the thing would be at least halfway to beauty—maybe all the way. We shall indeed be surprised at the result of attempting to give plain answers to questions such as these. Beauty will burst upon us unawares. There was a poster used for the last exhibition of French industrial art which showed the smoke of factory chimneys twisting and curling up into the air to form a rose. It was a graceful bit of symbolism. And out of a regard for rightness of things—and that is all that our questions mean—must spring, without any doubt, beauty. And to the right thing that little extra touch of love is so easily added, that bit of decoration which emphasises rather than hides structure, that flourish which a true pride forces out of the craftsman. And out of that extra touch of love indeed springs all loveliness. No rules can define it. No rules can teach you how to recognise it. It just comes.

These attempts to illustrate my meaning in words are clumsy and laboured, as compared with an object-lesson. Luckily at the present moment there is in the Dorland Hall, in Lower Regent Street, an exhibition of British Industrial Art in relation to the Home, to which many of you can go, in the spirit of criticism which my friends and I have tried to awaken in you. The exhibition is novel in one important particular. The things that are shown have been selected. Not everything that manufacturers have offered has been put in. Manufacturers have generously co-operated, but all the things shown have been chosen by independent people with one object in view, to display the level of attainment in design of British industry at this time, and to prove that this design is alive and progressive and moving in a common direction, whether it be in textiles, or pottery, or furniture, or glass, or other material. The time is ripe for such a review. These talks are but one sign of the revived interest in things. I do not pretend that everything in the exhibition is perfect. Quite the contrary. It is there for fair and reasonable criticism. It is there for you to practise on. Some things you will like and praise; other things you will not like, and condemn. But please, whether you praise or condemn, do it with understanding. There you can see the steel and wooden chairs that I have told you of, the cocktail cabinet, the glass in many shapes and colours, even the frying-pan. There you can see much more which will help you to appreciate good design. You must be left to your own devices, but if I have stirred you to questioning I have accomplished all that I can. It little matters what I have said, whether it be right or wrong, so long as the manner of saying it has provoked you to use your mind with your eyes.

6.4   Is Modern Architecture on the Right Track?
by Reginald Blomfield and others

Architecture, which of all the arts lends itself most easily to public criticism, has undergone an admittedly remarkable transformation in the last twenty years. The question which springs uppermost in the minds of those who see great new buildings rising in their midst must be: Are we entering on a new era of great architecture; or, on the other hand, is architecture disappearing as an art, as a result of new constructional methods? We have accordingly asked a number of architectural experts to answer this broad question, which we have tried to translate into the following specific queries:

(1) Is the engineer making the architect unnecessary today?
(2) Has functionalism in building gone too far?
(3) Can the English town and city ever properly assimilate the new architecture?
(4) Is the new architecture ugly?
(5) What will the next generation think of the ultra-modern style of present-day buildings, including the ultra-modern home?
(6) Are we likely to evolve in the near future a new style of architectural ornament?

Sir Reginald Blomfield

Some of us had hoped that Modern Architecture, having gone off the deep end, might come to the surface again with a clearer vision of what architecture really means, and has always meant hitherto. We realised that the modernists had got rid of a lot of unnecessary trappings, and were making a laudable effort to bring architecture back to its essentials. Unfortunately, they appeared to have an inadequate perception of what those essentials are, and in their zeal for 'functionalism' or whatever they call it, they are simply killing the art of architecture. The art critic of one of our daily papers recently assured its readers that in future professional painters will confine themselves to making patterns, and, following the same line of thought, our modernist architects would seem to limit architecture to factory design. They are handing over the art to engineers, and greatly as I admire the ability of engineers within their own province, their incapacity in matters of aesthetics is notorious, and indeed is recognised by themselves. The modernists are selling the fort of architecture.

Yet, after all, architecture is an art and from time immemorial it has been regarded as one of the greatest. Beautiful buildings, the Parthenon for instance, the Pantheon, Chartres, or St Paul's have moved men and women more profoundly than any but the very greatest masterpieces of painting and sculpture; but who is going to be moved, except to resentment, by buildings such as Herr Mendelsohn produces in Germany or M. Corbusier in France, or by buildings of steel and brick that purport to be made of concrete, buildings cased in steel and glass, buildings that appear to follow no principle but that of contradicting everything that has ever been done before? I suggest that our modernists are wrong in principle. (1) They definitely ignore the past. They no longer study it, and in this deliberate ignorance it is easy for them to cut adrift, and start afresh on their own. They have some excuse in the nineteenth century, that disastrous interlude in the arts, which, though it had men of genius, undid the work of the eighteenth century, and landed us in our present chaos. But civilisation is far too old and complicated for a clean sweep. It runs back for thousands of years, and in all those years man has been building up certain instinctive preferences or prejudices, if you like, which lie at the back of consciousness. These may be stamped upon for a time, but they will inevitably play their part again, and though our modernist may prefer 'Olympia' to the Parthenon, I do not think that the future will endorse his preference. The modernist asks us to suppress all our acquired and inherited instincts, and hand over our minds to him as a *tabula rasa* on which he is free to write what he likes, but in the first place we are not at all certain that he has anything to write that is worth writing, and in the second place we may prefer to be masters of our own minds. The next generation, or the next but one, will assuredly wipe the slate clean. (2) In the second place the modernist view of architecture, its translation into mere functionalism, is absurdly inadequate as a conception of architecture. Its procedure, apart from merely fashionable imitations of that new manner as practised on the Continent, appears to be the selection of some one practical condition of the building to be designed, and the sacrifice of everything else to this one element. Light, for example, is wanted in all buildings, therefore the modernist designer fills all one side of his rooms with a window, and not content with this he repeats this feature in a series of horizontal bands from end to end of his façade; and having thus complied with what he takes to be the essential element of his design, rests on his oars and expects us to admire the result. Yet it is inexpressibly tiresome, and ignores the fact that the value of light has to be considered in relation to shade, and that all light is only a degree better than all shade. It is assumed that if a building provides the accommodation required, is lit and aired and stands up and keeps the weather out, this is all that is required of the architect. It is no doubt all that is required in factories, which are the source of inspiration of most modernist buildings. But a factory is not a house nor is it a municipal building, nor are the steel tube furniture and the general suggestions of a lavatory in modernist houses pleasant to the eye. The modernist carries his work no further than a stage well within the competence of the engineer, and he leaves off at the very point at which he ought to begin. It is here that I part company with the modernists, not for their dismissal of Gothic tracery and classical orders or meaningless ornament, or for their use of steel and reinforced concrete or any other material suitable for building, but because they insist in our regarding architecture, no longer as an art, but only as a branch of engineering. I do not wonder that at a recent mock trial Mr Chesterton accused artists of doing their best to madden the world by their quick changes. Fifty years ago it was the fashion to say that the only way to become an architect was to work with one's own hands; now it is the fashion to say, leave it all to the engineer. A study of history would have broken down either theory, but of the two 'the last state of this man is worse than the first', because it cuts at the very root of architecture, an art of which the aim and ideal is to translate practical conditions into terms of ordered beauty.

These considerations lead me to give the following answers to your questions.

(1) The architect is more than ever necessary, and he should work hand in hand with the engineer, taking over the work where the engineer stops.

(2) Functionalism has gone too far, in that it has misconceived the purpose of architecture, and by turning its back on the past, has deprived itself of any adequate technique, and is running its head against deep-seated instincts which will beat it in the end.

(3) English towns and cities and our countryside cannot assimilate this new architecture. It is essentially Continental in its origin and inspiration, and it claims as a merit that it is cosmopolitan. As an Englishman and proud of his country, I detest and despise cosmopolitanism.

(4) The new architecture makes no appeal to me except in those cases where the designer shows that he is not wholly unconscious of the great architecture of the past.

(5) What the next generation may think it is impossible to say at the rate we are going; but unless we are heading for chaos, I think the new architecture will go the way of other fashions. What is good in it will be absorbed, and the rest of it relegated to the dustbin.

(6) As to ornament, if the new architecture is really great, it can do without any ornament at all.

Charles Holden

(1)   I would say that both the engineer and the architect have a long way to go before either can supplant the other. An engineer who has the imagination to discover the expressive possibilities of his own constructive medium would be a public benefactor; the same applies equally to the architect. Under right conditions the work of the engineer and the architect should be harmonious and not antagonistic.

(2)   It depends on what is meant by functionalism; the style or fashion of functionalism, or the principle of functionalism. If the style or fashion, I would say that it will have the life of a fashion and that it will be done to the death by its own devotees; on the other hand the principle of functionalism will never go too far, for it is the vital force behind every great constructive period the world has known—the lintel, the arch, the dome, and the vault. Functionalism, which introduced all these in their turn, will no doubt find a suitable idiom for the girder and the stanchion and for the reinforced concrete frame. That is indeed the exact significance of the present movement in the architectural world.

(3)   History shows that the world has assimilated in the past the various manifestations of the vital principles of functionalism which possessed the structural stability necessary for survival, and I have no doubt that it will continue to do so.

(4)   Generally, where the design is true to the constructive principle and where the designer has a real pleasure and pride in every phase of his work, he will not rest content until he has extracted, to the extent of his capacity, all the latent beauty that lies within the scope of his project and in the materials he employs. We need have no fears on the score of ugliness where these conditions obtain.

(5)   The next generation will, if it is wise, be looking after its own biological needs. It will, I hope, respect the true and condemn the false irrespective of period or fashion.

(6)   History is the best guide and indicates that it may take one hundred years or more to develop any distinctive form of architectural ornament.

An architect needs a long view; I regard the present phase of extreme simplicity as comparable to a piece of ground which is allowed to lie fallow for the benefit of future crops. In the meantime our architecture is gaining in significance by the elimination of non-essentials. Architecture is not embroidery, it fulfils a fundamental human need, and it is in the fulfilling of this need with pride and pleasure in the truthful expression of its various functions that we convert building into a fine art.

To sum up on the broad question, 'Is modern architecture on the right track?' I would say that the architecture of today is in a most interesting state of transition, a state of adventure and of trial and error, maybe, but a state which is healthy and stimulating, and I see no reason for depression.

Truth is the most fruitful source of inspiration; it shows us a road with a destination and with more destinations beyond, to infinity; it will not land us in a *cul-de-sac*.

Professor A. E. Richardson

In the last century the conflict of opinion was between architects who favoured classic and those who advocated Gothic. It is now between those who decry and those who affirm engineering. Such controversies may be exciting, but they do not help in the creation of an ideal. It is therefore high time for the public to realise the status of architectural education and the important part the profession serves in everyday matters. For the purposes of this article, time would be well employed discussing the need for reform in the development of towns, or, better still, the elimination of the slums, but that would not be germane to the issue before us. Architecture is not a controlling force; it is an expression of multitudinous facts. Its resultant qualities depend almost entirely on the stimulus it receives from public demands. At the present time only a very small proportion of building work can claim to have architectural value, for the speculative builder and the opportunist have conjointly deceived the public. The issue of the moment is not how to improve the best, but how to prevent a repetition of the nondescript, especially the cheaper, forms of housing. This great difficulty has been partly solved by the architects of Amsterdam and Stockholm, but is not clearly understood by authorities and the public in this country.

The reason for indecision in matters of design is not far to seek. In recent years directing mediocrities have discovered architecture to be a subject for facile pens, and to literary interference has been added the harmful influence of photography. Fashion after fashion has been encouraged and the convenient label 'modernism' has been employed. In the philosophy of building two leading theories are representative; the first is truth, the second is artistry in structure. Within these headings can be included a host of attributes which vary according to the ability of executants. In other words there is no disputing about taste. In so far as it is fashionable, 'modern architecture' is definitely on the wrong track.

While youth favours adventure in design, middle-age profits steadily by experience, and old age is desperately conservative. Meanwhile the mass of humanity is hurled forward by mechanical and economic changes, and misled by the dubious slogan of progress. It is clear that the general motives already mentioned inspire the actions of architects, but thoughtful men hold tight to the precepts of their intensive training, and very rightly so. In actual practice adventure becomes commonsense, experience ripens into genuine artistry and conservatism at least shows care for the future. This process has always been in action; it is inevitable, it is logical and it is true. What then is the position of the architect who is an artist, a planner and capable organiser? He is not likely to hand over his stock-in-trade to the engineer, who is trained on entirely different lines. It can be said that architecture is the chief of the plastic arts; it has a mighty past and a splendid future, and at all times it has filled a great space in the story of humanity. There is no question of a duel between the architect and the engineer; both are highly skilled, both regard co-operation as essential to the success of specific undertakings. But the formula of engineering cannot be applied to every phase of architecture: it would be a monotonous world if this were to be the case. Whatever changes in the social system may occur in the future, architecture will continue to exist, its spirit will be constant, not only to the outlook of the moment but to those abstract and human qualities which have accompanied it through the ages. The engineer today not only recognises the skill of the architect as a deviser, but he is anxious to be a co-executant in the subordination of structural and functional facts to the harmony of an architectural idea. On the Continent, particularly in Germany, it is now realised that 'functionalism' is not everything, and haste is being shown to retrieve false moves. The surest test of architectural effect is the viewpoint of the man-in-the-street, which is seldom taken into account. The average man and woman have grown accustomed to reverence ancient buildings; they admire the aspect of old towns and villages. The venerable cathedrals and parish churches appeal to the intuitive sense of English people. On this account also it is doubtful whether undue disturbance of pictorial values by cubist designs will find favour. By all means let us have up-to-date buildings, by all means let us encourage invention; but there is the responsibility of maintaining artistic harmony. Why not take a lesson from Amsterdam and construct entirely new quarters while preserving the best of existing amenities? In all my travels I have never encountered finer modern buildings than those at Stockholm. Here the new working-class flats are models of good taste. They are spaciously arranged, they are free from unnecessary ornament, and without exception they are delightful to look upon. The Swedish architects are neither dull nor extravagant. They have not sought for a newer form of architectural ornament, they have not burked tradition nor ignored the claims of structural truth. In Stockholm the merits of brick and stone have obtained equal recognition with the employment of reinforced concrete. There is almost a total absence of advertisements, and the litter of commerce is reduced to a minimum. Is it too much to hope for similar changes in England?

To my way of thinking the chief trouble before the learned societies and educational bodies is neither the direction of architectural taste nor the encouragement of involved thinking, but the emancipation of democracy from the enormities of shoddy building. Better by far the universal adoption of concrete for terrace groups in the suburbs than the serrations of 'mock' Tudor which perpetuate Victorian snobbery.

W. Curtis Green

That this question is being discussed by a journal so widely read as *The Listener* is evidence of an awakening interest in architecture, an art that, in spite of neglect and apathy, is very much alive today, within very confined limits.

It is probably true that some ninety per cent of the building of today has no affinity with architecture. It is merely building: some of it may be quite good building, it may even be the work of legally qualified architects, but that does not in itself lift it into the realm of architecture. Architecture is building *plus* that finer quality that comes from descent from and kinship with the ages. It is an affair of the spirit, the carrying on of the tradition of a living art. It is not only the satisfying of the material needs, but of the intellectual and spiritual aspirations of mankind.

It is also probably true that there can be no such thing as 'new' architecture, except in so far as it can be true that a man can be a 'new' man. To say that is to say that a man has suddenly been enlightened and sees the purpose of life for the first time. Such an awakening may be happening; it is devoutly to be hoped for, and there is evidence of a stirring of the dry bones among many of the younger and more vital of our architects. The trouble is that these men are so seldom employed. The great public who build are for the most part unaware that there is no economic reason for their money to be spent on ugly and uninspiring building. They do not realise that their houses, their churches, their schools, their offices, their public buildings, could all be additions to the commonwealth, adding beauty and enjoyment to everyday life, instead of being the reproach and eyesore that most building is today. To build with the right materials intelligently costs no more than to build with the wrong ones without proper guidance. The engineer can never make the architect unnecessary. Where the engineering problem is the dominant one the architect is still necessary. The great Power Station at Battersea has, by the intelligent co-operation of the architect, Sir Giles Scott, with the engineers, been transformed into something that gives pleasure by its dignity and expression of power. Reinforced concrete, one of the most recent and useful contributions to modern building, the highly skilled work of engineers, makes building generally of the most depressing character, unless it be controlled and modelled by the architect. The engineer by training and by the necessity of his calling is preoccupied with structure and the material side of building. The architect by his calling weaves together material things, the work of scientists, engineers, and craftsmen, so that they may supply the needs and bring harmony and comfort of mind and body out of the complexities of modern life. And here is the danger of the tendency to be in the fashion: each created thing is new, but fashion is a succession of clever novelties; a work of art is the product of its age, but its spirit is inherited.

Functionalism is only one of the properties of architecture. Extravagance and over-emphasis are the negation of art. In so far as the younger school of architects is preoccupied with architecture their work will be on the right track. Theories are useless; knowledge of architecture can only be acquired by study of the actual thing. Too much modern work shows a complete neglect of tradition. The trend to simplicity, cleanness of line, directness of planning, absence of cheap and meaningless ornament is in the right direction; these qualities are all to be found as contributory in any of the acknowledged masterpieces of architecture.

Where buildings lack the greater qualities of imaginative design they will be swept away by later generations with neither compunction nor regret, to give place to new buildings which may perhaps have these qualities—if they are wanted.

E. Maxwell Fry

Is modern architecture on the right track?—I should like to frame this question in another and less immediate form. It is of little use to peer into the future for an architectural Moses bearing new tables of the law. It cannot be as simple as that. If the answer lies in the future we shall have to wait for it. But if we have left any tracks so far we shall find them in the past, of which we are to ask, not whether we are on the *right* track, but in what ways and to what extent was the central stream of architectural impulse diverted by the upheaval of the nineteenth century. That a rupture took place is not now questionable. England ceased to produce good architecture, good metal work, silverware, furniture, and glass after the first quarter of the nineteenth century. Why?

Because the national way of life was broken. The eighteenth century way of life was not necessarily good, but it was complete, whole. The Industrial Revolution, coming suddenly, offered strange powers, at variance with the old way of life, and for a hundred years the philosophers were cheated, and life was a warring divorce. Art, and architecture with it, lost touch with reality, and flew to this and that palliative, shrinking from the acceptance of the truth that machinery and factories and towns are the business of those that think and create as well as of those who act. The Gothic revival, the arts and crafts movement, Edwardian revival of revivals, gentleman's Georgian—all these are manifestations of a wish to escape from the reality of industrialism. They represent the extent of the divergence from the eternal creative stream.

Modern architecture has turned the hate of machinery,

and of steel and concrete, into love. By doing so it has recognised and assimilated the virile structure of the nineteenth century, that made ships and locomotives beautiful. It is, therefore, become whole. It responds wholly and naturally to the reason of things, and rejoins the stream of real tradition.

'Well building has three conditions', wrote Sir Henry Wotton in the eighteenth century: 'Commodity, Firmness, and Delight.' The revivalists, one and all, reversed the order in trying to fit architecture into the figure of their day-dreams. They *felt* overmuch, as men with a grievance against the order of life. Their architecture had a sort of *feeling*, but was not reasonable. For 'commodity' read 'function'; for 'firmness' read 'structure'; and 'delight' still arises from the satisfaction of these two conditions; not as a thing added, but of the thing itself.

The nineteenth century established a new order unlike anything that went before. Eight million people became forty millions; stage-coaches became railways; inns became hotels; towns, cities. Why solve these new programmes with old formulas? Of what use to us is a St Pancras Station of which half is Gothic and half engineering, that is to say, pure structure? Why deal any longer with dead styles when we have an architecture that can solve *all* the problem of a railway station, functionally, structurally, wholly?

If modern architecture responds to the three conditions there is nothing further to fear. Whether it is ugly or beautiful, is not within the competence of men whose taste has been maimed by the last century to judge. If it can satisfy these conditions its final acceptance is inevitable and we and the next generation will discover its beauties.

As to the jumbled, fused, maltreated English town—is there anything it cannot assimilate? Surely the purity of modern architecture at its best can only bring repose to the confusion of fruitless nineteenth-century ornamentation, order into unplanned chaos, and standards of excellence where none exist. The conflict of the styles is over now. Our job as architects is to establish firmly the *order* of constructive architecture so that it serves society completely—and to raise its standards. Others coming after may do what they wish in addition. Whether they will care for what we do is beside the point, since our job is for the first time in a hundred years clearly defined, and within the power of modern architecture to satisfy completely.

Frederic Towndrow

Oscar Wilde once said that if you want to know what a nation is like, look to its architecture. This is profoundly true; for, strange as it may appear, architecture never lies: it is only art that tells the truth. For whereas painting and sculpture may be employed upon the slightest provocation with so little excuse, architecture requires sums of money for its execution. And whereas drama and poetry are subject to individual genius and passing fancies, architecture is the result of a community of effort; of client, architect, and builder, and the multifarious sources from which materials and equipment are obtained. Moreover (and this is most important), it is largely an unconscious art: it reveals without our being aware that it does reveal. In fact, try as we may to avoid it, architecture shows us as we really are, with a most uncomforting precision.

And what does contemporary architecture in Great Britain reveal? It shows the British as a nation which works largely by habit, a people slow to grasp the reality of new conditions. The British do not reason or theorise about a thing; they just 'feel' about it, and do it in a sort of way that pleases most of their countrymen. Around us we see buildings designed in the ancient classical styles with columns, pilasters, cornices, and small rectangular windows arranged in pretty patterns according to ancient usage and obsolete methods of construction. These buildings to most Englishmen seem quite normal, but they reveal a state of mind which more properly belongs to a period of thirty to forty years ago—before the modern use of steel and reinforced concrete and the modern desire for light and air.

Thus the great mass of English people are suffering from this time-lag between what they really need and what they 'feel' they like. In the course of time they will come to realise that what they really need in planning and economy can only be obtained in the strange-looking buildings of the new architecture; and then they will come to admire them just as they admire the motor-car and aeroplane and all the things that do their job. As a matter of fact it is perhaps too early to say exactly what the Englishman will think of the new 'scientific architecture' (I use this expression 'scientific architecture' in preference to 'modern' or 'functionalist') because there are only about a dozen really scientific buildings in this country, and only about half a dozen architects—if that—who understand the philosophy or ideals of the movement. There is Joseph Emberton's Royal Corinthian Yacht Club at Burnham, and his new offices for Messrs. Beck and Pollitzer at Southwark Bridge. In domestic architecture very little has been done; there are two new houses by George Checkley at Cambridge, one by Amyas Connell at Amersham, one or two—not more— by different architects throughout the country, and a house by myself—an early effort—in Essex. In a public way there are the B.B.C. studios by Wells Coates and others, there is the interior of the Horticultural Hall by Howard Robertson, there is the work of Thomas Tait—especially the new Freemasons' hospital at Ravenscourt Park (which is a most attractive building in red brick), and the work of Charles Holden in the new Underground extensions on the Piccadilly Line. One has only to look at these new stations, signal boxes, and railway buildings at Southgate, Cockfosters and Enfield-West to be convinced as to the justice and beauty of the new architecture. When he sees them

even the dullest Englishman will become caught up in the inevitable movement of modern architecture. There is no longer any question: the battle has been won; it is just a matter of time to see whether the battle has not been won too easily.

At this stage I had better define what I mean by 'scientific architecture' (or 'modern' or 'functionalist', whichever word you like to use). It is the architecture which is the result of intense reasoning in planning and structure. It arises absolutely from causes; and these causes are not in architecture but in modern life and modern methods of construction. Thus there is no such thing as a 'modern style'. On this we must be most emphatic, for style implies the idea of an accepted external expression which may be imposed upon the organic nature of the subject. The scientific school of thought, in its purest form, is definitely opposed to this idea of a set external expression; it is entirely an intellectual method of approach to the problems of building. Therefore it is not committed in any way to the use of reinforced concrete, or white plaster, or horizontal windows, or angular shapes, or flat roofs. These, where they occur, should be the result of causes in service and structure which happen to be operating at the moment. Where the needs are different then the results must be different. For instance one may have a building that is no less modern because it has stone walls and a tiled roof, assuming that there is some reason in logic for the extra expense of stone walls and a tiled roof. Flat roofs are employed not because they look 'modern' but because under most conditions they are cheaper and more serviceable.

It is in this *attitude of mind* in relating logical cause and effect that the scientific architect differs from his predecessors. He says to himself, 'I must be reasonable, and if the result appears ugly or strange then I must not change it at the expense of reason'. Yet fortunately (for him) he has found, as the designers of the aeroplane and the dynamo have found, that the searching for fitness produces beauty. In fact, this is the greatest discovery in modern thought, a discovery the old architects never dreamed of, for they did not have our modern machines to give them the clue.

Thus we need not ask ourselves whether this new architecture appears to us as beautiful or not. Given the right state of mind we increasingly think of beauty in terms of fitness. The question we must always ask is not whether these buildings appear beautiful, but whether they are fit for their function. And within this function we must include—to the right extent—the human desire for orderliness, brightness, and colour. Upon this ground only, of complete and inclusive fitness, may we appraise or criticise the new architecture. If it fails at all it fails in respect of its lack of fitness.

(1) It may be argued that what we have here is engineering and that the engineer will make the architect unnecessary.

The reply to this is that it does not matter very much whether the man who designs our buildings in the future calls himself an architect or an engineer; he may be either. The point that does matter, however, is that he must be trained in such a way that he is both architect and engineer; that is to say, he must have the architect's imaginative sense of planning, the architect's sense of form and colour, with the engineer's knowledge of structure. A high degree of imagination (such as only the architect possesses at the moment) is necessary in planning, so that a man may conceive an immense number of alternatives, all of them possible, from which to select the most practical. Moreover, in a building, with our still limited scientific knowledge, there are still a large number of things which cannot be established on a calculable basis by facts and formula. Here the intuitive capacity of the architect is able to step in and save the engineer from the blunders of miscalculation.

(5) It is difficult to say what the next generation will think of what we call the 'ultra-modern style' and the 'ultra-modern home'. They will probably look upon it as something experimental, and perhaps as rather old fashioned. More than likely, several generations ahead, there will be sentimentalists who will go into rhapsodies over an 'olde-worlde-functionaliste cottage'. Generally it is reasonable to suppose that the ideals of the modern architect will be more acceptable to the next generation than they are to the present one. At any rate, young people now in their teens and twenties are tremendously keen about the new architecture.

(6) However, the most difficult question of all is as to whether this new architecture will, in the future, evolve a new style of architectural ornament. It is impossible to answer this question, for one cannot be certain whether future generations will require ornament upon buildings in the sense that our fathers required it. It is possible that they will delight solely in the logical and intellectual qualities of a building, and may find quite sufficient pleasure in its mechanism, its space, and its comfort. No doubt in this there will be a strong demand for colour, and artificial lighting, and possibly for symbolic sculpture. It is uncertain whether there will be any need for ornament in the old sense of that word.

M. H. Baillie Scott

(1) Certainly not! Architects who combine practical ability with artistic sensibility are more than ever necessary to combat the invasion of the spirit of materialism which threatens the world of building today. For this spirit, if unchecked, will end by destroying utterly the rural beauty of the countryside, and by making this beautiful land of ours—this land which our fathers knew so well how to adorn by their buildings—into a habitation fit only for robots and the slaves of the machine. Mr Goodhart-Rendel, in his admirable Oxford lecture last month,

expresses concisely the essential function of the architect. 'It is now generally agreed', he said, 'that the fine art called architecture differs from the useful art called engineering in that it involves aesthetic choice, which engineering does not. There are few structural problems that have not several solutions equal in utility; from these solutions architecture chooses that which best serves her artistic purpose. She is also free, in the opinion of most people, to choose, for her own ends, any slightly less useful solution that actually is useful enough.'

(2) I think this question might better be 'Can functionalism go far enough?' I have never met a functionalist, but imagine that believers in such a narrow creed must be rather dull and tiresome people of strictly limited intelligence. It would be interesting to know if they realise that this much-vaunted new doctrine was invented in the Garden of Eden, and has been practised in every work of man since the world began. Not only man, but birds and bees and beavers are primarily functionalist builders. But man has always been something more, and it is this *something more* which raises his work above that of the beasts of the field, for all these build in three dimensions only. It is man alone who can add the fourth dimension of wonder, beauty and delight. May I quote again from Mr Goodhart-Rendel? 'It has always seemed to me odd', he said, 'that the least interesting of all these dead and bottled ideas, the one labelled "functionalism", should have arisen and spread in the years when ordinary people first began to be interested in the subconscious mind. You would have supposed that anybody who realised how much hidden wisdom and how much forgotten but still influential experience may lie behind the apparently unreasoning choice made by an artist—you would have supposed that anybody realising this would be especially wary when measuring art by the yard-stick of conscious thought. Conscious thought may, and should, test as far as it can the results of artistic impulse; it may, and should, be allowed to annihilate what it can prove to be emotionally insincere or misdirected. But the unconscious thought behind the impulse may be far subtler than any conscious process by which it can be tested, and often truer also. No reasoning can determine the entasis of a column.'

(3) Again, certainly not! The 'new architecture', if I may judge from most of the examples I have seen, is as violently at variance with the spirit of the old town as it is with the countryside which it disfigures and desecrates. The particular charm of an English town derives very largely from its expression of national and local character, influenced no doubt originally by climate, habit, and the special technique of the material available. The new style apparently owns no such allegiance; it has neither ancestry nor kindreds; it cannot be on speaking terms with its neighbours, for it does not know their language.

(4) Whether any architecture, old or new, is ugly or

not depends entirely on the powers of the architect in each case. Almost any style of architecture may be made beautiful by a sensitive and inspired artist or ugly by a blind materialist. The best examples in the new manner have come from architects who have trained their perceptions by the study of old work; the worst from those who find the new style an easy way of expressing their ignorance and contempt of all that stands for beauty in building. (5) and (6) Questions of this kind can only be answered with any degree of confidence by those who, like Mr H. G. Wells or 'Old Moore', possess the gift of prophecy. Hitherto students of history have sometimes predicted successfully its inevitable repetitions. But the progress of modern science may have entirely upset the recurring cycles of history. If, as we may hope, the new generation has not entirely lost that love of home which used to be so deep-rooted in the hearts of our countrymen, it is difficult to imagine how the modern machine-made substitute for English building can prove worthy of their devotion. And, as regards ornament, I think it is highly probable that there may before long be a revulsion from the present tendency to abolish everything which may clothe and beautify the bare structural facts of our buildings, and that grace and comeliness may once more be recognised as essential to good building.

To sum up: modern architecture is wrong in so far as it concerns itself merely with practical utility and scorns the nobler human qualities which building can express. It is wrong, too, in ignoring the splendid building of the past, and in its attempts to get a transitory cheap notoriety by aiming at novelty for its own sake. We should try to do the best we can quite irrespective of the calendar. Whatever forms our modern buildings may take, those alone will have survival value which represent an organic development of the art of building and are deeply rooted in our great tradition. Modern architecture is wrong, too, in its impudent claim to a monopoly of practical efficiency. It often, indeed, signally fails in this respect, more especially in not recognising that the fundamental purpose of the house is to afford an adequate protection from external conditions of temperature and weather. Its flimsy flat roofs, thin walls and too extensive glass areas are quite unsuited to our climate.

Joseph Emberton

'Is modern architecture on the right track?' That depends upon what the expression 'Modern Architecture' covers. If such buildings as South Africa House, or the Shell Building—I mention these because they are the latest contributions to London's bigger buildings—probably not. On the other hand, if the expression is limited to those new forms such as the Van Nelle Factory, Rotterdam, which have been developed in Germany, France and Holland, the answer is very definitely 'yes'. Architecture is not a matter of aesthetics. It is a matter of reason. Architecture should be the servant of man, and not man the slave of architectural tradition. Architecture should be so developed as to increase man's fitness and competence, besides adding to his pleasures.

To insist that the forms of buildings constructed of concrete or steel shall bear the same appearance as their more primitive predecessors in brick and stone, is to prejudice the usefulness of modern science, at the same time producing buildings which have no relation to our time and which can play no part in history. This prostitution of good building, which makes its form subservient to the idiosyncrasies of individual architects, cannot have that sense of inevitability which is the most characteristic impression created by the great buildings of the past, e.g., Salisbury Cathedral or the Parthenon. My main reason for believing that we are getting on the right track is because the best modern architecture is adopting precisely the same principles as were employed in the design of these magnificent remains from the past.

The problem of the mediaeval builder was to enclose spaces as large as possible with small stones. The natural result was the arch, the vault, the buttress and the pinnacle —all functioning parts; not features added for the sake of decoration or symmetry. Surely there can be no reason why steel or reinforced concrete should not produce their own characteristic forms in the solution of the more complex problems of today? The usefulness of the cantilever surely should not be discounted on account of aesthetic prejudice.

The heavy Norman pier became the much more slender one in later Gothic times for no other reason than that with his increased knowledge of the bearing capacity of stone, the builder found he could economise in space. Why therefore should we not accept the more attenuated form of a steel or reinforced concrete column, and effect further economy, instead of encasing it with thick walls of stone for no other reason than to make it look like something which it is not? Thousands of tons of stone are still quarried and brought to London, to destroy valuable and useful space by this expensive form of camouflage, and consequently Regent Street is full of large rusticated piers—mostly hollow—where shop windows would be much more useful.

I believe that the only way to achieve good architecture is to employ the most appropriate materials which scientific development has produced in providing such buildings as will give the utmost service to man without any aesthetic prejudice whatsoever—'To follow the argument wherever it may lead'. In doing this, besides increasing the competence of man, we shall add to his pleasure by producing new entities—buildings which will bear a definite relation to our time, which could not have been built five years ago, and should not be built five years hence. Thus architecture would become a living thing. The buildings would bear some relation to each other, and not represent a collection of individual architect's ideas as to the most appropriate arrangement of antique ornaments. The growth of architecture would then be interesting, and although the different units comprising a street may have been erected at different times, there would be the same harmony as exists between Henry VIII's Chapel and the rest of the Abbey. It is true that the new characteristic forms are not very companionable when side by side with the so-called traditional forms, but is not that the misfortune of our time? In any case, we cannot go on for ever imitating Italian palaces or French châteaux.

It is perhaps interesting to compare architecture with other structures which our age has produced. Take for example the aeroplane, motor-car, liner or omnibus, for it seems to me that a building is as much a machine to work in, or to live in, as these are for transport. These have all produced beautiful—or, at least, satisfactory—forms, without much thought having been given to aesthetic effect. In many cases the quality of beauty is directly related to efficiency. We react naturally to these new virile forms, but our taste for real architectural form has been so prejudiced by affectation and superficial camouflage that we are shocked at the sight of a real healthy structure.

(1)   The engineer is not making the architect unnecessary today. Both are essential in the design of a modern building. The engineer makes the structure, and the architect arranges it to achieve maximum usefulness. There is not time in a man's life to do both with any degree of competence. Although an architect requires a considerable knowledge of structure, the less an engineer knows about architecture the better, for an engineer's results should be achieved by calculation and should be exact, whereas those of an architect are only partly by calculation and mainly by discretion.

(2)   Functionalism cannot go too far until a building can function too well, but the over-emphasis of function may.

(3)   If an English town or city must live, it must assimilate the new architecture. Mud huts were replaced by brick cottages, so must the brick cottages eventually be replaced by concrete and steel. Man's increasing reliance on machinery will determine this. One day we shall take as great a pride in the things we do ourselves as those done by our ancestors.

(4)   That the new architecture is only considered ugly by the prejudiced is indicated by the fact that it is almost invariably accepted by the youthful.

(5)   'Ultra-modern' is a horrid label, and indicates eccentricity which is detrimental to anything. Modern architecture, being based on reason rather than sentiment, will appeal to the reason of future generations. Such reliance could not be placed on architecture based on sentiment.

(6)   Let us purify our structures before we begin to think of ornament, and we shall probably find that they need but

little decoration. Who would put an ornament on the Schneider Cup machine? Few require much ornament on a well-designed motor-car, but mascots are very desirable on an inferior design.

Christian Barman

The one thing that everybody notices about the newest architecture is that it is so very different. For generation upon generation we have had a sequence of ideas and forms moving by indistinguishable stages like the growth of an animal or a plant. Suddenly it is as though an entirely different animal or plant had appeared. 'It's a trick!' you hear people say, and the remark is understandable. To talk about a chrysalis is not quite playing the game; and, besides, the last thing the younger architects want to do is to write down the architectural past as a puppyhood state. We know only too well that there are achievements behind us that we shall never have a chance to equal. But we also know that there are tasks in front quite unlike the tasks that were laid on our predecessors. And it is the exceptional nature of these tasks that demands exceptional action on our part. Architecture has to be different because today the job it has to do is so entirely different.

Now and again the lives of individuals as well as institutions are interrupted by happenings calling for sudden, portentous action. The level country, shall we say, in which years or centuries were passed, has led to a mountain range, and not to cross this range means defeat. But the stock phrases for this kind of happening are mostly taken from military life, where years of meaningless routine are sharply and terrifyingly punctuated with battles in which the future of a nation may be at stake. We architects believe that architecture is about to live through one of these exceptional moments. In the military jargon, we believe that architecture is like an army that cannot maintain itself another day without engaging in battle. And we fearfully surmise that the outcome of the battle will deeply affect not only the future of our own art but the whole future of human life on earth.

What is this battle all about? There is a question that is on everybody's lips today: 'Can human society', we ask, 'assimilate the machine?' The machine came into the world over a century ago, but so far it cannot be said that the process of assimilation has gone on very satisfactorily. The machine has given us motion, and the power of motion has been fairly successfully distributed among mankind. It has not only helped us all to move ourselves about much more easily than before, but by giving us quicker means of clearing away our waste products it has made collective human life cleaner and healthier. On the main fabric of this life, however, the machine has had little effect so far, and that little has been, on the whole, destructive. The new power has yet to be turned into useful human good. The new energy still remains to be utilised.

We are drifting from the metaphors of war into metaphors of the stomach, but the image is useful. When an animal has swallowed a quantity of food there arises for it the crucial question: 'Can I pass this food through the lining of my alimentary canal?' If the food cannot be digested it will not do the animal any good. On the contrary, it may do a great deal of harm unless it is properly dealt with. And in order to deal with it properly, the animal has to rely on the enzymes or ferments which make digestion possible. We believe that architecture is one of the enzymes without which it is impossible for the machine to enter into the body of modern society to the benefit of that body. No doubt there are other enzymes that are needed just as much, but we do not believe that any amount of these can make up for a lack of the architectural stuff.

After all, when a man has provided himself with food, he spends most of his remaining energy building up a decent visible and audible human environment. Here he is a maker indeed. And if machine civilisation is to go on, it is in this, the greatest and finest activity of man, that the machine will have to be most fully used. The machine has shown itself capable of providing abundant light and heat for everyone, but we are still very far from having worked out the right kind of light and the right kind of heat. And this is only the beginning. In smaller physical objects, like textile goods and vessels for eating and drinking, we can see the influence of the machine at work. Here, it is true, we find there is a great deal more to go round than there used to be. But these things are only little pieces of the architectural frame, the budding of a single leaf on a great tree, the single swallow that does not make a summer. The past has taught us that our furniture and our teapots are a part of architecture, and without an architecture that is right none of the lesser objects can be right. If the structure of our towns and buildings continues on its present plan and refuses to admit this new thing that is no longer new, the result will be catastrophe. The justification of the new architecture is that its ferment may yet manage to turn the machine into something that will nourish the life of man and make it bigger and richer.

Wells Coates

Your question, 'Is Modern Architecture on the Right Track?' has about it the authentic irritating twang of the platform moralist. I am a little shocked that THE LISTENER should sponsor so dreary a catechism.

It is evident that the modern architectural scene is here viewed as a jostling Hyde Park hustings affair, with all the texts and pretexts in friendly disarray.

'Is the new architecture ugly?' 'Has functionalism in building gone too far?' 'Is the engineer making the architect unnecessary today?' One after another these amphibiological questions are to be seen raising their twin-heads above the noisy throng of listeners. . . . And from the next stall the ghost-cry: 'Is education dangerous?' 'Has the B.B.C. been allowed to go too far?' 'Is the Prime Minister making the politician unnecessary today?'

England went off the gold standard in architecture about a hundred years ago. In spite of the most strenuous efforts of the banker-architects to stabilise the currency, we are still suffering from the effects of an architectural period of inflation, followed by a depreciation of all real *architectural* values.

Many individual fortunes have been made by speculative builders during this distressing period.

In this atmosphere of crisis, there are those who exhort us dully to return to some old, or gold standard—or at the least to some paper-imitation token-currency of architectural style with all its promises to 'Pay Bearer on Demand' the things that other people have desired.

Then there are those who are all for 'pegging' architectural currency at some arbitrarily determined present-day level—grudgingly including in their reckoning only those new values that have been accepted in the most *respectable* banking circles. Under the banner of Polite Compromise, these architects pay lip-service to every kind of snobbish, fashionable, or profitable conjunction of styles. Thus, Swedish elegance may be seen to be grafted on to British competence, to form one more bright individual 'style'.

A great deal has been written and said about a managed currency—a planned architectural economy—on the part of those whose interests lie all ahead and who are prepared for a break with the Past rather than be destroyed with it. The new policy starts from consumer's needs—and capacities to pay—and consumer's rights, in relation to all the available data of production: facts, figures, materials, of the present structure of society.

The new architectural currency is being designed in two materials: first, human needs, and the necessity for a new dimension of Plan and Order in the arrangement and aspect of life; second, the new resources of technology, a multitude of details, processes and conditions of great complexity.

You ask if modern architecture is on the right track, and you ask questions based on stylistic premises, framed with circumlocutions such as 'ultra-modern', 'functionalism', etc., which are barren, meaningless, *trackless*, to the contemporary architect, who is not the least concerned with predetermined, presupposed, preconceived shapes or styles as such.

To retain your railway symbol—I should say that the new architecture is travelling on two parallel permanent ways: the one is the way of Science—the science of the *inside* of things, science the *identifier*, measurer, and calculator; the other is the way of Art—which is the science of the *outside* of things: art the *differentiator*, selector, and maker. For Architecture—the surest and completest art—is both science and art, moving on parallel lines.

Architecture Symposium—A Summing-Up

Sir Raymond Unwin, Past President of the Royal Institute of British Architects, sums up the symposium on the question 'Is Modern Architecture on the Right Track?' that appeared in our issue of July 26

To sum up with fairness is difficult because those who have spoken for tradition have been so ready to admit that 'the modernists had got rid of a lot of unnecessary trappings and were making a laudable effort to bring architecture back to its essentials'; while some advocates of modernism have relied on very doubtful assumptions.

The fundamental difference between architecture and engineering construction is hardly fully brought out on either side. To me the difference seems of the order of that between useful noise and music. Some of the reasoning seems like a suggestion that we should enjoy the tapping of the typewriter or the racket of the road drill more than music because they are more useful.

A building only becomes architecture when, in addition to satisfying efficiently all the uses for which it is intended, it is also capable of giving pleasure by reason of the form which it takes and the harmony with which its parts and colours are combined.

Man through his ear is pleased, and may be deeply stirred, by notes when sounded in certain definite relations; he would be pained if the same notes were merely jangled haphazard. So through his eye man is delighted, and may be much moved, by certain combinations of line, form and colour; but he will be wearied or pained by a mere jumble of parts or inharmonious relations. True relation to use may be an important element in this harmony, but that does not justify the confusion of use and beauty in architecture.

The modernist movement in seeking forms of building more in accord with present or foreseeable conditions and modes of use, has a very strong case, which, however, may be weakened if its advocates seek to identify this great movement with assumptions of doubtful validity or relevancy. The assumption that ferro-concrete has yet established itself, in comparison with other methods of construction, as an equally efficient, suitable or even economical mode of building for general purposes, has so little warrant as to suggest that love of a new style of design adapted to that construction may be at least one parent of the thought. That, however, is a comparatively minor matter.

A more serious assumption underlies the stress laid on the need to subordinate design more completely to the growing material and mechanistic aspect of the uses, methods, and mass production of parts, which it is claimed will dominate the future. Sixty years ago such a forecast

of future tendency might have carried conviction. Then mankind was struggling with a scarcity of products and the prospect of unlimited increase in the numbers needing them. The satisfaction of elementary material needs then still presented a problem only to be solved, if soluble at all, by unremitting devotion to mass production. The outlook today, however, is quite a different one; the population problem is rapidly solving itself; and the present difficulty as to material goods seems to consist rather in finding consumers for the masses of them which can easily be produced.

Architecture has to satisfy man as a whole, and cannot be attained by undue concentration on his physical needs or even on science. The excessive stressing of use, and the relegating of other elements of enjoyment to a quite subordinate place, finds little warrant in human need. A phrase is appropriately quoted that 'Well building has three conditions, Commodity, Firmness and Delight'; but the gloss which seeks to eliminate independent existence from the third, would hardly have pleased its author! Can we really maintain that those structures which have given the most widely diffused delight owe everything to the first two, even if described as function and construction? The needs of man which are purely physical and material are not many, as Diogenes demonstrated long ago. Nine-tenths of his desires are the product not of his bodily frame but of his active and inquisitive brain, his strong and varied emotions, his retentive memory and vivid imagination; among these desires, a liking for beauty takes equal rank. Without venturing on the less understood sphere, where the use of the word 'spirit' might be deemed appropriate, all will agree that each man develops a unified personality arising from the combined result of all the parts and faculties just named, according to the varied measure of his endowment with each of them. Architecture must appeal to the whole of this complex nature. The suggestion that a house is as much a machine to work in or to live in, as an omnibus is one for transport, seems to ignore about three-fourths of the feelings and reasons which in fact determine either the choice of a dwelling, or the enjoyment of living in it. Let every dwelling be convenient and well equipped with efficient apparatus, certainly; but that is the beginning, not the end of design. It is the special function of the architect to transform the sanitary family stables or economical human warehouse into homes, with all the content of comfort and beauty which that old English word implies.

That tradition tends more or less to obstruct desirable innovation is true enough: it also puts a check on changes which are due to mere fashion, a check of special value in regard to anything so permanent as buildings. Perhaps even more important is the great heritage of enjoyment which it preserves and the valuable guide which it gives to that balance of qualities most generally appreciated by our race; a balance which is by no means the same for different peoples, and therefore not best secured by any cosmopolitan average.

Fitness for use is rightly stressed as an important element in the beauty of buildings, whether fully apparent or only to be intellectually appreciated, but to stress it as an only or an all-sufficient element is surely for the architect to abdicate to the constructional engineer. Association with past pleasure is but one of many elements; one whose influence increases as men grow older. It is quite natural for tradition to mean more to the old than to the young, for it has been reinforced by many pleasant associations. The young, free from this influence, may recognise more readily the beauty of novel forms or fresh combinations and relations.

There is indeed great need for the modernist and the innovator in architecture as in many other spheres. Our streets are littered with examples of the passing fashions in building which have troubled the last sixty years. If, however, we are to regain the right path, we must not start with our faces directed as far east of it as the hardened traditionalist faces west.

If the discussion is to be summed up in a fresh set of answers to the questions, I would suggest the following:
(1) *Is the engineer making the architect unnecessary today?* Certainly not! Though some of the writers show a tendency to abdicate in favour of the engineer through failure to realise the essential difference in their functions and methods.

(2) *Has functionalism in building gone too far?* If and so far as it is regarded as the sole end of architecture it certainly exceeds its province.

(3) *Can the English town or city ever properly assimilate the new architecture?* So far as the new is architecture, and not mere building, due regard for harmony with surroundings forms an essential element; with such regard the new can be assimilated.

(4) *Is the new architecture ugly?* Much present building, whether the style be new or old, is ugly: but ugly architecture is surely a contradiction in terms.

(5) *What will the next generation think of the ultra-modern style of present day buildings, including the ultra-modern home?* If ultra-modern may be taken to indicate an extreme form of certain recent tendencies, founded on the assumption that ferro-concrete is henceforth to be the general building medium, then the next generation will be likely to look upon such buildings as examples of a passing fashion.

(6) *Are we likely to evolve in the near future a new style of architectural ornament?* Probably, for men of all races and in nearly all times have delighted to adorn their productions with some refinement of form, play of colour, or enrichment of surface, having often a further content of meaning or symbolism, and going beyond anything needed to fit them for function: doubtless they will continue to do so; and will adapt the adornment to any changes in the character or form of building.

6.5 For and Against Modern Architecture
by Reginald Blomfield and Amyas Connell

Sir Reginald Blomfield

I understand we are here to talk about architecture, you as a modernist, I as a traditionalist, so the first thing I must do is to explain what I mean by traditionalist.

He is one who has no use for sudden breaks and catastrophes, but is intent on maintaining the continuity of art. He values not the letter but the spirit of the past, for he is no revivalist, and he will avail himself to the full of all the resources of modern science that suit his purpose. A traditionalist, as I understand him, is the only reasonable modernist, because he does not limit his art to the conceptions of his inner consciousness, and takes into account the wisdom of the past.

But there are modernists *and* modernists. One sort I have just suggested to you. The other sort—and I hope I am not mistaken in assuming this to be your position—deliberately turn their backs on the past, determined that what has been done once shall not be done again, and that everybody shall do what he likes in his own way. This movement had its origin in much loose thinking in France and Germany, it has spread like a plague to this country, and unless brought back to the straight and narrow path of sanity, it is likely to land the arts in bankruptcy, and the artist in the madhouse. In a little book published this year I attacked it under the name of *Modernismus*, and as I expected, this study was received by the modernismists with howls of execration. Mr Baty in THE LISTENER, and Mr Boumphrey in the *Spectator* (names, by the way, rather suggestive of their critical attitude) had not a good word to say for it, and the young lions of the architectural press, with the honourable exception of the *Builder* and the *Carpenter and Builder*, were furious. I was represented as obstinate, prejudiced, a revivalist, a grave-digger, and I wonder they did not say 'body-snatcher' as well. But I gathered that some of my shots must have got home between wind and water, and that, like the Priests of Baal, the young men were reassuring themselves by loud cries that their idol was still unbroken.

In order to avoid confusion, I shall call these extremists not 'modernists', but 'modernismists'. Now, I will ask you to consider the theory of architecture on which they found their practice. It is based on three assumptions, which in my opinion are very dangerous fallacies. The first is, that anything which answers the purpose, for which it is made, is *ipso facto* beautiful. The second assumption is that nationalism is a thing of the past, that all art is to be cosmopolitan, and the individual is to disappear, lost in the collective action of innumerable and undifferentiated units. The third assumption is that the restraints of reason and of commonsense can be swept away—anybody can do anything he likes in any way he likes, no matter whether the result is wholly unintelligible, because either he, or his friends, or the art-critic of the day, will be there to explain the hidden mystery.

Now take the first assumption, that efficiency equals beauty. It is quite obvious that a thing may be perfectly efficient for its purpose, yet exceedingly ugly—a sewer for example, or a pig-sty. Even a motor-car, admirably adapted as it is for racing through the country and killing people by the way, is not beautiful, unless by 'beauty' is meant something wholly different from what it has always been supposed to mean since the dawn of civilisation. This assumption really means the abnegation of the whole idea of beauty. In future nothing will be either beautiful or ugly; the thing will just be there, rousing no emotion, calling for no comment. It is a blank and dreary outlook. Surely you would not say that this crude utilitarianism is a complete account of the art of architecture?

Let me say at once that we need not trouble our heads about specific styles, such as Gothic, or Classic, or the sixteenth century, or the eighteenth century, and so on. 'Style is the man.' Some people will always be impressive because they have got something to say that is worth saying, and know how to say it, and it is this, and this only, that constitutes style; quite a different thing from 'styles'.

Now in any building that can rank as architecture, I think you will agree with me that there are, broadly speaking, three essentials. First, the plan must meet the practical purposes for which the building is erected. Second, the building must be well built, no settlements in the walls, no cracks in the ceilings, no waste of material. So far, an experienced builder or a competent engineer would deal with the matter, but there is a third essential, and it is the presence or absence of this element that will decide whether a building is or is not a work of architecture, and that is the way in which its imaginative possibilities are realised and dealt with, whether in the result the building gives us the aesthetic satisfaction that is derived from subtle proportion, fine composition, the sensitive use of material, the exact adjustment of detail to its purpose. It is this third essential element that the modernismist architects have either forgotten or ignored. They have sold the fort to the engineer and the builder, admirable men in their way, but not architects. So far has the process of abdication gone that it is even suggested that the materials used will dictate the design; reinforced concrete, for example. But in practice this theory has failed. You will recollect that the design of the famous Observatory at Potsdam was supposed to be inspired by reinforced concrete, but the supply of steel rods having failed, it was finished equally well in brick, and when it comes to covering in the walls of a steel-framed building with black plate-glass, the theory of inspired and inspiring materials becomes ridiculous. I regret to have to say it, but it seems to me that the real inspiration of these frantic experiments is a thirst for notoriety in the first instance, the desire to startle at all costs, followed up by the irresistible instinct of sheep to follow their leader. Moreover, many of these modernismist buildings are not efficient; where is the efficiency of those tiers of solid concrete balconies, the latest trick of design? These balconies are just receptacles for rain and dirt, which can only be cleaned out through the rooms behind or on the heads of the people below, and they shut out the most valuable part of the light from the rooms underneath. Again where is the efficiency in the grotesque figures that are scattered about on the facades of modernismist buildings, such for example as those seen on a recent important building in the west end of London? They are not pleasant to look at, they are irrelevant to the design and construction of the building, and they cost a lot of money, probably leading, later on, to a further expenditure on their total erasure. I ask you, why do our brilliant young modernismists go out of their way to startle and annoy the peaceable man in the street? The painters with their visions of their own insides, and the sculptors with their shapeless lumps are bad enough, but one need not go to the galleries, whereas there is no escaping these terrible façades.

The second assumption which I mentioned is the claim that the art of the future is to be cosmopolitan. The race, the nation, and the individual, are to have in it no place at all. Art is to be standardised, so that, in the words of the late Herr Cohen-Portheim, 'In twenty years there will be one style of architecture compulsory for the whole of Europe'. This is Hitlerism or Bolshevism *in excelsis*—strangling literature and the arts. Yet what is it that we look for in works of art and literature? Is it mass production that 'servile mass mentality' which, as General Smuts said at St Andrews, is 'the greatest human menace of our time'? Is it not rather the individual message of one rare mind, keenly sensitive, more far-seeing than the rest, gathering up into itself what many feel in a vague and uncertain way, but are unable to put into intelligible terms? For myself, I am for the hill on which I was born. One should learn on every hand, but I have no use for this cosmopolitanism, and this suppression of the individual artist, and I object not to modernism with which, in its drive for simplicity of statement I have every sympathy, but to modernismus, because it repudiates the past and does away with all standards of values, and because it is based on fallacies that cut at the very root of art.

I hope, Mr Connell, you won't mind this plain statement of a position held by many beside myself. It is now for you to go in and hit my bowling out of the ground. I will only send down one last ball, which I hope may prove a shooter. Over eighty years ago, Heine, most brilliant and sensitive of men, wrote these words in his 'Confessions'— 'What disquiets me is the secret dread of the artist and scholar, who sees our whole modern civilisation, and the fruit of the noblest work of our ancestors, jeopardised by the triumph of communism.' Whether it is communism or not, modernismus is a vicious movement which threatens that literature and art which is our last refuge from a world that is becoming more and more mechanised every day.

A. D. Connell

You have admirably demonstrated, Sir Reginald, the old truth that in a few minutes fallacies can be uttered which may take a lifetime to demolish. I cannot therefore hope to deal with all those contained in your statement. So let us take first your final point, as being typical of your approach to the problem of architecture. Some of our listeners who have used a match to light their after-dinner cigarette will probably recall that, only a few years ago, we feared to use the first matches, looking upon them as Lucifers, instruments of the devil. Now this was quite an irrational and instinctive fear, and I would suggest that you too are too instinctively frightened to participate fully in the inevitable progress of modern civilisation. You are afraid of the present phase of evolution because you can neither understand nor use it. So you protect yourself with a philosophy which pretends that it does not exist. You have told us you dislike the machine, but what you really seem to dislike and fear is efficiency, and fear is the basis of your misunderstanding. I suggest that you look upon modern architecture with a vision distorted by fear, and that fear has trapped you into making absurd conjectures about what you call the assumption upon which the modern architect founds his practice, that it has prevented you from relating science in a rational way to the problem of human needs; and, further, this instinctive fear and inability to see clearly the evolution of modern architecture has led you to the familiar device of invoking prejudice—out comes your red herring, and you couple modern art with Bolshevism, Hitlerism, Communism and what not.

After this it may seem strange to you that I agree with you on one very important point, your definition of a modern architect. The modern creative artist does pre-cisely aim at maintaining the continuity of art. He endeavours to use intelligently the accumulated experience of the past by understanding its spirit and trying to apply that to the changing conditions and the needs of society. Not like your self-styled traditionalist, who merely copies the letter. Would it surprise you to learn, or do you wilfully ignore, the fact that many of the most modern architects know almost as much about ancient architecture as you do? Thus the modern does not believe in sudden breaks and 'catastrophes', he believes that the process of development of art, as one of the expressions of this civilisation of ours, is a logical evolution (though I grant you that the nineteenth century was an unfortunate break in the tradition). He believes that architecture, as one of the many branches of human activity, changes its forms through the ages with the changing forms of society. It changes, too, with the progress of science—the acquisition of new materials—new methods of production and construction. Therefore he does not, and I even suspect that you do not, refuse to ride in a motor-'bus because it is not drawn by horses: nor does he try to design it as an imitation stage-coach. So where we do part company is in the translation of these beliefs into architectural forms.

I suggest to our listeners that your definition of the aims of modern architecture is not only arbitrary but false. And though you would no doubt like me to accept your definition in order that you might then proceed to demolish it, I do not myself as a modern architect maintain that anything which serves its purpose is *ipso facto* beautiful, and I do not think that you will find that many other architects do. They believe rather that, in general, the greater the efficiency the better the design. Or, if I may put it another way, an architect who is functioning as an architect should have as his aim perfect efficiency. But as he works towards this aim, under its discipline, the desire for beauty which is part of the make-up of every human being, finds its expression; and he creates a beauty which has grown naturally out of the practical task that he set himself to do. Whatever you may say about sewers and pig-sties— and I may remind you that one of the greatest architectural engravings is of the great sewer in Rome—the modern man does get aesthetic pleasure from the most highly specialised forms of efficiency, such as a modern locomotive, a de Havilland Comet plane, the *Blue Bird* motor-car, the new liner *Queen Mary*, and no less from a highly efficient modern house, built with modern materials: that is really all there is to it. He finds in them the beauty that arises from the elimination of everything that is not essential.

And, by the way, what I have said in no way 'sells the fort' as you rather ingenuously put it, 'to the engineers and builders'. If they interpret the acquired wisdom of the past in a more reasonable way than the architect, then let us call ourselves engineers, for it is obviously immaterial what label we apply to something that is well done. The modern architect, rather than limit his function to dressing up buildings in fancy dress, has expanded it and now co-ordinates his own activities with those of the scientist, the engineer, and the manufacturer. They are allies, not enemies. And because a few of the architects of today are, consciously or unconsciously, traitors to the spirit of our age, that does not damn modern architecture as a whole. You get charlatans in every movement.

Now, Sir Reginald, I cannot understand your contention that modern architecture ought not to be cosmopolitan, nor why cosmopolitanism should exclude the possibility of individualism in art. Would you accuse people of cosmopolitanism and lack of national character if they used the invention of a Swiss doctor in combating disease? Or will a piece of Bradford cloth cease to be English because the dye for its colouring was invented by German scientists? Does not your own work directly evince the influence of French designers?—of the eighteenth century? What I am suggesting is that the modern architect is rightly cosmopolitan in so far as he is using the achievements of modern science and technical progress in various countries, and applying them to the needs and conditions of his own land. This cosmopolitanism, however, is—as was the cosmopolitan classicism of the eighteenth century—not an end in itself. It will lead inevitably, indeed it is already leading, for those who can see with unbiased eyes, to an essentially national inflection of the idiom. Any schoolboy can pick out an English from a French or American motor-car or locomotive, just as any first-year architectural student can distinguish a German from an Italian eighteenth-century palace.

And just as national characteristics are not submerged by internationality, so, too, individuality cannot help emerging from even the simplest and most impersonal architectural forms.

You deplore at one moment that 'the individual is to disappear, lost in the collective action of innumerable and undifferentiated units' and at the very next you complain that 'anyone can do anything he likes in any way he likes'. I think I may leave your two arguments to answer each other, and simply emphasise that modern architecture is in the highest sense traditional because it is not content with repeating out-worn and vulgarised forms. It is concerned with the spirit, and from its understanding of the spirit of the past it is able to create, not superficial imitations in this or that style, but living successors in the true line of descent. For even if we grant, and I do grant freely, that antiquity has created forms which have a permanent value, why should that exclude the possibility of a new and unprecedented beauty yet to come?

You have said some hard things about modern architecture, chiefly, it is true, about architecture I should hardly describe as such: but no matter. Let me reinforce your vocabulary of invective by reminding you that though modern architecture is denounced as cultural Bolshevism by the leaders of Nazi Germany, and is disdainfully dismissed by the leaders of Bolshevik Russia as 'the decadent capitalist style of West European bourgeoisie': yet, on the other hand, it has recently been adopted as the official Fascist style in Italy. In short, your appeals to prejudice amount to very little.

I admire you, Sir Reginald, for a loyalty to your native hill; 'home-keeping youth hath ever homely wit'; or, if you want something less cosmopolitan than Elizabethans, it was, I believe, Sancho Panza who greeted every fresh surprise in life with the remark 'I come from my own vineyard, I know nothing'. An honesty of incomprehension which he never sought to cloud with abuse of what was new.

Sir Reginald Replies

Taking it by and large, your answer amounts to this, that I am panic-stricken and don't know what I am talking about, indeed, that I am a sort of Sancho Panza, without the humility and modesty of that honest man. But this is not argument and you must permit me to say that you are beating the air, not me. I have been waiting in vain for any conclusive answer to the views I have advanced. Some of these you have adopted yourself, others, with I am sure the best intentions, you have misrepresented.

You begin by representing me as terrified, even panic-stricken by modernismus, but I am not in the least. I have thought a good deal about this movement for some years past, and have come to the conclusion that its manifestation in architecture is only one symptom of a disease which in recent years has been attacking literature and all the arts, and I have sufficient faith in humanity to believe that in due course this disease will run itself out, and people will recover their senses. As to modernistic architecture, I have said repeatedly that there is this element of good in it, that it has wiped out meaningless detail, and has attempted to reduce architectural expression to the simplest possible terms; but I also say it has thrown overboard elements of essential value, it has thwarted ingrained and permanent instincts, and in the process of 'almost ultimate elimination', to use your own terms, it has eliminated architecture.

Whether this movement is Hitlerism or Bolshevism, Fascism or Communism, is immaterial. Its ravages are worse in painting, sculpture, music, prose and verse than in architecture, because there must always be the restraint of fact in architecture, but the frantic things we see in our Galleries, the horrible noises that we hear on the wireless, the packing-case buildings that we see disfiguring the landscape, and the gratuitous eccentricities that disturb us in the streets, all spring from this insidious and dangerous germ.

You are evidently uneasy about the dogma that

'efficiency equals beauty', and this, if I may say so, is a sign of grace. Indeed you seem to throw up the sponge when you say that 'no modern architect of your acquaintance has ever suggested that anything which served its purpose was *ipso facto* beautiful'. Really, Mr Connell! How about the writings of M. Corbusier and Herr Bruno Taut, the teaching of the Architectural Association, and the pronouncements of that enthusiast for 'efficiency', Mr Frank Pick? 'Efficiency equals beauty' is the war-cry of the modernismists, their one attempt in theory to justify their strange aberrations.

Then again, you accept my point that man never has been and never will be content with mere utilitarianism. You say bravely that man 'cannot escape his instinct to impart beauty to anything he makes', and that is exactly what I have been at particular pains to establish, both in my book and elsewhere, and it is because I am convinced of the truth of this that I am also convinced that modernismus has taken the wrong turning in architecture, that it is defying instincts that cannot permanently be suppressed. It is not a mere question of substituting one style or manner of design for another, it is a question of the attitude of the artist towards his art. The modernismist is endeavouring to establish a standpoint of his own invention which, if it were to prevail, would again mean 'the ultimate elimination of art'.

In regard to cosmopolitanism, you do not seem to have grasped my meaning. I was careful to point out that the traditionalist would, of course, avail himself of all the resources of applied science that suit his purpose, whether they were the discoveries of a Frenchman or German or anyone else, but that is not the cosmopolitanism to which I referred. The danger to which I call attention is the standardisation of building, its reduction to one type, so that, as Herr Portheim said, wherever we went we should find 'one style of architecture compulsory in the whole of Europe'. Surely under these conditions the individual would be swamped in the universal flood. This is not contradicted by what I said elsewhere 'that anyone can do anything he likes in any way he likes', because in this I was referring to an entirely different matter, namely, that when there is no standard of values, no accepted technique, no rules and no referee, there is nothing to prevent anyone from standing on his head and saying 'What a good boy am I!'

I am unable to follow you when you claim for modernismus that it 'draws vital sustenance from the living unstylistic spirit of tradition'. That is what it ought to do, but in my opinion it not only fails to do, but declines to make any efforts to do, because it has clamourously insisted that it has done with the past and all its ways. Do you really think that the architects of the Parthenon, the Pantheon, St Sophia, St Peter's in Rome or St Paul's in London approached their problems from the point of view from which a modernismist would approach his—would they have been content to provide so many covered-in areas with no thought beyond immediate efficiency?

You have asked me to indicate what sort of modernism I do like. I will give you an instance, the great Church of St Esprit on a difficult site in Paris, designed by M. Paul Tournon, and not yet completed. M. Tournon has followed the motive of St Sophia, still the finest church in existence, a vast central dome with shallow aisles and exhedrae at the ends. The result is admirable, both for liturgical efficiency and architectural effect. The outer walls are all in brick, the whole of the rest is constructed in reinforced concrete and could not be constructed in any other way. Here you have exactly what a modernist building should be. It makes skilful use of the latest resources of building, it is perfectly efficient, and yet there is in it a hint, an echo of that older music which I want to find in the work of our modernists.

No, Mr Connell, I fear there is a wide gulf still between us; and I regret this the more, because, as I was careful to point out in my little book, there is abundant evidence of ability in the younger generation, and quite apart from this I believe that better work on reasonable lines is being quietly done in this country than in any country in the world. But this work is not that of modernismus, and it is not revivalism, it is work that moves steadily forward on lines laid down long ago—that deals with the problems of the present without forgetting that we are the heirs of a great historic past. What I hope is, that our young men will think again and turn before it is too late, and I commend to their attention that famous saying of Lord Bacon, 'It were good that men in their innovations would follow the example of Time itself, which indeed innovateth greatly, but quietly and by degrees scarce to be perceived'.

6.6   Modern Architecture in England by Berthold Lubetkin

The general feeling among American architects appeared, at least until recently, to be that in their own country there was little or no hope for the immediate development of modern architecture. They felt that terrific real estate interests, combined with a rather conservative attitude, at least in domestic work, toward new building technique, formed almost insurmountable obstacles to the would-be modern architect. But the last five years have brought very considerable changes in the sphere of modern architecture, changes which are enough to shake any convictions as to the future course of events, enough to prove that the strangest reversals are not only possible, but likely.

In those countries which had been considered the most conservative, and therefore the most difficult ground for the modern architect, the modern movement is making great progress, while in others, which had been looked upon as the promised land of architectural development, a tremendous reversal has taken place. In Germany, once the foremost country in constructive innovation, the prevailing political regime has banished modern constructional methods and the external characteristics of modern architecture. The flat roof has become the symbol of revolt, the mark of political unreliability; to design horizontal windows is to attract the attention of the secret police. A very similar situation exists in Austria and central Europe. In Russia, on the other hand, any attempt to design buildings of a light and joyful appearance is interpreted as an attack on the proletariat, by depriving him of the monumental proofs of his new-found material prosperity. France and Czechoslovakia have long been paralyzed by economic crises.

This reversal of the old order is so complete that it is not surprising to find that England has become almost the only country in which modern architecture can flourish in comparative freedom. This circumstance has naturally attracted many foreign architects, fleeing from political restrictions or economic stagnation in other countries. A paradoxical situation arises; England, which had so long lagged behind the continent in accepting new architectural and technical ideas, now leads the world in this domain. But in England the price which has to be paid in fighting for each innovation represents an enormous amount of creative energy. Each step on the road to progress is a struggle against conservatism and prejudice, as we shall see later.

As in the case of Albania, which has the most up-to-date telephone system in the world, the last country to adopt technical improvements usually introduces the most modern; according to this precedent, England, whose architectural history is so full of adaptations and improvements of foreign ideas, might be expected to possess the most mature modern architecture. Unfortunately, several factors have combined to retard the attainment of this goal.

One of the most important of these factors is just that influx of architects from abroad which might have, and in some ways has, proved so happy for English architecture. In many cases, architectural models have been transplanted in time and in space in such a way as to render them meaningless. Architects, who in the recent past, had made great contributions to the development of the modern movement on the continent, found themselves uprooted by political and social changes. Transplanted to another country, they were likely to continue their work in too unbroken a sequence, not realizing that the sociological conditions were so very different as to invalidate such a lack of flexibility. Their ideas, methods, and stylistic approach of a few years ago died with the surroundings which gave birth to them, while the evolution of architecture has given rise to some new problems, new requirements and new methods of solutions.

In fact, the whole architectural scene in England is fundamentally different from that of other countries. While in England a considerable interest has long been taken by the general public in matters of town and country planning and architecture, this public interest is not of a kind that would favour progress. The general interest in planning is a purely negative and conservative one, and results almost exclusively in efforts on the part of the public to preserve existing amenities and old buildings simply as museum pieces or artificial settings. There is little or no interest in progress, in fact any attempt at alteration of the existing conditions calls forth violent protest, and is accepted, if at all, as a necessary evil.

Another characteristic of the English situation, the outcome of the public's attitude, is the building legislation. It is required that every design should be submitted to the local authority for acceptance or rejection, purely on grounds of amenity. Not unnaturally, this committee, composed as it is of local business men, often builders, is usually opposed to architectural innovations. It is extremely difficult to appeal against the decision of a local authority, and the waste of time involved is so great that their rejection is generally a death sentence to any project. This unwillingness to accept any change, aesthetic or technical, is also seen in the regulations governing construction, to which every building must comply. These building regulations, based on the standards of sixty years ago, make no allowance for modern technique, and result in extremely clumsy and out-of-date methods of construction. These in turn have their influence on the building industry as a whole. It is difficult to persuade manufacturers to execute modern designs, for they prefer to adhere to the old 'safe' models which they know by heart. The actual building is also influenced; foremen, knowing that the safety factors stipulated by law are ridiculously large, do not insist on careful workmanship (this particularly in the case of reinforced concrete), with the result that the general standard of execution and finish has become very low, and is now behind that of the rest of Europe.

The result of this tremendous body of prejudices and obstructions, supported as it is by the authority of the law, has been to lend a disproportionate importance to very small points. To obtain permission to build a flat roof is in itself such an achievement that it is likely to overshadow, in the mind of the architect, the significance of his original conception. The result is that at present it is almost impossible to judge objectively the aesthetic qualities of a building. So much has to be taken into consideration, that the only firm criterion is that of function, and we see a return to the functionalist doctrine, which was probably believed in less by its own originators than by any of those who came after. This is hardly to be wondered at in a situation where one cannot, for instance, criticize an obvious coarseness and over-heaviness in the structural members of a building when one knows that it is only due to the local surveyor's abysmal lack of knowledge of reinforced concrete construction.

Often unable to apply any exacting standard of aesthetic values in the criticism of buildings which they know to have been executed only after a long struggle with un-educated and unsympathetic officials, architects and critics are forced to regard buildings from a standpoint which, in more favourable conditions, they would never have dreamed of adopting. If modern architecture is to make the progress of which it is capable, it should go without saying that every building fulfills the purpose for which it is intended; this should be the starting-point, not the ultimate criterion. But a mass of repressive regulations and a lack of intelligent constructive criticism have brought us to a position where this elementary requirement is almost our only yardstick in judging the value of buildings. It is clear that in these circumstances the greatest necessity is architectural criticism; such criticism, if it existed, would serve a twofold purpose; first to educate the public, and through them to remove the outside obstructions to architectural progress; and second to clarify the ideas of the architects themselves, and to provide them with that common intellectual basis which for the moment is so sadly lacking.

Unfortunately, energetic criticism, such as could achieve these ends, is almost entirely lacking in England at the moment. This is no mere accident, but is to a great extent due to the fact that the entire architectural press is so influenced by the present libel laws that it can do little more than give a short technical description of the buildings illustrated. In these circumstances, the architects have been forced to organize themselves for purposes of education and propaganda.

The first of such groups to be formed was the MARS (modern architectural research) Group, in which were centred the hopes of the more advanced sections of architects in this country. Unfortunately, this group has, during the three years of its existence, gradually become less and less of a vital force. One reason for this appears to be a consequence of the lack of criticism we have just examined. Approaching their problems without much clarity of thought, and having far less in common with one another than they had imagined, these architects have never overcome the initial difficulty of formulating their own definition of modern architecture.

In a time of crisis, they might have been able to give more time and attention to the problems of organization and programme, but as the whole life of the group has corresponded with a period of specially intense building activity, just those architects who might have made valuable contributions to the group as a whole have been most fully occupied with their own work. In consequence, the members have been unable to agree on any fundamental issue, and as a result, the volume and importance of their work has been steadily decreasing

A newer organization, which at first sight would appear to have little connection with specifically modern architecture, is the Architects' and Technicians' Organization. This group came together on a purely social and political basis, and is not actually concerned with any stylistic questions, but while its main interest is in such problems as housing, it may perhaps lead to some amelioration of the architect's position. For it is impossible to separate the broader issues of town and regional planning and housing from the whole body of building legislation, and a concentrated attack on this front based on purely utilitarian grounds, might result in a reform of the law and of its administration, which would have important repercussions on the conditions of architectural work. This may seem hard to achieve, but at least it is a far more realistic and promising line of attack than any idealist grouping of modern architects can hope to be.

6.7a   A Client on his House by Geoffrey Walford

180   JOURNAL OF THE ROYAL INSTITUTE OF BRITISH ARCHITECTS   19 December 1938

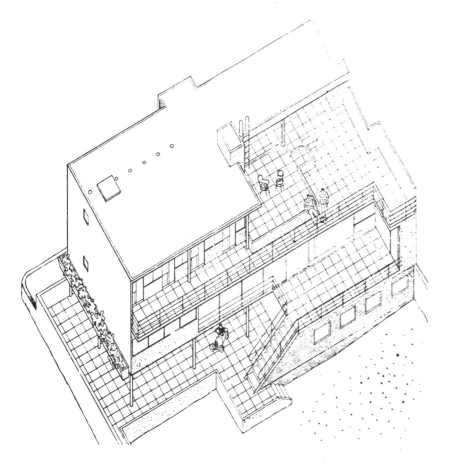

Above : Garden front

Left : Axonometric

The illustrations show the children's bedrooms on the top floor opening on to the roof terrace, the large horizontally sliding windows of the first floor living room, and the children's playroom and covered terrace on the ground floor

The building is of monolithic reinforced concrete, and is rendered externally with a scraped finish in varying tones of browns

Brickwork is used to enclose portions of the ground floor. The terraces are paved with concrete slabs and the roof is surfaced with asphalt. This side of the house receives sunshine until about 11 a.m.

6.7a   A Client on his House by Geoffrey Walford

19 *December* 1938   JOURNAL OF THE ROYAL INSTITUTE OF BRITISH ARCHITECTS   181

A CLIENT ON HIS HOUSE

No. 66 FROGNAL, HAMPSTEAD.   Architects: CONNELL, WARD & LUCAS [*AA. & L.*]

By GEOFFREY WALFORD

I have some doubt on the value of an attempt on the part of the " building owner " to account for the building which represents the result of his efforts. Our powers of analysing our motives and reactions are unfortunately in the realm of sheer speculation. So complex are the threads that constitute the sum total of experience of each individual, so varied are the contacts of individuals connected with any new building, that no case can be more than a law unto itself.

However, the comments of many who have seen this house, the overheard remarks of many who stop in the street to stare in bewildered amazement, and the violent opinions that have been expressed seem to indicate that some attempt at explanation may be of interest. It may seem surprising to some that this building is not symptomatic of exhibitionism, nor of iconoclasm, nor is it the result of any particular liking for operating theatres or for the decks of ships—that is, so far as I am aware. It may seem more surprising that to me it represents the logical conclusion to nothing more mysterious than the problem of how to live.

It may be that most, or possibly all, creative work springs from some frustration or restriction. The problem of determining the organisation and mode of living necessarily involves the acceptance of some restrictions and the escape from others. The individual can determine the problem, so far as it is affected by the building forming his environment, by accepting or adapting what others provide for him, or by creating a building in accordance with his own solution of the problem. Moreover, the problem is one that goes further than the determination of mere accommodation and the use of space. It includes the determination of a background and environment of emotional significance.

In this particular case the desire to solve the problem with a new building sprang from impatience with the compromise of adaption, both from the aspect of efficiency and background. The houses of a past age and the contemporary imitations called for an imitation of the more formal life of a past age, and involved a strain on personal effort and resources no longer necessary or of any apparent value. On the one hand a more precise use of space and a greater reduction of labour seemed possible. On the other hand, the use without pretence or shame of materials and methods

Left : Two views of the living room, looking towards the dining end. In the bottom photograph are the five curtain tracks which allow for curtain arrangement in fifteen colours. When not in use the curtains slide round the corner into a store. The slight increase in ceiling height marking the sitting area can also be seen

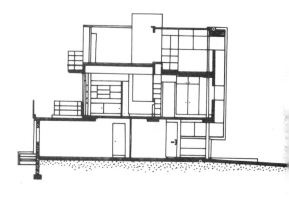

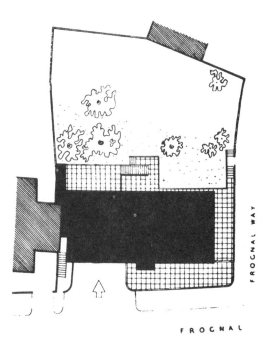

FROGNAL WAY

FROGNAL

SITE PLAN

SCALE OF FEET

19 *December* 1938   JOURNAL OF THE ROYAL INSTITUTE OF BRITISH ARCHITECTS   183

The four children's bedrooms on the second floor each contain a built-in wardrobe and a desk with a mirror on the underside of a flap top. The rooms are planned in pairs, with sliding doors between them, and can be used as double guest bedrooms when the children are away at school. The large terrace is covered on the West, and the central portion is slightly raised, giving extra ceiling height in the living-room below

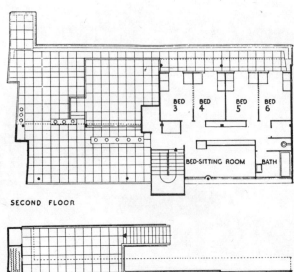

SECOND FLOOR

The first floor comprises a complete living unit for the owner and his wife. Sound-proofed floors render it free from interference from the children's rooms above and below. The living room, which is glazed from floor to ceiling along the whole of its East side, is planned in three areas—dining at the kitchen end, with easy access to the terrace for meals; sitting in the central portion, where the ceiling height is increased; and a grand piano and bookshelves at the entrance end. The windows slide horizontally, making it possible to throw half of the room entirely open. At the head of the external service stair outside the kitchen is a refuse chute to a dustbin on the ground floor

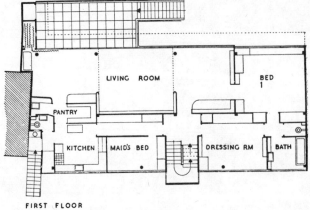

FIRST FLOOR

The ground floor comprises a large entrance drive under the house, a garage with covered access to the hall, and the children's playroom, glazed on three sides and opening on to a covered terrace. Adjoining the hall are a lavatory and cloakroom. The service entrance and dustbins are behind a screen wall

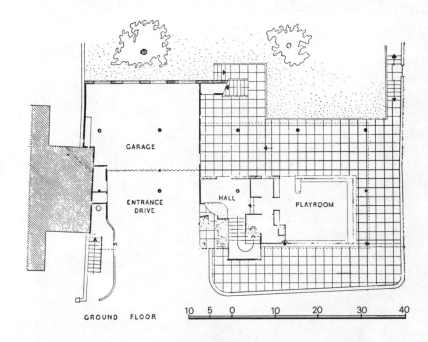

GROUND FLOOR

184   JOURNAL OF THE ROYAL INSTITUTE OF BRITISH ARCHITECTS   19 *December* 1938

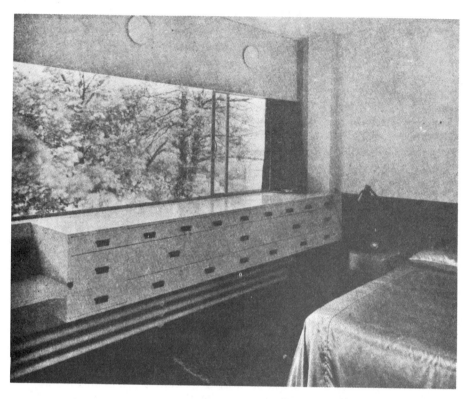

*Left : The owner's bedroom, adjoining the
living room and overlooking the garden*

*Below
Left : The kitchen*

Right : The owner's dressing room

*Above the windows can be seen the metal
discs screening the openings for permanent
ventilation*

now available seemed to offer the basis of a background sympathetic to existence in this age. In the distracting and stimulating conditions of work and pleasure outside the seclusion at home, my need is for relaxation, and for a background conducive to conversation, reading, music and reflection. I find simplicity and spaciousness of unbroken surfaces offer rest to the eye and to the mind. I find delight in the control of forms arising in the building itself and its appurtenances, rather than in superimposed effects. I find delight in the use of colour and in the play and variation of light. I find delight above all in the relation between house and garden, whereby the terraces and garden may be an extension of the interior of the house, and whereby the interior is screened rather than enclosed from the open air, trees and sky.

The plan of this house was governed by the requirement of accommodation for two people and four children in the school holidays, and for two people only in school terms. Isolation of the children's accommodation was desirable not only for the obvious benefit to them and to other occupants in the holidays, but for convenience of upkeep in their absence. Isolation by separate floors rather than by separate wings seemed to be the only solution for a house required to be in London. One floor, therefore, must constitute a complete living unit for two people and possibly one servant. The next consideration was garage and workshop accessible under cover for an owner driver, together with an entrance to house and garage under cover. The benefit of arrival and departure by car under cover seems so obvious as to be a necessity for town life unless chauffeurs or other servants are employed. This requirement, together with the complete living unit, appeared to cover too much site area ; consequently the living unit was placed on the first floor, which had other advantages for a town house. The detachment of the first floor from the garden could be overcome by a terrace over part of the garage with a flight of steps down to the garden. This first floor living unit had to consist of a living room, including space for dining, for piano and for bookshelves, a bedroom, dressing room and bathroom, a kitchen and pantry and a maid's bed-sitting room. The living room alone should be planned generously, the remaining rooms taking the minimum reasonable space. This layout on one floor gave the advantages of using the bedroom and dressing room as private sitting rooms, and of living without servants in the absence of the children. The space required by this floor governed the area of the house. It gave space on the ground floor, of which approximately half was available for the covered entrance, garage and an outside stair to a back door at first floor level, and of which the other half provided a playroom and covered space open to the garden for the children, and a small entrance hall and cloakroom. On the second floor approximately half was taken by bedrooms and bathroom for the children and for a possible children's maid, together with box-room, linen cupboards, etc. The children's four bedrooms, moreover, could be used as two double spare rooms for guests by the provision of sliding partitions. The remaining half of the second floor was available for roof terrace opening straight off the top of the staircase and off the children's bedrooms. Thus all floors in the house were accessible to terraces in the open air.

It was particularly required that all heating and domestic supply of hot water should be by electricity on account of cleanliness and of the abolition of all stoking and of the carrying and storage of fuel. This requirement limited the possible areas in London for a site, as in many areas the cost of electricity is prohibitive for such extensive use.

This plan was conceived in anticipation that a site in London would only afford light and air on the front and back, and not on the sides. The site was found subsequently and although it proved to be a corner site the plan required no modification. The western boundary appeared to be obvious for the street front, and the eastern outlook was more attractive than the southern. Moreover, in this position all trees on the site were preserved.

The plan of this house was formed without any preconceived idea of what the house would or should look like. I held a conviction that design was not a matter of erudition in style nor of aptitude for repeating the fine effects of other ages, but simply a matter of sensibility for structure, for the placing of masses and weights, and for materials. It seemed that reinforced concrete would be the most suitable structural material, in view of the open spaces required under the first floor, the desire for unbroken length of window and the freedom of placing internal partition walls without sacrificing precision of planning. Moreover, only a few designers in this country appeared to accept frankly reinforced concrete as a material and structural method different from that of any form of masonry, and their work appealed to me as having that structural quality which, personally, I find missing in nearly all other contemporary work with the exception of that of some engineers. I felt confident, therefore, that the plan in the right hands could be translated into a pleasing building. I may say frankly that in my opinion that confidence has been confirmed, and the experience has proved to be one of great interest. The plan was accepted and carried out without sacrificing one inch of my carefully measured detail requirements. The considered and deliberate placing and emphasis of line and surface, and the selection of variation in colour and texture, both externally and internally, followed sympathetically the structural forces or the separate entity of walls, fittings or other varying forms.

I can only regret that this building should offend the susceptibilities of some people and be beyond the comprehension of others. To me it has proved to be an experience of intense interest and delight.

6.7b   66 Frognal by Connell, Ward and Lucas

28.10.38   THE   ARCHITECT   &   BUILDING   NEWS   99

6   FROGNAL,   HAMPSTEAD,   N.W.3
ARCHITECTS :   CONNELL,   WARD   AND   LUCAS,   AA. R. I. B. A.

THE SITE AND GENERAL LAYOUT.—The small site of ·165 acres is within three or four miles of the centre of town. It was therefore to the owner's advantage to make the fullest possible use of the available ground space, a fact which controlled the general form and construction of the house. The ground level runs right in under the house, at the front, so that a shelter for cars can be provided without waste of ground space, and also at the back, where a covered terrace, which forms in effect an integral part of the garden, occupies the space under the living room, which otherwise would be covered by building. On the roof there is a roof garden.

ORIENTATION.—It will be seen that the rooms in the house face east and west, there is no outlook to the south. This arrangement was preferred for the following reasons : the owner particularly required the lighting of each room to be from one side only ; it was considered that rooms on both sides of the house should obtain sunlight, and that the principal bedrooms and the living room should have the morning sun ; the most secluded and private outlook possible on a corner site was desirable for the living room and the principal bedrooms, and it will be seen that this has been achieved, the outlook being across the garden and in amongst the trees.

As a result, it has been possible to provide the living room with a window 45 ft. long and 8 ft. high, half of which slides completely away, making the room virtually a part of the garden if desired.

Further, no other orientation or layout would have been possible without sacrificing some of the existing trees, all of which have been preserved.

INTERIOR   ARRANGEMENT.—Internally the house is arranged so as to provide distinct separation between the first floor, which forms a complete living unit for the owner and his wife, and the top floor, which contains the four children's bedrooms. When the children are away at school, the top floor can be put out of use. For accommodation of visitors, the children's rooms can be converted by means of sliding partitions into guest rooms. On the ground floor, again quite separate, is a playroom for the children. By this means and by the use of special sound-proofing methods, the different parts of the house mentioned above can be kept free from interference by noise.

DOMESTIC WORKING.—The house is heated by electricity, under thermostatic control ; water heating and fires are electric also, so that there is no solid fuel on the premises, no dirt and none of the labour required in making fires or stoking boilers. The materials for floors and walls were chosen with particular attention to the question of cleaning, and the fittings throughout the house were designed primarily for convenience in working, as it is intended that the house should be run with the minimum of domestic help.

SECTION
THROUGH
PLAYROOM

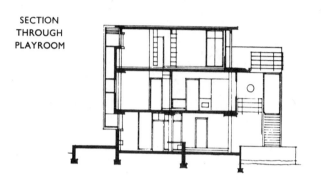

With the exception of chairs, tables and beds, there is no furniture in the house which is not built-in, and each piece of built-in furniture is designed to suit the particular requirements of the owner.

PROGRESS. — There was considerable objection to the building of this house by authorities, by architects, by adjoining owners, by estate owners, and by certain local residents ; but thanks to the very patient and reasonable attitude of certain of the authorities, and to the help of many of the local residents, these obstacles were eventually surmounted, and the owner was able to obtain the house he required.

The roof is used as garden space, walls are faced with brown Colorcrete and the roof surface is Paropa.

NOTE: These pages from The Architect and Building News have been recast to avoid duplication with the R.I.B.A. Journal article. All the text and illustrations are from the the same article, but we have left some out. We have concentrated it all into pages 99–100 for ease of reference.

Eds.

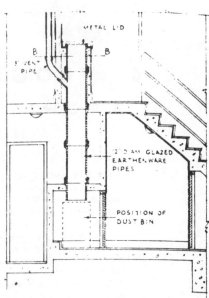

The staircase leads to the kitchen door, outside which is the rubbish shoot shown above.

Left, a view in the playroom, the walls of which are mainly window surface.

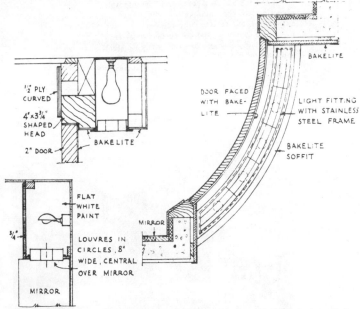

Over the windows and the front door pelmet lighting with louvred soffits is installed, as shown above. Right, the entrance hall.

Sources Acknowledgements

Grateful acknowledgement is made to the following sources for material used in this booklet:

Text

American Architect and Architecture for Berthold Lubetkin, 'Modern architecture in England', February 1937; *Architectural Review* for Berthold Lubetkin 'Architectural thoughts since the Revolution', May 1932, Berthold Lubetkin 'Recent developments of Town Planning in the USSR', May 1932, P. Morton Shand, 'Architecture and Engineering' November 1932, and P. Morton Shand, 'Concrete', November 1932, Reprinted from the *Architectural Review* published by Architectural Press, London; G. Boumphrey and Wells Coates 'Modern dwellings for modern needs' in *The Listener* 28 June 1933; A. Connell for R. Blomfield and A. Connell, 'For and against modern architecture' in *The Listener* 28 November 1934; S. Giedion 'Zur situation deutscher architektur' in *Der Cicerone*, Leipzig, Vol. XVIII, 1926; E. Halliday and G. Russell 'The living room and furniture', *The Listener*, 3 May 1933; H. Häring, 'Zwei Städte' in *Die Form* 1925-6; Harvard University Press for CIAM Town Plánning Chart © 1942, 1970 International Congresses for Modern Architecture; F. Pick, 'Meaning and purpose of design' in *The Listener*, 28 June 1933; G. A. Platz, 'Der Städtebau: die wirtschaftlichen und technischen grundlagen: das formproblem' in *Die Baukunst der neuesten Zeit*, Berlin, 1927; W. Riezler, 'Die Wohnung' in *Die Form* 1927; State Publishing House, Moscow, for 'Deklaratsiya' in *Pechat' i Revolyutsiya*, Moscow, June 1929; Union of Soviet Architects for 'Vopra i OSA' in *Sovremmenaya Arkhitektura*, 1929, No. 5, p. 171; Das Werk for H. Schmidt, 'Die Wohnung' in *Das Werk*, Basel, Vol. XIV, 1927.

Figures

1, 3 and 4 G. A. Platz, *Die Baukunst der neuesten Zeit* 1927, courtesy of Im Propylaen Verlag, Berlin; *2* Company archives Farbwerke Hoechst; *5 and 11* H. and B. Rasch, *Wie Bauen* 1928, Wedekind and Co. Stuttgart; *6–8 and 10 Die Form* Vol. 2 1927; *9* Le Corbusier, *Oeuvre complete*, courtesy of Artemis Verlag, Zurich; *13 Die Form*, Vol. 3 1928; *14–21b Architectural Review* May 1932, Vol. LXXI; *22a* Wendingen 3, 1923; *22b* L. Hilberseimer, *Groszstadt Architektur* 1927, courtesy of Verlag Julius Hoffman, Stuttgart; *Document 6.7a text and figures Journal of Royal Institute of British Architects*, 19 December 1938; *Document 6.7b text and figures Architect and Building News*, 28 October 1938.

Translations

3.1 and 3.2, Colin Chant; 4.2, Christopher Baggs.

History of architecture and design 1890–1939

A305 Plan-reading guide

Walls

1 Load-bearing, usually brick or masonry
2 Partition wall
3 Cavity wall of brick or breeze block usually marked as **1**
4 Low wall or garden wall outside main building
5 Wooden partition
6 Movable wooden screen
7 Wooden or metal balustrade

Apertures

8 Glass framed by wood and metal from floor up
9 Door
10 Window set in a wall
11 Niche in wall
12 Fireplace

Overhead

13 Indicates a change in ceiling level or overhang of upper floors
14 Indicates an important structural beam overhead

Entrances

15 Main entrance
16 Alternative entrance for servants or to garden
17 Fitted furniture – seat, dresser
18 Fitted cupboard with double doors

Roofs

19 Projecting roof seen from above (sloping roof)
20 As above but flat roof

Stairs

21a Spiral stair (ascending in direction of arrow)
21b Straight stairs ascending in direction of arrow
22 Stairs down to basement

Circulation

23 Indicating areas of circulation in a house (corridors, passages etc.)
24 Paved areas on verandas and terraces

Supports

25 Wood, stone or concrete pillar
26 Steel stanchion
27 Flue for fire or boiler
28 North point

HALL OR H	–	Hall
LIVING OR LR	–	Living or sitting room or parlour
DINING OR DR	–	Dining room
BED OR BR	–	Bedroom
DRESSING OR D	–	Dressing room
NURSERY OR N	–	Nursery
BATH OR B	–	Bathroom
WASH OR W	–	Wash house (clothes)
KIT OR K	–	Kitchen
SC	–	Scullery
WC OR	–	Lavatory
STORE OR S	–	All forms of storage – coals, pantry, linen cupboard
SPACE	–	An empty space over a room below

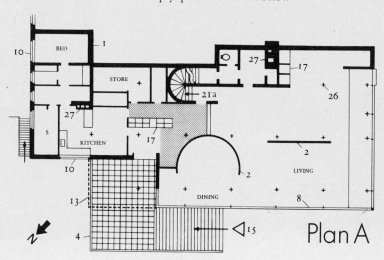

Plan A

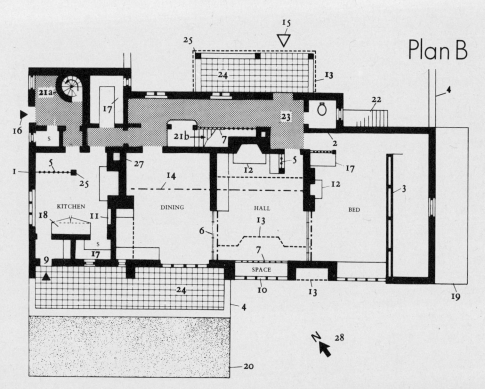

Plan B

Notes for reading plans

1   Find any photographs of the interior or exterior of the building (in the course unit or elsewhere in books) and locate the views on the plans. If there are section and elevation drawings, relate these to each other and to the plan. The more visual information at your disposal, the more you can discover from the plans.

2   Bearing these other illustrations in mind, start at the main entrance or front door on the plan (▷) and work through all the rooms. Note the handling of circulation (lobbies, corridors, etc.), and the interrelationship of the main rooms, the use of the stairs, the relationship of upper and lower floors and changing ceiling or floor levels. For houses, note arrangements for eating, cooking (servants or mistress of the house?), relaxing (by day, by night), heating, working, entertaining guests, sleeping, children and washing clothes. You will only be able to work all this out if you think hard about the clues offered by the plan and make intelligent guesses.

3   Satisfy yourself that you understand the basic structure of the building: load-bearing walls (brick, concrete, stone, wood) or frame construction (steel, wood or reinforced concrete frame) with infill. What do the upper storey walls rest on?

4   What kinds of power does the building use? Coal, gas, electricity, wood? For heating, cooking, washing, cooling, lighting (and are they independent?). Look for chimneys and fireplaces and information in your course units. Look for clues in photographs of the interiors if possible.

5   Note the effects of site and sun: views from the main rooms, the effect of sunlight on the exterior and on the internal lighting at different times of the day. What about privacy?

6   Make a note if you decide there must be missing information: missing floor plans (basement or attic), missing sections or elevations. Does it look as if these are important? Is it worth searching for more information?

7   Has the building survived in its original condition? Additions, demolitions, weathering of surfaces, replacement of surfaces, windows, doors, etc. Watch out for tell-tale signs of changes in the plans and illustrations, i.e. do the photographs tally precisely with the plans? Are the plans or photographs recent or original? Remember architects often change a building during construction.

Assessment

1   How does the building compare with others of a similar type which you know well at first hand? Is it typical? Is it abnormal? Would you like to live/work/play in it?

2   How would you categorize the overall aesthetic effects: open or closed space, looking in or looking out, light or dark inside, restful to live, work or play in, or stimulating and unusual, monumental or simple? Does the building have an idea, or theme and is it followed through effectively?

3   What strikes you as unusual about it? What is its place in the history of this kind of building, or in the history of architecture as a whole? Is it a good or bad building in your opinion?